Inklings of Heaven

This book is dedicated to Matt
in gratitude and love

Inklings of Heaven:

C. S. Lewis and Eschatology

Sean Connolly

GRACEWING

First published in 2007

in the United Kingdom by:
Gracewing
2 Southern Avenue, Leominster
Herefordshire HR6 0QF

ISBN 978 0 85244 659 1

Typeset by
Action Publishing Technology Ltd, Gloucester, GL1 5SR

Contents

Foreword

by Walter Hooper

When most of us think of C. S. Lewis we think of Aslan, and other fruits of his Christian faith. But for half his life he would have been embarrassed by the connection. The main reason for his many years of unbelief concerned his understanding of mythology. In his autobiography he said that, when he was reading the Classics at the age of fourteen, editors took it for granted that pagan religions were a 'farrago of nonsense, though our own, by a fortunate exception, was exactly true.'[1] 'No one,' he complained, 'ever attempted to show in what sense Christianity fulfilled Paganism or Paganism prefigured Christianity.'[2]

No one, that is, until Lewis was getting on for thirty-three years old. Writing to his old friend, Arthur Greeves, Lewis told of the evening of 19 September 1931 when his friends, J. R. R. Tolkien and Hugo Dyson – 'the immediate human causes'[3] of his conversion – helped him see that whereas pagan stories 'are God expressing Himself through the minds of poets, using such images as He found there ... the story of Christ is ... a true myth ... *It really happened.*'[4]

Because he wrote so convincingly about the Faith it is diffi-cult for many people to believe Lewis *meant* it when he described himself as 'the most reluctant convert in all England'.[5] 'Amiable agnostics,' he said, 'will talk cheerfully about "man's search for God". To me, as I then was, they might as well have talked about the mouse's search for the cat.'[6] Years

---

[1] C. S. Lewis, *Surprised by Joy: The Shape of My Early Life*, p. 47.
[2] Ibid.
[3] C. S. Lewis, *Collected Letters of C. S. Lewis:* Volume II: *Books, Broadcasts and War 1931–1949*, p. 501.
[4] C. S. Lewis, *Collected Letters of C. S. Lewis:* Volume I: *Family Letters 1905–1931.* p. 977.
[5] *Surprised by Joy*, p. 178.
[6] Ibid, p. 177.

later a member of Billy Graham's *Decision* magazine urged
Lewis to admit that he had 'made a decision' at the time of his
conversion. 'I would not put it that way,' he replied, 'I was
decided upon. I was glad afterwards at the way it came out, but
at the moment what I heard was God saying, "Put down your
gun and we'll talk."'[7]

Thereafter Lewis used every opportunity that came along to
emphasise that his only reason for believing in Christianity was,
simply and solely, because it is *true*. In an account of his life
written as a blurb for one of his books, he insisted: 'I am not
the religious type. I want to be left alone ... But since the facts
seemed to be the opposite I *had* to give in.'[8] 'The great difficulty,' he told some clergyman, 'is to get modern audiences to
realise that you are preaching Christianity solely and simply
because you happen to think it *true*.'[9] 'To me,' he wrote to the
Anglican nun, Sister Penelope, 'the real distinction is not
between high and low but between religion with a real supernaturalism and salvationism on the one hand and all
watered-down and modernist versions on the other.'[10] 'I am,'
he said to others, 'a dogmatic Christian untinged with
Modernist reservations and committed to supernaturalism in
its full rigour.'[11] And, finally, in a well-known passage in the
Preface to *Mere Christianity*, Lewis distinguishes Christianity
from anything merely personal. 'I am not writing,' he said, 'to
expound something I could call "my religion", but to expound
"mere" Christianity, which is what it is and was what it was long
before I was born and whether I like it or not.'[12]

If anyone is likely to imagine that all this was a matter of
giving dry assent to a set of propositions, let him think so no
longer. Lewis has told us that during his atheist years the 'two

---

[7] C. S. Lewis, *Essay Collection and Other Short Pieces*, p. 553.
[8] Roger Lancelyn Green and Walter Hooper, *C. S. Lewis: A
Biography* p. 170.
[9] C. S. Lewis, 'Christian Apologetics,' in *Essay Collection*, p. 148.
[10] *Collected Letters II*, p. 285.
[11] C. S. Lewis, 'On Ethics', in *Christian Reflections*, ed. Walter Hooper
(London, Geoffrey Bles, 1967; Fount, 1998), p. 55.
[12] C. S. Lewis, *Mere Christianity: A Revised and Amplified Edition, with a
New Introduction, of the Three Books, 'Broadcast Talks', 'Christian
Behaviour' and 'Beyond Personality'*, p. ix.

hemispheres' of his mind 'were in the sharpest contrast. On the one side a many-islanded sea of poetry and myth; on the other a glib and shallow "rationalism". Nearly all that I loved I believed to be imaginary; nearly all that I believed to be real I thought grim and meaningless.'[13] With his conversion his two outstanding gifts – Reason (the capacity for logical, rational and analytical thought) and Imagination (a 'truth-bearing faculty')[14] – were reconciled, and thereafter operated as one. Putting it another way, Reason is a way of Telling while imagining is a way of Showing. Lewis proved to be good at both: sometimes Reason – telling – worked best, as in *Mere Christianity* and *Miracles*; sometimes Imagination – showing – worked best, as in his interplanetary novels and the *Chronicles of Narnia*.

At this point I feel compelled to bring in something that has been growing in my mind for the last dozen or so years. Before his conversion he could write well, and he was more ambitious than at any time in his life. But apart from two volumes of verse, nothing happened. I believe the whole thing can be summed up in five words: *Lewis had nothing to say*. It really does appear that when Lewis cared more about God than being a writer, God *gave* him things to say. I use the word 'gave' advisedly, but I think God *gave* Lewis and Tolkien – 'sub-creators' both – the books we love so much. If I seem to be claiming too much, let me say that I meant the same thing Lewis meant and said in a letter to a friend: 'If every good and perfect gift,' he said, 'comes from the Father of Lights[15] then all true and edifying writings, whether in Scripture or not, must be *in some sense* inspired.'[16]

Sean Connolly reminds us at the beginning of his book that Lewis was not a professional theologian and that he left us no system of theological thought. Lewis believed strongly that, whatever his talents, 'the questions which divide Christians from one another often involve points of high theology or even of ecclesiastical history ... [and] ought never to be treated

---

[13] *Surprised by Joy*, ch. XI, p. 161.
[14] C. S. Lewis, Letter to T. S. Eliot, 2 June 1931.
[15] James 1:17.
[16] C. S. Lewis, Letter to Clyde Kilby, 7 May 1959.

except by real experts.'[17] 'I should,' he insisted, 'have been out of my depth in such waters: more in need of help myself than able to help others.'[18] What we have instead is a mixture of Lewis's various geniuses – for science fiction, for theology, for literary criticism, for theological satire, for fairy stories – operating as one and illuminating one another.

If I may be forgiven some autobiography, let me say that almost no pleasure is greater than looking back on those precious months in 1963 when I was with Lewis almost daily for about three months. What impressions did I form of him? I never thought of him as a theologian. His conversion to Christianity had gone so deep that I could not have imagined what he would have been like before it happened. In a word, his faith was so blended with everything else that it was no more noticeable than that he had two hands. The gift he feared he had lost was 'seeing pictures' of the sort that led to his interplanetary novels and the *Chronicles of Narnia*. He could not complete a story later published in its incomplete form as 'After Ten Years'[19] because he couldn't 'see' what was to follow. If I were forced to separate the geniuses that made up C. S. Lewis, I think I'd say that the don, the academic, was perhaps the most memorable. This was because of his constant defining of terms and his pursuit of truth. But in the end, he was not several people, but one.

And that is what makes this such a truly great book. When Sean Connolly first began talking about it with me I feared that I would see – as so often – the separation of Lewis's writings. It has not happened. The author brings together, with what seems the greatest ease, the interlocking threads of Lewis's thought. The book is a logical and brilliantly clear illumination of outstanding gifts that came together when C. S. Lewis's Reason and Imagination were forever reconciled.

[17] *Mere Christianity*, p. viii.
[18] Ibid.
[19] It is found in C. S. Lewis, *The Dark Tower and Other Stories*.

Introduction

Heaven loomed large for C. S. Lewis. This might seem a strange thing to say of a man who famously, during the early years of his adult life, dismissed any such belief as wishful thinking or mere mythology. Perhaps it is stranger still of one who, for the first year after his conversion from atheism, continued to reject speculations about immortality and ever afterwards – even once a committed Christian – remained suspicious of organised religion's penchant for using paradise as some sort of a moral bribe. Nevertheless, in Lewis' fiction, poetry, apologetics, and even his English criticism, heaven loomed large. Indeed, if heaven is to be believed in at all, he argued towards the end of his life, then how can it loom less than large? 'How can it, except by sensual or bustling preoccupations, be kept in the background of our minds? How can the "rest of Christianity" – what is this "rest"? – be disentangled from it?'[1]

I often wonder if the deepest spiritual malaise of our contemporary culture (for which read our western, consumerist society) isn't the loss of that heavenward gaze. We no longer need – or at least we don't think we do – the promise of a better age to come because we are all too busy building those better times in the here and now. How can our want of heaven compete with our want of winning the lottery when the latter seems so much more tangible, so much more real, so much more likely? How can we be expected to hope for a hereafter when we live in such a scientific and technological age and much of the mental furniture that went alongside heaven's traditional imagery has been brushed aside? At worst we're left with featureless white rooms and floating about on clouds; at best, with the anticipation of some sort of syrupy family

---

[1] C. S. Lewis, *Prayer: Letters to Malcolm* pp. 113–14 (Letter 22).

reunion or the intellectual's nirvana – the abyss, or Nothingness, which seems to appeal to so many in today's product-stuffed world. But can these really compete with the 'Be this' and 'Buy that' pressures of the everyday life we live? Unless we're particularly prone to the spiritual or unless we're facing imminent death or suffering the loss of a loved one, heaven has become an anachronism: the realm of the religious and no one much else. The danger is that in our concern to secure the present moment we have forgotten the future. Or, to put it more precisely, in our everyday efforts to make safe our own futures, we have stopped thinking about – I ought to say, stopped desiring – the only real Future there can be: life with God.

The biblical data tells a very different story. So much of the Bible speaks about our relationship with God in terms of longing, of desire, of yearning. God's reign is depicted by our hunger and thirst being satisfied, by rich harvests being reaped, by luscious pastures and flowing waters springing forth, and by safety and security being provided. Isaiah, in particular, presents the Age to Come as a time of mountains overflowing with wine, of banquets being thrown, of free corn given in abundance. This imagery arose from a peoples living in a desert culture, whose nation state was constantly under threat, and whose livelihoods – and indeed, lives – could be wiped out by a single bad harvest, or a plague of locusts, or a drought, or a war. Their future with God was not to be a bodiless alternative to their corporeal experience here and now, but the very fulfilment of it: the giving, by God himself, of their every desire and need. Then there is the sexual imagery: the erotic love poems of the Song of Songs, for example; the relationship between Yahweh and his people being described as like the intimacy of a husband and his wife. Again, all far removed from the sort of cerebral, disembodied search for meaning so popular with many of the New Age trends that pass for spirituality these days. The religion of ancient Israel was unashamedly a religion of the heart, the stomach and the loins. In the New Testament, too, we find a similar focus on the future: on the hope for an age when God will come to reign and be all in all (Cf. 1 Corinthians 15:28), when wrongs will be righted and the downtrodden be lifted up (Cf. Luke 1:51–55), when death will have lost its sting (1 Corinthians 15:55) and the whole of creation as we now know it will be made anew (Revelation 21:5). And in both Old and New Testaments what is significant is that this future is *longed* for. It is surely no accident, then, that the Church's Advent antiphon speaks of the coming Christ as the 'Desire of all nations'.

Mother Teresa once identified the West – by which she meant those of us living lives of comparative affluence – as suffering from a far greater poverty than anything she and her companions had experienced in Calcutta. We face a poverty of spirit, she believed, because we have lost our pressing need of God and become self-sufficient. Using the language of the Old Testament we might say we find ourselves living in the Land and being secure – always a fatal first step to following false gods. And she has a point. When we have so much – and let's face it, compared to those who have to walk six miles a day just to find water, we do – and when we are told that it is the world that offers us our every desire, what meaning can religion's hope for heaven ever hold? What future can we expect?

In this book I want to explore eschatology – the study and science of the End Time – not just as some kind of an academic discipline, although a rigorous, disciplined and intellectual approach is essential if we are to avoid the sugar-sweet solutions that society tends to offer in answer to life's most fundamental questions. But I also want to awaken in us a *desire* for the End Time, because I believe that this eschatological desire is to be at the heart of our faith and our friendship with God. And for that reason I aim to explore eschatology using the work and writings of C. S. Lewis as a kind of lens. It might seem something of a spurious claim to suggest that Lewis was an eschatologist when the word eschatology hardly ever appears in the corpus of his published writing, but nevertheless I boldly make the claim: C. S. Lewis was an eschatologist. Here was a man who was not a classically trained theologian, who wrote no systematic theological treatise, and who time and again referred to himself as a layman and an amateur, as one theologically uneducated and even unlearned. Yet here was a man, English scholar, broadcaster, children's writer, and Christian apologist, whose later life became very much caught up in the business of heaven. Together with his brother

Warnie, with his friends, J. R. R. Tolkien, Charles Williams, and many others, C. S. Lewis made up an intellectual group which called itself the 'Inklings'. The joke, of course, was a literary one but it could just have easily being eschatological. For Lewis, above all, the heaven-directed was never lacking. His work is wrought with the sense of another world, more solid and of a deeper reality than we can even begin to comprehend. He captured perfectly the truth that we have an inkling of that Something More – if only we would realise it – in every longed for, aching, yearned after, itching and unsatisfied moment of our lives. Lewis' work – and thus this book – is not just about eschatology. It is about an eschatological desire that drives our Christian faith and calls us to communion with God.

Chapter 1

C. S. Lewis and the Eschata

Where to start when studying the end: this is the initial question facing any eschatology. Do we start with the Last Things themselves: heaven and hell, judgement and purgatory, the parousia and the end of the world? Or do we start where we are, examining ourselves from the perspective of those promised ends? Given the danger of relegating eschatological theology to something akin to a mere theological appendix, contemporary eschatology – at least post-Moltmann[1] – seems to have all but avoided any synthetic presentation of the *eschata*. The emphasis has tended to be largely on the dynamics with numerous theologies of hope and liberation, and with various examinations of the End Time as it impinges on the here and now. An initial glance at the work of C. S. Lewis, however, suggests that he produced an eschatology that was chiefly characterised by its concern with the descriptive data. This is unsurprising for one whose theological work was unsystematic and largely apologetic. What do we mean by heaven and hell? What is purgatory? What sort of judgement will Christians face? These were the relevant questions for Lewis' particular audience. In a later chapter I will show how a closer reading of the Lewisian texts demonstrates quite a detailed understanding

---

[1] By this I mean post 1965 and the publication of *Theologie der Hoffnung*. However it should be noted that the publication in 1995 of *Das Kommen Gottes: Christliche Eschatologie* marked a new phase in Moltmann's endeavours by complementing his work on the eschatological dynamic with a thorough examination of the descriptive content of eschatological theology. See Jürgen Moltmann, *The Coming of God: Christian Eschatology*.

of the eschatological dynamic but, for now, I want to focus on Lewis' picture of those Last Things; I want to step beyond the stable door, so to speak, and see what Lewis presents there.

Death

It is sometimes said that death is the great leveller: that because of the inevitability of the end of life there lays a basic equality written into our mortality. This might be so, but the same cannot be said about dying. Inequalities of income or education, of diet and/or basic medical care, can and do make all the difference when it comes to the actual process of letting go of life. Death and dying are not the same thing and these disparities of influence and affluence, as well as something even as dull as demographics, can cause a substantial shift in the way we might die and, indeed, the very reason for our death. There can be an inequality, too, in the manner with we which we approach our impending demise. The pagan's promise to live, drink and be merry for tomorrow we might die stands in stark contrast to the Benedictine understanding of life as a school in which one is preparing for one's death. Even for the person of religious faith, the approach to death and dying can be somewhat ambiguous. Do we long to shuffle off this mortal coil, or do we cling to life and look to prolong it at any cost? Do we accept death theoretically at least but then, rather more practically minded, deny dying? It is just possible that we might find ourselves filled with trepidation at the prospect of a painful end, or frightened by the frailty of our faith (are we really so sure about the afterlife?), or unnerved at the notion of finally coming to meet our creator face to face. The Lutheran theologian, Jürgen Moltmann, once wrote that everyone who lives with any degree of awareness knows that death is 'not only *an* event in life: it is *the* event – and that all our attitudes to life are attitudes to the death of this life of ours'.[2] C. S. Lewis once remarked, in his beautifully written *A Grief Observed*, that it is hard 'to have patience with people who say "There is no death" or "Death

2 Jürgen Moltmann, *The Coming of God*, p. 50.

doesn't matter". There is death. And whatever *is* matters.'[3]

In the Old Testament it is true to say that we find a complex and developing concept of the meaning of death. The scripture scholar, Gerhard Von Rad, has traced the gradual encroachment of death's domain upon the land of the living in ancient Hebrew thought. Human weakness, illness, imprisonment, and oppression by one's enemies all came to be seen as some kind of death. In cultic terms, death denoted abandonment by God. By the time of Qoheleth the certainty of death for all – be we clean or unclean before the Lord – has given rise to a somewhat tragic outlook on life. 'All is vanity,' decries the preacher, since ultimately everyone will end up with the same, indifferent fate. For the Hebrews of biblical times, then, death has become much more than a mechanism by which life is ended: it has become the sacrament of human melancholy, meaning that it now symbolises and makes present the whole range of human suffering and futility.[4]

C. S. Lewis himself observed, in a personal letter written to an elderly American correspondent in 1959, that there were only three things to be done about death: desire it, fear it, or ignore it.[5] Whilst the third alternative, he believed, was the

---

[3] C. S. Lewis, *A Grief Observed*, p. 15.

[4] Gerhard Von Rad, 'Life and Death in the Old Testament', in *Bible Key Words*, Volume 14: *Life and Death*, p. 18. See also Gerhard Von Rad, *Old Testament Theology*, Volume 1: *The Theology of Israel's Historical Traditions*, p. 387.

[5] C. S. Lewis, *Letters to an American Lady*, p. 84. Interestingly the Sacred Congregation for the Doctrine of the Faith was concerned with precisely this 'third alternative' as subtly undermining the faith of Christians. Its letter, *Recentiores episcoporum synodi* of May 1979 stated: 'Even though, generally speaking, the Christian is fortunately not yet at the point of positive doubt, he often refrains from thinking about his destiny after death because he is beginning to encounter questions in his mind to which he is afraid of having to reply, questions such as: Is there really anything after death? Does anything remain of us after we die? Is it nothingness that is before us?' Sacred Congregation for the Doctrine of the Faith, 'The Reality of Life after Death', in *Vatican Council II*, Volume 2: *More Post Conciliar Documents,* p. 501. The Dominican theologian Anton Van der Walle depicts this fearful 'head in the sand' approach to death with a reference to Tolstoy's *The Death of Ivan Illyich*. Cf. Anton Van Der Walle, *From Darkness to the Dawn*, p. 3.

most uneasy and uncertain of them all, his own position was undeniably a blend of the first two. On the one hand he was able to reassure the grieving Sheldon Vanauken that death is the process we must undergo to be perfected: an act of consummation rather than termination. On the other hand, as he accepted in *The Problem of Pain*, desiring death is not necessarily always the admissible response. If we cannot honestly allow ourselves to desire death, we must at the very least accept it, he believed. 'It is natural for us to wish that God had designed for us a less glorious and less arduous destiny, but then we are wishing not for more love but for less.'[6] What is perhaps of greater significance, however, is Lewis' conviction that whatever ambivalence we might hold towards our own mortality, death itself can be said to be ambivalent. It can be both holy and unholy, our ultimate discredit and our only hope. Death is the thing 'Christ came to conquer and the means by which he conquered'.[7] This ambivalence is given form in Lewis' allegorical apology for Christianity, *The Pilgrim's Regress*. There, towards the end of the story, the principal character, John, sees the face of Death and realises that, paradoxically, the only way to escape is to die. Being told that he ultimately has two options, to jump or be thrown, to give in or to struggle, John hesitantly opts for the first. 'Then I am your servant and no more your master,' the voice of Death contends. 'The cure of death is dying. He who lays down his liberty in that act receives it back.'[8] As Lewis understood it, then, death can either be the definitive act of self-surrender before God or the final lost battle in a futile life of attempted self-sufficiency. Paul Ford, commenting on Lewis' children's story *The Last Battle*, has suggested that the stable door around which much of the tale takes place can be read as a metaphor for death. 'On this side of the door,' Ford notes, 'death is terrifying, black and unknown; but on the other side of the door lies the glory of Aslan's country.'[9] It seems to me, moreover,

6 C. S. Lewis, *The Problem of Pain*, p. 28.
7 C. S. Lewis, *Miracles: A Preliminary Study*, pp. 131–2.
8 C. S. Lewis, *The Pilgrim's Regress: An Allegorical Apology for Christianity, Reason and Romanticism*, p. 209.
9 Paul Ford, *Companion to Narnia: A Complete Guide to the Enchanting World of C. S. Lewis' The Chronicles of Narnia*, p. 130.

that this 'Last Battle', just like the apocalyptic literature found in the Book of Revelations, is actually a reminder that the manner of our death denotes a basic disposition: put crudely, it signals which side we might be on. As Karl Rahner explained it, 'Death is not something which happens to a man alongside much else. Death is the event in which the very man himself becomes his definitive self.'[10] If we have come to define ourselves by our relationship with the divine, then death is not something to be feared. Death, for Christian eschatology at least, is more than merely a sacrament of human melancholy. It is the sacrament, yes, of our helplessness before the infinite, but also of our hopefulness in our Creator Lord.

Death and Sin

An important theological consideration of any concept of death is its association with sin. The Second Vatican Council (drawing on scriptural texts such as Wisdom 1:13; 2:23–24, Romans 5:21; 6:23; James 1:15) was clear in its reception of the Church's ancient teachings that death is the consequence of sin. *Gaudium et Spes*, for example, stated that, had he not sinned, man would have been immune from bodily death.[11] It was St Athanasius, amongst others, who had argued that once death had entered creation through sin, God could not simply eradicate it without undermining his own consistency. As God had warned that eating of the tree of knowledge would bring death, so it must do so if the divine word was to hold true. Our redemption, then, would require another way by which death could be overcome, he argued.[12] Karl Rahner made the point that this traditional teaching does not imply that without sin human beings would continue their biological life indefinitely, but rather that the nature of death as we now know it, with its

---

[10] Karl Rahner, 'Death', in *Encyclopedia of Theology: a Concise Sacramentum Mundi*, p. 329.

[11] Vatican II, *Gaudium et Spes*, 18. See also the Sixteenth Council of Carthage in 418 (DS 222), the Second Council of Orange in 529 (DS 371) and the fifth session of the Council of Trent in 1546 which produced a decree on Original Sin (DS1511).

[12] Cf. St Athanasius, *On the Incarnation*, pp. 2, 7.

terrible sense of pain and loss, of darkness and doubt, is the result of our sinful rebellion.[13] In other words, what should have been, without concupiscence and sin, the ending of man's biological life and the transformation to his 'definitive condition before God by means of a free act engaging his whole life' has become instead a tortured, darkened, and painful letting go before God. If sin is basically the refusal to meet God on his terms, then how much more painful becomes the moment in death when there really is no other choice but to meet him in such a way? A helpful illustration of this doctrine of sin and death is found in *Mere Christianity*, with Lewis' analogy of the obstinate toy soldier. The toy soldier made of tin is destined to become real and this means turning tin to flesh. But the soldier isn't interested in becoming real; he likes being the toy. 'All he sees is that the tin is being spoilt,' suggests C. S. Lewis.[14] The process by which a willing toy soldier would have happily submitted to the transformation becomes, for the obstinate toy soldier, a moment of death and destruction to be feared and shunned. In other words, through sin a sort of obstinacy has entered creation which theology calls 'death'.

The Council of Trent, however, appears to offer a somewhat deeper appreciation of this connection between sin and death. Not only is death a consequence of our sins, Trent suggested, but it also puts us further at the mercy of evil. By our sinful rebellion against God we are expelled from paradise *and* we lose that holiness and justice with which we had once been constituted. We have rebelled, therefore, and are now a set of rebels; and, as such, we find ourselves at the mercy of all the other rebels within creation. Trent also spoke of death as a punishment imposed upon us by God for our sins.[15] C. S. Lewis expanded upon this idea with the notion of remedial action and divine punishment understood as divine mercy. '[Death] is also the means of redemption from sin, God's medicine for Man and His weapon against Satan,' he noted in

---

[13] Rahner, 'Death', p. 329.
[14] C. S. Lewis, *Mere Christianity*, pp. 148–9.
[15] Cf. Council of Trent, 'Decree on Original Sin', in *The Christian Faith in the Doctrinal Documents of the Catholic Church*, p. 508.

Miracles.[16] Lewis posited here that without the necessary surrender in death – without the trauma of the rebellious creature being forced at some point to face its creator – the consequence would be an immortality of ever increasing pride in which man would fall ever deeper into sin and ever further away from God. To understand why Lewis believed that left to ourselves without death we would necessarily become more sinful it is important to remember his stated position on the character of sin itself. Sin of its very nature, he believed, breeds sin 'by strengthening sinful habit and weakening the conscience'. Thus he argued: 'Good and evil both increase at compound interest'.[17] The remedy of death, then, consists in its causing a break, or breach, in the cycle of concupiscence and human sin.

Death and Immortality

The full gamut of Christian eschatology, of course, does not end in death. Indeed, for the Christian soul, dying is just the beginning and there is a whole world beyond the stable door to be explored. In his diary entry for 24 May 1922, Lewis noted: 'Like me [Owen Barfield] has no belief in immortality.'[18] This was prior to Lewis' re-conversion to Christianity (and Barfield's to anthroposophy) of course, but what is interesting is Lewis' admission that even for a year after his conversion the doctrine of immortality still played no part in his thinking. By the time he had come to write *Mere Christianity* C. S. Lewis had accepted the Christian assertion that individual human beings are to live forever, but yet, it seems, he still felt a certain disdain for the subject. The problem, he perceived, was that there was a real danger of the divine not being central to this doctrine: of immortality rather than God becoming the goal. For Lewis, the centre of Christian faith and doctrine was not a hope for ongoing existence but 'the thirst for an end higher than natural ends; the finite self's desire for, and acquiescence in,

[16] *Miracles*, p. 135.
[17] See *The Problem of Pain*, p. 94 and *Mere Christianity*, p. 109.
[18] C. S. Lewis, *Letters of C. S. Lewis*, ed. W.H. Lewis, p. 163.

and self-rejection in favour of, an object wholly good and wholly good for it'.[19] Lewis never disputed the Christian understanding of the immortality of the soul. Indeed, he asserted: 'The earliest Christian documents give a casual and unemphatic assent to the belief that the supernatural part of man survives the death of the natural organism. But they are very little interested in the matter.'[20] What was of interest to Lewis was not pure longevity of human existence but quality of life. In the face of promised resurrection Lewis argued that 'immortality simply as immortality is irrelevant to the Christian claim'.[21] This position is echoed in the recent eschatology of Jürgen Moltmann:

> The immortality of the soul is an opinion – the resurrec-
> tion of the body is a hope. The first is a trust in something
> immortal in the human being, the second is a trust in God
> who calls into being the things that are not, and makes
> the dead live.[22]

Judgement

Karl Rahner's conclusion that death is the defining moment of human life – the event by which we recognise what has become the basic disposition of our days – leads us to the notion of judgement. If it is true to say that the modern mores of Western, consumerist society prefer to take that most uneasy and precarious of all the options and somehow try to sanitise death, then how much more of a truism is it to presume that the same society has no place at all for any concept of eternal judgement. If death is to be disregarded at least until its demands can no longer be ignored – for example, with the loss suddenly of someone we have loved, or the onset of a terminal disease (made worse by a poor prognosis) – then its effects, for

---

[19] C. S. Lewis, 'Religion without Dogma?' in idem, *Compelling Reason: Essays on Ethics and Theology,* p. 86.
[20] *Miracles,* pp. 29–30.
[21] Ibid. p. 155.
[22] Jürgen Moltmann, *The Coming of God,* p. 65.

those of us now living, can still be lessened. We will assure one another with places of comfort and peace, and speak appreciatively of the dead and the dying as if they had not only done no wrong but, indeed, could do no wrong. Even Christian ministers, preaching their funeral homilies, are not exempt from this sidestepping of eternal judgement, preferring instead (as the International Theological Commission complained back in 1992) to present paradise as some sort of a quasi-automatic consequence of death.[23] And yet, if death does indeed define us, there must be a manner of judgement – some kind of a verdict – on the life we have hitherto led. As C. S. Lewis once put it: 'What may be upon us at any time is not merely an End but a Judgement.'[24] And again: 'That will not be the time for choosing: it will be the time when we discover which side we really have chosen, whether we realised it before or not.'[25]

The theme of judgement in Christian eschatology finds its roots in certain aspects of Judaic messianism. Dermot Lane has sketched out the development in pre-Christian Judaic thought of prophetic and apocalyptic eschatology. The prophetic strand of Old Testament theology, developed from around the eighth century BC onwards, points to the 'Day of the Lord' when God will act in this world decisively and deal with his people's enemies with vengeance and just retribution. The apocalyptic strand, a later development from around the second century BC, takes up this notion of God as the people's defending champion but gives it an other-worldly aspect, understanding the 'Day of the Lord' as the moment when eternity comes crashing into our temporal experience and produces the inauguration of the End Time. 'This new dimension of Jewish faith points beyond life in this world,' comments Dermot Lane, 'implicitly critiquing a purely prophetic, this-worldly form of hope.'[26] By New Testament times, these prophetic and apocalyptic strands have combined

[23] Cf. International Theological Commission, 'Some Current Questions in Eschatology', in *The Irish Theological Quarterly*, p. 237.
[24] C. S. Lewis, 'The World's Last Night', in idem, *The World's Last Night and Other Essays,* p. 111.
[25] *Mere Christianity,* p. 54.
[26] Dermot Lane, 'Eschatology', in *The New Dictionary of Theology,* p. 331.

into a hope for deliverance which finds its expression in the notion of the coming reign of God. Within this context, then, the Early Church attempts to make sense of the message of Jesus of Nazareth and to understand his subsequent passion, death and resurrection. The atmosphere of the first Christian communities is pervaded with the strong sense that Jesus had fulfilled this expectation of deliverance – that he had definitively inaugurated God's kingdom – and with the even stronger anticipation that he would soon return to bring about the completion of that kingdom and with it the end of time. In early Christian eschatology, therefore, there is to be found both a this-worldly and an End Time element. What is interesting, however, is the seeming shift in the model of judgement from what Judaic and early Christian theology portrays as the coming of God as a defending champion at the end of time to what later eschatology perceives to be a rather more personal verdict in death upon the conduct of our earthy lives. In his commentary, *Reflections on the Psalms*, Lewis contrasted this very difference, although perhaps concluding rather too simplistically that whereas one belonged exclusively to the eschatology of ancient Israel, the other could be categorised as a concept of Christianity. For Christians, he argued, the day of judgement is perceived to be a day of wrath, one from which we pray for God to deliver us. The Judaic position, on the other hand, is one of universal rejoicing. Using the image of a courtroom to illustrate divine judgement, Lewis commented that Christians take a criminal case scenario, with themselves in the dock looking to be found not guilty. Jews, on the other hand, view judgement in terms of a civil case, with themselves as plaintiffs petitioning for justice.[27] The Christian seeks acquittal, the Jew vindication. The truth of the matter, of course, is rather more subtle and both ancient Israel and Christianity contain elements of each model of eternal judgement: God as a fearful, supreme judge and God as a powerful, defending champion.[28] However, it is true to say that medieval theology witnessed a movement away from

---

[27] Cf. *Reflections on the Psalms*, p. 8.
[28] Cf. Is 13:9; Ezk 7:19; Zp 15:1, for example, with Ps 76:7–8; 2 Th 1:5–6; 2 P 2:9; Rv 6:9–10.

the social and universal characteristics of eschatology in favour of an individual emphasis. Lewis' distinction can be made, to some extent at least, within the comparison of the eschatology of ancient Israel and the early Christian Church with later Christianity and especially the scholastic era, in which eschatology was demoted as a whole to some sort of a theological appendix. As Josef Neuner and Jacques Dupuis have argued, this privatisation of judgement (and, indeed, of most of eschatology) was due, in large part, to the delayed parousia and the need for theologians to make sense of individual death and the pious practices that were growing up around it.[29] Nevertheless, the co-existence (and indeed, for modern eschatology, the necessary restitution) of these two models of judgement is important if we are to grasp thoroughly the classical differentiation between what is sometimes called particular and universal judgement. With the shift towards an overly individual emphasis on judgement (at the expense of the defending champion model), there is a danger of not only the social and ecclesial implications of divine justice being ignored but also of a negation of the full force of what universal judgement might mean. The question quite naturally arises: if, at my death, I have already been judged and found worthy (or indeed unworthy), what more is to be said of me? Is universal judgement merely a re-run of that personal judgement within the hearing of everyone else? On the other hand, if we are to understand particular and universal judgement more accurately as two aspects (or even two parts) of a single process which entails both a personal liability and a social responsibility, which incorporates both particular and communal concerns, and which brings together the concepts of Christ's coming both as defending champion and supreme judge, then we have not only a much richer understanding of eschatological judgement but also a much closer incorporation of the biblical data from which the doctrine is drawn. This single process approach, however, does not necessarily mean to say that particular and universal judgement are the same thing, nor that they must take place at the same time; merely

---

[29] J. Neuner and J. Dupuis, *The Christian Faith*, pp. 937–8.

that they belong essentially to the same process of salvation.

One of Lewis' best known depictions of judgement clearly uses Matthew 25:31–46 as its source. In *The Last Battle* Lewis narrates how all the Narnian creatures come before Aslan the Lion, forced finally to look at him face to face. Only one of two reactions is possible, the author concludes. Either the characters recognise their Lion (and their Lord) and are filled with utter love, passing to his right and beyond him to the new Narnia within Narnia. Or else they fail in their recognition and see before them only a terrible beast and, being filled with fear and hatred, swerve to his left into the eternal darkness that is his shadow.[30] Not only are both the gospel pericope and the scene from the end of the Narnia Chronicles examples of universal judgement: 'All nations will be assembled before him,' says Jesus of the coming of the Son of Man in Matthew 25:32; all the creatures of Narnia come face to face with Aslan, even those who had already died.[31] Not only does Lewis match up with Matthew the specific reference of sides for the saved and the damned: 'He will place the sheep on his right hand and the goats on his left,' writes the Evangelist in Matthew 25:33. But what is at the core of both texts, and what should be at the core of any Christian understanding of judgement, is that concept of recognition. The repetitive question put forward by those destined for salvation and those heading to perdition is the same in each case: 'Lord, *when* did we see you?' The point the Evangelist is making is that if we can't come to see Christ in the poor and the put upon, in the sick and imprisoned, we will not find ourselves recognising him in the last days either. Interestingly, in both the gospel account and in Lewis' allusion to it there is a intermeshing (or even a muddling) of what we should strictly perceive to be elements of particular and universal judgement. Christ (or Aslan in *The Last Battle)* stands at once as both defending champion for those who recognise him and as dread Lord to those who do not; the scene of judgement is both publicly universal and highly personal. Both accounts are a graphic reminder of Karl Rahner's point concerning the pitfalls of theological definition.

---

[30] Cf. C. S. Lewis, *The Last Battle: A Story for Children*, p.144.
[31] Ibid. p. 146.

'There can be no justifiable attempt – or demand,' he once wrote, '– to indicate neatly and clearly which particular elements in the consummation of the individual belong to one or other of two definitely distinct events.'[32]

Elsewhere C. S. Lewis depicts judgement differently and, needless to say, makes use of different biblical sources for his theological interpretation. In *The World's Last Night*, for example, he warned: 'We shall all know and all creation will know too: our ancestors, our parents, our wives or husbands, our children. The unanswerable and (by then) self-evident truth about each of us will be known to all.'[33] This follows the image given in Revelation 20:11–12 of a sort of public airing of personal shortcomings. It echoes a theme Lewis had used earlier in his writing career with his suggestion in *The Problem of Pain* that salvation might consist not in the obliteration of our sinful shame but rather in the bearing of that shame forever; a burden for which we will exult because it shows to all the enormity of God's goodness and mercy.[34]

An important aspect of the Lewisian concept of judgement is his defence of traditional imagery. Although Lewis himself admitted, 'I do not find that pictures of physical catastrophe – that sign in the clouds, those heavens rolled up like a scroll – help one so much as the naked idea of Judgement,'[35] nevertheless he held on to the importance of their effect for our theological imagination. 'What do you suppose you have gained by substituting the image of a live wire for that of angered majesty?' he asked in *Letters to Malcolm*. 'You have shut us all up in despair; for the angry can forgive, and electricity can't.'[36] I suspect that this emphasis on the value of traditional biblical imagery arose from Lewis' own experience of lacking it as a child. Reflecting back upon his personal prayer for his mother just before her death, he confessed that he had approached God as some sort of a conjuror or a magician rather than as his Saving Lord, one who would perform the act

---

[32] Karl Rahner, 'Parousia', in *Encyclopedia of Theology*, p. 1159.
[33] 'The World's Last Night', p. 113.
[34] Cf. *The Problem of Pain*, pp. 45–6.
[35] 'The World's Last Night', p. 113.
[36] *Letters to Malcolm*, p. 93 (Letter 18).

required (saving his mother) and then leave well alone.[37] This grieving, desperate nine-year-old had adopted his own, perhaps even subconscious, analogy for God because he had lacked (or hadn't liked) the ones given in revelation. Even our abstract thinking is metaphorical, as Lewis was to learn in later life, and the danger with attempting to replace traditional images with what we think might be some kind of a modern and more literal clarification is simply that we are likely to substitute one set of images for another – and probably a poorer set. 'We must not smuggle in the idea,' Lewis warned his fictional friend Malcolm, 'that we can throw the analogy away and, as it were, get in behind it to a purely literal truth.'[38] We cannot. This premise is fundamental to understanding Lewis' contribution not only to eschatology but also to theology as a whole and to the area of Christian apologetics. It is a theme I shall return to in more depth in a later chapter.

Judgement and Purgatory

One important element in understanding Lewisian eschatology is his concept of our coming to perfection. Perfection is attained, Lewis argued, when God has made us truly lovable and this, in turn, is achieved through letting God love us. 'His love must, in the nature of things, be impeded and repelled by certain stains in our present character,' Lewis observed, 'and because he already loves us he must labour to make us lovable.'[39] Although this process of being made lovable occurs all through life, nevertheless it doesn't end with death. 'I never believed before,' admitted Lewis, reflecting on the death of his wife, ' ... that the faithfulest soul could leap straight into perfection and peace the moment death has rattled in the throat.'[40] It is helpful here to remember how Lewis understood the fruit of Christ's resurrection: what he believed to be the purpose of our redemption. By rising from the dead Christ

---

[37] Cf. *Surprised by Joy*, p. 15.
[38] *Letters to Malcolm*, pp. 49–50 (Letter 10).
[39] Cf. *The Problem of Pain*, p. 33.
[40] *A Grief Observed*, p. 37.

has renewed the whole of creation: 'a new chapter in cosmic history has opened'.[41] This creation of a new heavens and a new earth also demands a new humanity. God aims 'not simply to produce better men of the old kind but to produce a new kind of man,' Lewis wrote.[42] Life and death, then, are both part of the process by which we are to be re-made, through which, as Lewis described it in an article entitled *Man or Rabbit:* 'All the rabbit in us is to disappear – the worried, conscientious, ethical rabbit as well as the cowardly and sensual rabbit. We shall bleed and squeal as the handfuls of fur come out; and then, surprisingly, we shall find underneath it all a thing we have never yet imagined: a real man, an ageless god, a son of God, strong, radiant, wise, beautiful, and drenched in joy.'[43] Jesus meant what he said, contended Lewis: that those who put themselves into his hands will be made perfect as his heavenly Father is perfect: 'Perfect in love, wisdom, joy, beauty, and immortality. The change will not be completed in this life, for death is an important part of the treatment.'[44]

This idea that the transformation to perfection may well (and almost certainly must) continue beyond the grave opened Lewis up to the doctrine of purgatory. In *Letters to Malcolm* Lewis posed the problem:

> To pray for [the dead] presupposes that progress and difficulty are still possible. In fact, you are bringing in something like Purgatory.[45]

'Well, I suppose I am,' he concluded, but was then careful to distance himself from what he termed the 'Romish doctrine' rejected by the Protestant Reformation. Lewis perceived the late medieval and renaissance ideas of purgatory to be somehow at odds with authentic doctrine. As seen through the work of Dante, such a doctrine could be considered

---

[41] *Miracles*, p. 153.
[42] *Mere Christianity*, p. 178. Cf. Rv 21:1.
[43] C. S. Lewis, 'Man or Rabbit?' in *God in the Dock: Essays on Theology*, pp. 64–5.
[44] *Mere Christianity*, p. 171.
[45] *Letters to Malcolm*, pp. 103–4 (Letter 20).

'profoundly religious', as he noted in his study of English literature in the sixteenth century.[46] But Lewis was highly critical of the positions of both Thomas More and John Fisher who, he argued, over-stressed the nature of purgatorial suffering. Thomas More's presentation in his *Supplication of Souls* equated to nothing more than a temporary version of hell. John Fisher went even further, with his belief that purgatorial suffering actually blotted out the memory of God for the afflicted soul. The problem with these approaches, Lewis felt, was that 'the very etymology of the word *purgatory* has dropped out of sight. Its pains do not bring us nearer to God, but make us forget Him. It is a place not of purification but purely of retributive punishment.'[47] It ought to be stated here that, despite Lewis' understanding, the actual 'Romish doctrine' was somewhat more complex. Even by the sixteenth century the distinction between purgatory as a process of purification and purgatory as a means of satisfaction was less clear-cut than Lewis perhaps thought. Neuner and Dupuis have noted that by the mid-fifteenth century there was a careful balance being struck between 'the Western conception of satisfaction-expiation and the Oriental insistence on purification'. The Council of Florence, in its *Decree for the Greeks* in 1439, not only 'deliberately omits all allusion to fire and carefully avoids whatever could lead to the concept of purgatory as a place' but also stresses the cleansing purpose of any purgatorial penalties imposed as satisfaction for sins.[48] And it is striking that whilst the Council of Trent at its twenty-fifth session in 1563 did affirm the existence of purgatory, it markedly did not comment on its nature.[49]

---

[46] Cf. C. S. Lewis, *English Literature in the Sixteenth Century, Excluding Drama*, p. 163. This idea of the pain of purgation in Lewis' understanding is clarified by his notion of the relative value of pain. See *Letters of C.S. Lewis*, p. 418 (Letter dated 31 January 1952).

[47] *Letters to Malcolm*, p. 104 (Letter 20).

[48] J. Neuner and J. Dupuis *The Christian Faith*, p. 944. (n. 2308). Indeed, Lewis did concede that Fisher might not actually mean what he said: or, if he did mean it as presented, that it didn't necessarily do justice to true Catholic doctrine. See *English Literature in Sixteenth Century*, p. 163.

[49] Cf. Council of Trent, *Decree on Purgatory*, in J. Neuner and J. Dupuis, *The Christian Faith*, n. 2310.

One of theology's most remarkable presentations of purgatory, even to this day, comes from the visions of St Catherine of Genoa (1447–1510) and it is a presentation that contrasts sharply with those of More and Fisher. St Catherine's *Purgation and Purgatory*[50] describes the soul as voluntarily choosing purgatory so as to prepare itself fully for union with God. There is no sense of compulsion, except that of the beloved's compulsion in wanting to look her best for her lover. As the *Purgation* puts it:

> As for paradise, God has placed no doors there. Whoever wishes to enter, does so. All-merciful God stands there with His arms open, waiting to receive us into His glory. I also see, however, that the divine essence is so pure and light-filled – much more than we can imagine – that the soul that has but the slightest imperfection would rather throw itself into a thousand hells than appear thus before the divine presence.[51]

This position, notably one that contributed to the 'Romish doctrine' of the early renaissance period, is remarkably similar to Lewis'. The souls in purgatory endure suffering, certainly, but suffering understood as the pain of realising that something in them might be displeasing or unattractive to God. Again, as the *Purgation* notes:

> Not that those souls dwell on their suffering; they dwell rather on the resistance they feel in themselves against the will of God, against His intense and pure love bent on nothing but drawing them up to Him.[52]

In *Letters to Malcolm*, C. S. Lewis argued that the true Christian position on purgatory resurfaces from its Romish aberration of the renaissance period in John Henry Newman's *Dream of Gerontius*. 'There, if I remember rightly,' Lewis comments, 'the

---

[50] Sometimes known as the *Treatise on Purgatory*.
[51] Catherine of Genoa, *Purgation and Purgatory: The Spiritual Dialogue*, p. 78.
[52] Ibid. p. 79.

saved soul, at the very foot of the throne, begs to be taken away and cleansed. It cannot bear for a moment longer "With its darkness to affront that light." Religion has reclaimed Purgatory.'[53] One suspects the scholars might be right in their assumption that Newman's *Dream* has Catherine's *Purgation* as its inspiration.

It might seem surprising that Lewis, coming from a Reform tradition within Christianity, was prepared to accept purgatory at all. And yet there are a number of unavoidable references in his work. In a letter to an American lady, Lewis imagined purgatory to be a large kitchen in chaos. For women the challenge would be to leave things alone while for men it would be for them to do something about it.[54] In *A Grief Observed* Lewis speculated that the dead might need a time in which to mourn the living, in which they learn to let go of their loved ones living on this side of eternity. Perhaps this mourning period might be part and parcel of their purgatorial sufferings, Lewis mused.[55] In *Reflections on the Psalms*, Lewis suggested that purgatory might consist of having to hear our own voices; of finally being forced to listen to ourselves as we really are, rather than being allowed to go on clinging to the self-deluding images we carry around with us throughout our lives.[56] Another image that Lewis provided a number of times is the image of purgatory as being like the moment at the dentist when one comes to rinse out one's mouth. 'The rinsing may take longer than I can now imagine. The taste of this may be more fiery and astringent than my present sensibility could endure. But More and Fisher shall not persuade me that it will be disgusting and unhallowed,' as he wrote in *Letters to Malcolm*.[57] The adoption of this doctrine, it seems to me, is as much out of Lewis' personal experience as anything else. His instinctive prayer for the dead – 'The action is so spontaneous,

---

[53] *Letters to Malcolm*, p. 104 (Letter 20). Cf. John Henry Newman, *The Dream of Gerontius*, p. 68.
[54] Cf. *Letters to American Lady*, pp. 105–6 (Letter dated 31 July 1962).
[55] Cf. *A Grief Observed*, p. 43.
[56] Cf. *A Reflections on the Psalms*, p. 7.
[57] *Letters to Malcolm*, p. 105 (Letter 20). This image is also found in *Letters to American Lady*, p. 84 (Letter dated 7 July 1959) and *A Grief Observed*, p. 38.

so all but inevitable, that only the most compulsive theological case against it would deter me,'[58] he comments not long before he dies – and in particular his grief over the death of his wife, Joy, lead him to reflect more deeply on how God might be loving us into perfection. Of Joy's death (and, indeed, of his mother's) Lewis makes the comparison with a landfall rather than an arrival: the journey for them has still to be completed.[59] And, as he noted strongly in *Letters to Malcolm:* 'Our souls demand Purgatory, don't they? Would it not break our heart if God said to us, "It is true, my son, that your breath smells and your rags drip with mud and slime … Enter into the joy"? Should we not reply, 'With submission, sir, and if there is no objection, I'd rather be cleaned first.'"[60]

Perhaps Lewis' most powerful representation of purgatory is to be found in his short story, *The Great Divorce.* Here Lewis portrayed a grey town existing in what seems like perpetual twilight (although a rumour abounds that nightfall may come at any moment) and populated by shadowy, argumentative ghosts. It stretches out for millions of miles because its inhabitants continually squabble and move to live in newer and empty streets, further and further away from one another and from the only bus stop from which they can (should they so choose) travel to heaven. The realisation that what the reader (and narrator) had assumed was hell might be something else comes about in a dialogue with a heavenly George MacDonald. Having discussed the possibility of the damned making the trip to heaven, the dialogue continued:

> If they leave that grey town behind it will not have been Hell. To any that leaves it, it is Purgatory. And perhaps ye had better not call this country Heaven. Ye can call it the Valley of the Shadow of Life. And yet to those who stay here it will have been Heaven from the first.[61]

It is important to realise here that Lewis is not introducing the notion of free human choice after death. A close reading of the

[58] *Letters to Malcolm,* p. 103 (Letter 20).
[59] Cf. *A Grief Observed,* p. 30.
[60] *Letters to Malcolm,* pp. 104–5 (Letter 20).
[61] C. S. Lewis, *The Great Divorce: A Dream,* p. 61.

text shows that purgatory is not presented as a time of indecision in which the soul is invited to decide definitively for or against God and beatific vision. Prior to the publication of *The Great Divorce* in 1946 Lewis had already noted: 'Finality must come some time, and it does not require a very robust faith to believe that omniscience knows when.'[62] In the imagery of *The Great Divorce*, then, for those souls who are saved the journey

[62] *The Problem of Pain*, p. 102. Lewis refers to limbo in this passage but does not expand his thinking on the idea here. There are other references to the subject in his work (see C. S. Lewis, *Screwtape Proposes a Toast and Other Pieces*, pp. 5, 7 and *Letters of C. S. Lewis*, pp. 318–19 (Letter dated 5 April 1939)). From these sparse references it can be concluded that Lewis was thinking of the technical theological understanding of limbo as a place of natural beatitude. He does not concern himself at all with the issue of infant limbo and it seems unlikely that this concept played any serious part in his eschatological worldview. *The Catechism of the Catholic Church*, whilst acknowledging that 'the Church does not know of any means other than Baptism that assures entry into eternal beatitude,' nevertheless asserts: 'God has bound salvation to the sacrament of Baptism, but he himself is not bound by his sacraments.' Thus, 'as regards children who have died without Baptism, the Church can only entrust them to the mercy of God'. Moreover, 'The great mercy of God who desires that all men should be saved, and Jesus' tenderness toward children . . . allow us to hope that there is a way of salvation for children who have died without Baptism.' Interestingly the Catechism makes no mention of infant limbo. Cf. *The Catechism of Catholic Church*, pp. 1257, 1261. Of what is sometimes called the 'Limbo of the Fathers', the Catechism – whilst not using the term – acknowledges that prior to the death and resurrection of Christ the term hell (*Sheol* in Hebrew and *Hades* in Greek) is used to describe the destiny of all the dead 'who are deprived of the vision of God'. Such is the case 'whether evil or righteous, while they await the Redeemer'. The descent of Christ into hell is 'The last phase of Jesus' messianic mission, a phase which is condensed in time but vast in its real significance: the spread of Christ's redemptive work to all men of all times and all places, for all who are saved have been made sharers in the redemption.' Cf. ibid. pp. 633, 634, 635. For a fuller treatment of the theological concept of limbo see Zachary Hayes, 'Limbo', in J. Komonchak, M. Collins, and D. Lane, *Dictionary of Theology*, pp. 585–6. Perhaps it should also be noted that, as Hayes points out, 'the hierarchical Magisterium has offered no clear, definitive position on the matter of limbo' and that 'In a number of very recent discussions of eschatology by some greatly respected theologians, the question of limbo is not brought up. This is the case with Schmaus, Ratzinger, Vorgrimler, and Nocke.' See Zachary Hayes, *Visions of a Future: A Study of Christian Eschatology*, p. 120.

from the self-obsessive grey town, the pain of encountering the solidity of the real country, the assistance and persuasion of the saints sent to meet them, and their final journey into the mountains of deep heaven are all parts of the process by which they are gradually being made ready for their eternal destiny. Purgatory prepares and purifies them for the beatific vision. For the damned, however, even though they may make the trip to the Valley of the Shadow of Life, they will inevitably find only suffering and disappointment and will return to the town of shadows to live in abject isolation: all of their experiences will be hell. As Lewis said at the end of *The Great Divorce:* within time there are possibilities and 'the choice of ways is before you. Any man may choose eternal death. Those who choose it will have it'. But in eternity 'there are no more possibilities left but only the Real'.[63] We are back to the Lewisian concept of perfection: the need to be remade into a new kind of man. At death the myriad choices we have made will crystallise to form our fundamental choice: we have either chosen to allow God to love us as he wills, or we have not. Purgatory, far from being any process of additional choice on our part, is rather the painful procedure by which we give up self-love and let God love us more: the method by which we are re-made and in which heaven is allowed to grow within us. It is the time when 'the tiresome business of adjusting the rival claims of Self and God' will be dissipated 'by the simple expedient of rejecting the claims of Self altogether', the final stage in our development when 'the old egoistic will has been turned round, reconditioned, and made into a new thing'.[64] Unsurprisingly, it is in keeping with Lewis' distaste for the retributive visions of purgatory presented by More and Fisher that he emphasises the process as a purification from, rather than a satisfaction for, sins.

Judgement and Morality

In *Screwtape Proposes a Toast,* a short follow-up article to his famous and very successful *Screwtape Letters,* C. S. Lewis attacked what he regarded as the dumbing down and levelling

---

[63] *The Great Divorce,* pp. 114–15.
[64] C. S. Lewis, 'Three Kinds of Men', in *Compelling Reason,* p. 31.

out of human living, such as would produce a society of moral mediocrity. 'What I want to fix your attention on,' he wrote, 'is the vast, overall movement towards the discrediting, and finally the elimination, of every kind of human excellence – moral, cultural, social, or intellectual.'[65] And it is interesting that Lewis chose to make this social critique within the context of our eternal destiny. The problem Lewis felt he was witnessing was the discouragement of individuality. This reluctance to be an individual, he believed, meant that for some people 'their consciousness hardly exists apart from the social atmosphere that surrounds them'.[66] And whereas great sinners, albeit egotistic individuals, were at least capable of genuine guilt and heart-felt repentance, the conformist was far more likely to allow 'a hard, tight, settled core of resolution to go on being what it is' to form at the centre of his being.[67] The real issue with such mediocrity was that God does not call us to be mediocre. The eschatological implications of such a social critique are important for our understanding of the Lewisian position on judgement. Lewis posited an intrinsic unity between moral action in this life and personal judgement in death. All moral actions (and, indeed, inaction) not only reflect our free choices as lived out here and now, but also point to and make present the ontological and eternal choice that we have been granted by our creator. In time, then, we see freedom as the right to choose from any number of actions: we can do this rather than that. In moral terminology we might say: we do right rather than wrong (or vice versa). However, Lewis argued that freedom is actually an ontological category: it is the freedom to be. And so the free choices we perceive ourselves as undertaking in time are actually a reflection (or projection) of the creature we choose to be. As Lewis pointed out in *Mere Christianity:*

> People often think of Christian morality as a kind of bargain in which God says, 'If you keep a lot of rules I'll reward you, and if you don't I'll do the other thing.' I do

---

[65] *Screwtape Proposes a Toast*, p. 12.
[66] Ibid. p. 5.
[67] Ibid. pp. 6, 13.

not think that is the best way of looking at it. I would much rather say that every time you make a choice you are turning the central part of you, the part that chooses, into something a little different from what it was before. And taking your life as a whole, with all your innumerable choices, all your life long you are slowly turning this central thing into a heavenly creature or into a hellish creature.[68]

The danger with this concept, of course, in that it could be interpreted as Pelagian: that we choose to become heavenly or demonic entities entirely by ourselves. This would be a misreading of Lewis' position. Lewis is clear that human freedom is always to be understood in relation to God and divine freedom. If we choose to be God's creatures, allowing him to love us and forgive us as he wills, then his love and forgiveness will indeed transform and perfect us. However, if we choose to deny our creatureliness before God, and if we reject his freely offered love and forgiveness, then we choose a self-contradiction and condemn ourselves to an eternity of frustration and unhappiness. As Hans Urs Von Balthasar once put it: 'If created freedom chooses itself as the absolute good, it involves itself in a contradiction that will devour it: the formal object that informs it – which is in fact absolute, self-positing freedom – is in constant contradiction with the finite freedom's pretentious claim to be infinite. This contradiction, if persisted in, is hell.'[69] Within this concept, then, personal judgement undertakes the function not so much of an extrinsic sentence passed upon us by a just judge, rewarding or punishing our actions in this life, but rather of an infallible verdict on what each one of us has become.

One consequence of this idea is that it counters the protest against a moralistic or moralising Christianity. 'The holiness of God is something more and other than moral perfection,' Lewis once wrote. On the other hand, it also affirms that although 'God may be more than moral goodness: He is not

---

[68] *Mere Christianity*, p. 76.
[69] Hans Urs Von Balthasar, *Theo-Drama: Theological Dramatic Theory*, Volume 5: *The Last Act*, p. 301.

less. The road to the promised land runs past Sinai.'[70] As Lewis said elsewhere: 'Christianity … leads you on, out of all that [morality], into something beyond. One has a glimpse of a country where they do not talk of such things, except perhaps as a joke.'[71] The moral order, rather than being the observance of an ethical code, is actually about becoming the type of individual God wants us to be. It has an ontological and eschatological function. 'We might think that God wanted simple obedience to a set of rules,' Lewis noted, 'whereas He really wants people of a particular sort.'[72] This notion is summed up well in the character of Emeth in *The Last Battle*. Emeth (whose name means 'Truth') encounters Aslan beyond the stable door and at first assumes he will be condemned for his life-long discipleship to the Calormene god, Tash. To his surprise, however, Aslan welcomes him into his country and calls him son. Although Emeth's religious belief system was wrong (following the false god, Tash) nevertheless his value system was entirely right. He was on the road to Aslan's country all along without ever realising it; he was becoming the sort of creature that Aslan intended him to be.

A second consequence of Lewis' moral eschatology is that it presents personal judgement essentially as self-judgement. Writing about Milton's presentation of Satan in his epic poem, *Paradise Lost*, Lewis observed: '[Satan] has wished to "be himself," and to be in himself and for himself, and his wish has been granted.'[73] Similarly, although this time the subject is not Satan but a fictional figure, 'X', Lewis noted: 'You see clearly enough that nothing, not even God with all His power, can make "X" really happy as long as "X" remains envious, self-centred, and spiteful.' Lewis continued, directing the narrative towards his readers:

> Be sure there is something inside you which, unless it is altered, will put it out of God's power to prevent your

---

[70] *The Problem of Pain*, p. 49.
[71] *Mere Christianity*, p. 124.
[72] Ibid. p. 66.
[73] C. S. Lewis, *A Preface to Paradise Lost*, p. 102.

being eternally miserable. While that something remains there can be no Heaven for you, just as there can be no sweet smells for a man with a cold in the nose, and no music for a man who is deaf. It's not a question of God 'sending' us to Hell. In each of us there is something growing up which will of itself *be Hell* unless it is nipped in the bud.[74]

Thus Lewis was able to say that hell is firmly locked but on the inside, and that one can't be *sent* to hell, one takes oneself there.[75] This aspect of self-judgement interlinked, as it is, with human freedom explains Lewis' suspicion of the universalist position. This argues that everyone (eventually), through God's goodness and mercy, will be saved – even the vilest and most unrepentant of sinners.[76] 'I would pay any price to be able to say truthfully "All will be saved"', Lewis argued, 'but my reason retorts, "Without their will, or with it?" If I say "Without their will", I at once perceive a contradiction; how can the supreme voluntary act of self-surrender be involuntary? If I say "With their will", my reason replies "How if they will not give in?"'[77] In other words, if a man refuses to allow God to transform him

[74] C. S. Lewis, 'The Trouble with X', in *God in the Dock*, pp. 70–1.
[75] Cf. *Preface to Paradise Lost*, p. 105; *The Problem of Pain*, p. 104; C. S. Lewis, *The Dark Tower and Other Stories*, p. 37.
[76] Note that at the end of *The Great Divorce* Lewis the narrator raises the subject with the heavenly George MacDonald, who was a famous proponent of the belief. In the text, Lewis leaves the question open, although there is the warning that the doctrines of universal salvation and predestination both carry the price of 'removing Freedom which is the deeper truth'. See *The Great Divorce*, pp. 114–15. The belief in universal salvation is not to be confused with the theory of *apokatastasis* condemned by an edict of Emperor Justinian and subsequently promulgated by the Synod of Constantinople in 543. Generally associated with Origen and later followers (although Dermot Lane notes that it 'can be found in varying degrees in Gregory of Nazianzen and Gregory of Nyssa') *apokatastasis* refers to 'a complete restoration' of demons and impious human beings at the end of time. See J. Neuner and J. Dupuis, *The Catholic Faith*, n. 2301 and D. Lane, 'Eschatology', p. 333. I shall return to this issue in a later chapter.
[77] *The Problem of Pain*, p. 97.

into a saint, how can he then become a saint? There is no question of God lacking mercy here. 'Honest rejection of Christ, however mistaken, will be forgiven and healed,' argued Lewis.[78] But if 'the happiness of a creature lies in self-surrender, no one can make that surrender but himself ... and he may refuse'.[79]

Heaven

'We are very shy nowadays of even mentioning heaven,' Lewis wrote in *The Problem of Pain*. 'We are afraid of the jeer about "pie in the sky", and of being told that we are trying to "escape" from the duty of making a happy world here and now into dreams of a happy world elsewhere. But either there is "pie in the sky" or there is not. If there is not, then Christianity is false, for this doctrine is woven into its whole fabric.'[80] Certainly heaven was a doctrine that was tightly woven into the fabric of Lewis' own worldview and one aim of his apologetics at least was to correct certain misapprehensions and misunderstandings concerning this subject. One example of this was his defence of the use of traditional imagery in describing the felicities of heaven. In *Miracles* Lewis distinguished four meanings of the word heaven: God himself, the beatific vision, the communion of the saints, and the sky or universe in which the earth exists. He argued that the New Testament writers' idea of heaven would have included all these meanings in an undifferentiated form. Their use of language shifted easily between the literal and the metaphorical. 'A man who really believes that "Heaven" is in the sky,' wrote C. S. Lewis, 'may well have a far truer and more spiritual conception of it than many a modern logician who could expose that fallacy with a few strokes of his pen.'[81] In an article responding to J. A. T. Robinson's position, which had challenged the traditional

---

[78] 'Man or Rabbit?' p. 63.
[79] *The Problem of Pain*, pp. 96–7.
[80] Ibid. pp. 119–20.
[81] *Miracles*, pp. 166–7.

imagery of God, Lewis wrote: 'We have long abandoned belief in a God who sits on a throne in a localized Heaven.'[82] Nevertheless, he felt it was not merely appropriate and acceptable but actually essential to use metaphorical language concerning God. Scriptural imagery is necessarily the symbolic attempt to express the inexpressible, he argued in *Letters to Malcolm*. The people who take such symbols literally 'might as well think that when Christ told us to be like doves, He meant that we were to lay eggs'. Yet these things 'not only cannot be asserted – they cannot even be presented for discussion – without metaphor'.[83] The point, then, is not to replace the analogy with an abstraction, but to ensure that the analogy is informed by the abstraction while the abstraction is enriched by the analogy. This interest in metaphor and language will be examined in more detail in later chapters but, as Lewis pointed out, 'Christianity claims to be telling us about another world, about something behind the world we can touch and hear and see,'[84] and either we accept that claim or we don't; but if we don't we have abandoned Christianity.

Heaven and Earth

Broadly speaking we can identify three major strands to the Lewisian picture of heaven. The first is the understanding that heaven is both the ground and goal of human existence. We see this idea most clearly in *The Problem of Pain* where Lewis presented the topic of a personal beatitude. 'Your soul,' he argued, 'has a curious shape because it is a hollow made to fit a particular swelling in the infinite contours of the Divine substance.'

> God will look to every soul like its first love because He is its first love. Your place in heaven will seem to be made for you and you alone, because you were made for it – made for it stitch by stitch as a glove is made for a hand.[85]

[82] C. S. Lewis, 'Must our Image of God Go?' in *God in the Dock*, p. 78.
[83] *Letters to Malcolm*, pp. 113–14 (Letter 22).
[84] *Mere Christianity*, p. 129.
[85] *The Problem of Pain*, p. 122.

This emphasis allowed Lewis to suggest that each of the saved 'shall forever know and praise some one aspect of the Divine beauty better than any other creature can'. For, as Lewis queried, 'Why else were individuals created, but that God, loving all infinitely, should love each differently?' One danger present in this particular approach is that it could tend to undermine the Christian concept of the communion of saints; that it privatises heaven, if you like, into a purely personal encounter with God. But, for Lewis, exactly the opposite was the case. A true communion of saints demands true individuality so that each soul can contribute something of its own. 'If all experienced God in the same way and returned Him an identical worship, the song of the Church triumphant would have no symphony,' Lewis reasoned; 'it would be like an orchestra in which all the instruments played the same note.'[86] This presentation of paradise as our eternal destiny is echoed in the many references of Lewis to 'another country' or our 'home country'. It is a particularly strong theme in the Narnia Chronicles and underscored by the character of Reepicheep, the valiant mouse in *The Voyage of the Dawn Treader* whose whole outlook is coloured by his desire to arrive at Aslan's Country.[87] But we find the motif of heaven as our ground and goal elsewhere too. In a letter to Don Luigi Pedrollo in 1954 Lewis passed on his condolences at the death of his erstwhile correspondent, Don Giovanni Calabria, and noted that Calabria had now 'happily passed over into his own Country'.[88] In an essay entitled, *On Living in an Atomic Age*, Lewis commented: 'We are strangers here. We come from somewhere else. Nature is not the only thing that exists. There is "another world" and that is where we come from.'[89] Given this sort of language, it is unsurprising to find that Lewis appears at times to be slightly disparaging about our earthly existence. In an increasingly secular world (and in,

---

[86] Ibid. p. 124.
[87] Cf. C. S. Lewis, *The Voyage of the Dawn Treader*, p. 162.
[88] C. S. Lewis, *The Latin Letters of C. S. Lewis: C. S. Lewis and Don Giovanni Calabria*, p. 99 (Letter dated 16 December 1954).
[89] C. S. Lewis, 'On Living in an Atomic Age', in *Compelling Reason*, p. 120.

arguably, an increasingly secularised Church) Lewis was keen to dismiss the idea of earthly utopias in favour of stressing the idea of the transcendent.[90]

The second strand in the Lewisian concept of heaven is the understanding of the beatific vision in terms of glorious consummation. In his sermon, *The Weight of Glory*, Lewis had again spoken of a desire for 'our own far-off country', a desire that expressed the reality that we 'are made for heaven'.[91] But in this text Lewis expanded his thinking to speculate about what that personal beatitude might entail. His starting point was the imagery of the New Testament and he began by delineating five basic types of scriptural promise concerning heaven. First, that the saved shall be with Christ; second, that the saved shall be like Christ; third, that the saved shall have glory; fourth, that the saved shall be feasted at a banquet; and fifth, that the saved shall have positions of heavenly power and influence.[92] Lewis was keen to note that this variety of celestial assurance was simply an attempt to say the same thing in a number of ways. 'Lest we should imagine the joy of his presence too exclusively in terms of our present poor experience of personal love,' he wrote, 'a dozen changing images, correcting and relieving each other, are supplied.'[93] Lewis then turned his attention towards the biblical notion of glory. Glory, he noted, made him think of either fame or luminosity. The former seems rather competitive while the latter raised the question: 'Who wishes to become a kind of living electric light bulb?'[94] In the course of his argument, though, Lewis took up both suggestions, proposing a heaven of iridescent splendour in which the saved bask in and reflect the divine approval of their creator. 'To please God,' Lewis explained, 'to be a real ingredient in the divine happiness ... to be loved by God, not merely pitied, but delighted in as an artist delights in his work or a father in a son', such is the weight of glory and our eternal destiny.[95]

---

[90] Cf. *The Problem of Pain*, pp. 92–3 and C. S. Lewis, *The Four Loves*, p. 132.
[91] 'The Weight of Glory', p. 28.
[92] Cf. ibid. p. 31.
[93] Ibid. p. 32.
[94] Ibid. pp. 32–3.
[95] Ibid. p. 34.

The third strand of Lewis' thought concerns the metaphysical proposition that heaven represents ultimate reality.
Interestingly, this idea is most prevalent not in any detailed
philosophical argument on Lewis' part but in a piece of speculative fantasy. In *The Great Divorce* Lewis used rich imagery to
make the point that what is heavenly is, of its essence, far
greater, much bigger, and more intense than any possible
finite reality. The contrast between the solid figures of heaven
and the ghosts of the grey town, whose feet are cut to pieces by
the very grass of the valley of the shadow of life, is just one
example. In *Miracles* Lewis had argued, 'The ultimate spiritual
reality is not vaguer, more inert, more transparent than the
images, but more positive, more dynamic, more opaque.'[96]
This was in reference to Old Testament imagery. In *The Great
Divorce* he was making the same point by contrasting finite
reality with the infinite. It is a metaphysical position that he
returned to again and again. In *Miracles* Lewis argued: 'Body
and personality are the real negatives – they are what is left of
positive being when it is sufficiently diluted to appear in
temporal or finite forms.'[97] And in his sermon entitled,
Transposition, he explained the position by the analogy of a boy
born in a dungeon whose mother attempts to teach him about
the world outside. With the aid of a pencil and paper his
mother tries to explain to him what the world of freedom is
like. But the boy gets confused and imagines reality to have a
pencil outline. To imagine reality without the pencil lines is to
imagine something somehow less.[98] Our earthly experiences,
then, are only a shadow of that heavenly reality for which we
are destined. It was in this context that Aslan in the Narnia
Chronicles referred to the 'Shadowlands'.[99]

Heaven and Hell

'If we insist on keeping Hell (or even earth),' wrote Lewis, 'we
shall not see Heaven: if we accept Heaven we shall not be able

[96] *Miracles*, pp. 95–6.
[97] Ibid. p. 95.
[98] Cf. C. S. Lewis, 'Transposition', in *The Weight of Glory*, p. 85.
[99] *The Last Battle*, p. 171.

to retain even the smallest and most intimate souvenirs of Hell.' Lewis made this claim in his preface to *The Great Divorce* in response to what he saw as the perennial attempt to wed heaven to hell – an attempt drawing on the mistaken premise that 'reality never presents us with an absolutely unavoidable "either-or."'[100] In Lewisian eschatology it is important to grasp that hell is an entirely parasitical concept. Even what we postulate about perdition is dependent upon our understanding of redemption and beatific vision. For example, if heaven is understood as the richness of variety, then hell is sheer monotony.[101] If heaven is full of music and silence, then hell contains sheer noise.[102] If heaven is celestial joy, then hell is humourless austerity.[103] If heaven is a communion in which true individuality flourishes, then hell is the destructive and devouring competitiveness of ego.[104] If, in heaven, ownership is forbidden and each soul is to be 'engaged in giving away to all the rest that which it receives', then hell is 'but the obverse of the self-giving which is absolute reality', a 'fierce imprisonment in self'.[105]

'The Dominical utterances about Hell,' argued Lewis, 'are addressed to the conscience and will, not to our intellectual curiosity.'[106] Karl Rahner expressed a similar point when he wrote: 'What Scripture says about hell is to be interpreted in keeping with its literary character of "threat-discourse" and hence not to be read as a preview of something which will exist some day.'[107] In other words, they function as stark warnings to make us repent rather than tell us details about what it might actually be like. Nevertheless, in *The Problem of Pain* Lewis did attempt to furnish us with at least three points concerning eternal perdition. Firstly, as has already been discussed in the context of judgement, hell is to be seen not as

[100] Cf. *The Great Divorce*, pp. 7–8.
[101] Cf. *Letters to Malcolm*, p. 8 (Letter 2).
[102] C. S. Lewis, *The Screwtape Letters*, p. 87 (Letter 22).
[103] Ibid. pp. 41–2 (Letter 11).
[104] Ibid. pp. 69–70 (Letter 18).
[105] *The Problem of Pain*, pp. 126–7.
[106] Ibid. p. 97.
[107] Karl Rahner, 'Hell', in *Encyclopedia of Theology*, p. 603.

a sentence imposed in punishment but rather as a verdict of what someone has become – or, perhaps, degenerated into. Secondly, hell is not a place as such but rather a state of sub-humanity. The damned has become an 'ex-man' precisely because its will is entirely centred on itself and it has lost control of its passions. It is nothing more than a collection of 'mutually antagonistic sins rather than a sinner'. [108] And finally, hell is not symmetrical to heaven. Perdition is not to be endured in the same way as heaven is to be enjoyed.[109] In *The Pilgrim's Regress* Lewis depicted hell as not purely the self-inflicted destiny of obstinate will but also as a sort of 'tourniquet', a final act of mercy on behalf of God to prevent the lost soul from eternally bleeding to 'a death she never reached'. As Lewis explained:

> [God] has put into the world a Worst Thing. But evil of itself would never reach a worst ... if it could, it would be no longer evil: for Form and Limit belong to the good. [Hell is] the tourniquet on the wound through which the lost soul else would bleed to a death she never reached.[110]

The purpose of these three points is, of course, to stress once again the absolute divorce – even at the level of ontological reality – of heaven and hell. As Lewis said, '[Hell] is in no sense *parallel* to heaven: it is "the darkness outside", the outer rim where being fades away into nonentity.'[111] The fictional speculation of *The Great Divorce* sums up better what Lewis has tried to say. Already I have commented on the difference between the solid realities of heaven as compared to the shadowy transparencies of the grey town. But, towards the end of the story, this difference is explored further and made more explicit.

---

[108] *The Problem of Pain*, p. 103. In *Perelandra* the hero of the story, Ransom, begins to refer to Weston as 'Un-man' because he has opened himself up to the evil influence and power of the Bent One and is now so unlike what one could call a man. Cf. C. S. Lewis, *Perelandra: A Novel*, pp. 110, 122.

[109] Cf. *The Problem of Pain*, p. 104.

[110] *Pilgrim's Regress*, p. 229.

[111] *The Problem of Pain*, p. 104.

Hell is 'smaller than one pebble of your earthly world', we are told. If a heavenly butterfly were to swallow hell and everything in it, it would have no taste. And if all the 'angers, hatreds, envies, and itchings' of perdition were put together and weighed against the least moment of heavenly joy, it would register no weight at all.[112] Although Lewis once asserted, 'I have met no people who fully disbelieved in Hell and also had a living and life-giving belief in Heaven,'[113] nevertheless he also insisted: 'We know much more about heaven than hell, for heaven is the home of humanity and therefore contains all that is implied in a glorified human life: but hell was not made for men.'[114]

The Parousia

In his essay, *The World's Last Night*, C. S. Lewis commented on some of the reasons for the apparent neglect of the doctrine of Christ's Second Coming amongst modern Christians: a reaction to previous over-apocalyptic emphases; an uneasiness about its apparent incongruence with certain evolutionary ideas; a distaste for a doctrine that proclaims the end of known existence. 'Yet it seems to me impossible,' he argued, 'to retain in any recognisable form our belief in the Divinity of Christ and the truth of Christian revelation while abandoning, or even persistently neglecting, the promised, threatened, Return.'[115] Certainly the doctrine has always held a central place in Christian theology and numerous commentators have noted how the Early Church was preoccupied with its imminence. However, Zachary Hayes has commented that it would be a send-up of early Christianity to regard the community as some sort of apocalyptic band waiting for the end of the world. He points to the Early Church's missionary zeal and the lack of a timeline for Christ's return as evidence of a more sophisti-

---

[112] Cf. *The Great Divorce,* p. 113.
[113] *Letters to Malcolm,* p. 73 (Letter 14).
[114] *The Problem of Pain,* p. 104.
[115] *The World's Last Night and Other Essays,* p. 93.

cated approach.[116] Karl Rahner defined the parousia as, 'The permanent blessed presence of Christ in the manifest finality of the history of the world and of salvation which is perfected and ended in the destiny of Jesus Christ.'[117] The important aspect of this definition is that it stresses the ongoing presence of Christ in our present time. The danger with talk of a First and Second Coming is the implication (at least at the imaginative level) that Christ has, in the meantime, gone away. Zachary Hayes comments on Rahner's position:

> In reality, the parousia emphasizes the saving presence of Christ to history ... In short, it symbolizes the consummation of history in God. It is in no way contrary to the scriptures or the official teaching of the magisterium when K. Rahner suggests that the parousia is better thought of as the world finally coming to Christ rather than as Christ returning to the world.[118]

Jürgen Moltmann similarly tackles this problem by distinguishing between three modes of Christ's presence: in the flesh, in the Spirit, and in glory. Only Christ's coming in glory is rendered by the term, parousia, which is the consummation of the other modes of presence. 'To translate *parousia* as "coming again" or "second coming" is wrong,' he argues, 'because that presupposes a temporary absence.'[119] In Lewis' thought we find the idea of the Second Coming as both an intervention and as a consummation. In *The World's Last Night* Lewis warned of 'a sudden, violent end imposed from without; an extinguisher popped onto the candle, a brick flung at the gramophone, a curtain rung down on the play – "Halt!"'[120] In this text Lewis' aim was apologetic and moralistic. He was attempting to defend and present the Christian faith and to make people think seriously about how they lived their lives.

---

116 Zachary Hayes, 'Parousia', in J. Komonchak, M. Collins, and D. Lane, *Dictionary of Theology*, p. 743.
117 Karl Rahner, 'Parousia', p. 1158.
118 Zachary Hayes, 'Parousia', p. 743.
119 Jürgen Moltmann, *The Coming of God*, pp. 25–6.
120 'The World's Last Night', pp. 100–1.

The dogma of the Second Coming is meaningless, he argued, if it does not raise in us the question: What if tonight is the world's last?[121] Elsewhere, however, he is not bound by such concerns. In *The Last Battle* Lewis depicted Narnian history as having reached a decisive crunch-point: who *is* Aslan? It is the question at the centre of the fierce battle around the stable door; it has been the essential question throughout the Chronicles; it is the very question used as the only criteria when Aslan finally arrives to judge. Aslan's parousia, then, is one of consummation. Of course intervention and consummation are not mutually exclusive. God's divine intervention in human history is precisely what brings that history to its consummation. And, as Lewis noted, God has already decisively intervened in the incarnation.[122] The parousia, then, is to be understood as the cosmic consummation of that historical intervention.

The Parousia and the General Resurrection

'Cosmological, biological, and physical speculations inquiring into the possibility of a resurrection,' argues Joseph Ratzinger, 'are not dealing with an object proper to their disciplines and are thus meaningless.'[123] It is a point similarly made by Lewis. 'We are not, in this doctrine, concerned … with waves and atoms and all that,' he noted in *Letters to Malcolm*.[124] Rather we are dealing with the metaphysical implications of Christ's resurrection and his offer of new life. As Ratzinger points out, 'The resurrection of Jesus became the guarantee and starting-point of the resurrection of Christians … He who belongs to the body of Christ is already encompassed in the sphere of the resurrection and by his participation in this body takes part in the resurrection of Jesus, in which death is conquered for him.'[125] In Lewisian terminology, the doctrine concerns the

---

[121] Cf. ibid. p. 109.
[122] Cf. *Miracles,* p. 113.
[123] Joseph Ratzinger, 'Resurrection', in K. Rahner, *Encyclopedia of Theology,* p. 1453.
[124] *Letters to Malcolm,* p. 115 (Letter 22).
[125] J. Ratzinger, 'Resurrection', p. 1452.

final implications for having become 'new men'. Christ, risen from the dead, is the blueprint for this new humanity. Not only is he the forerunner of our own resurrection but it is his risen life which will call us from our graves. Christ 'is the origin and centre and life of all new men', as Lewis put it in *Mere Christianity*.[126] This idea of the general resurrection as a consummation of Christ's resurrection is essential to Christian theology and is why the general resurrection is understood as being intrinsically linked to judgement and the parousia. As Ratzinger says of the evangelist John: 'He sees in Christ not only the resurrection, but also the judgement.'[127] In *Miracles* Lewis outlined some of the reasoning behind this Christian assertion. Jesus' own resurrection, he argued, was interpreted by the Early Church within the context of the Judaic belief in the 'Day of the Lord' – indeed, Lewis postulated that this was the only possible category within which the disciples could make sense of what had happened. This belief taught that there would come a time when peace would be brought to Israel and through them to the rest of the world. On that day, 'the righteous dead ... would come back to earth – not as floating wraiths but as solid men who cast shadows in the sunlight and made a noise when they trampled the floors.'[128] The Early Church, postulated Lewis, presented Christ's resurrection from the dead and ascension into heaven as the first movement in the advent of that Day. Thus at the end of time, with the parousia, the process of new life which had begun in Christ would be completed and all those who belonged to him would share in a general resurrection, signifying the establishment of God's reign without any further ambiguity. However, the disciples' experience of the resurrection of Jesus was far more than merely the experience of meeting someone who has come back from the dead. As Lewis pointed out: 'A wholly new mode of being has arisen in the universe.'[129] Therefore the general resurrection was also to be understood in terms of this new

---

126 *Mere Christianity*, p. 182.
127 J. Ratzinger, 'Resurrection', p. 1452.
128 *Miracles*, p. 154.
129 Ibid. p. 156.

mode of being and the consummation of God's kingdom to be understood in terms of the creation of a new heavens and a new earth. But, as Lewis warned: 'We know and can know very little about the New Nature.'[130] Nevertheless, Lewis did give himself over to speculation about what the general resurrection might entail and we find some interesting ideas in *Letters to Malcolm*. Here, once again, Lewis refuted any notion that the resurrection was merely a resuscitated corpse. 'What the soul cries out for,' he reflected, 'is the resurrection of the senses. Even in this life matter would be nothing to us if it were not the source of sensations.' He expanded this idea with the analogy of the memory, by which we 'already have some feeble and intermittent power of raising dead sensations from their graves'. Lewis argued that at the resurrection all our sense experiences are not merely restored but rather transfigured, such that 'Memory as we now know it is a dim foretaste, a mirage even, of a power which the soul, or rather Christ in the soul ... will exercise hereafter.'[131] The following example makes the point clearer:

> I can now communicate to you the vanished fields of my boyhood ... only imperfectly by words. Perhaps the day is coming when I can take you for a walk through them.[132]

Of course the danger with this speculation is that Lewis, who in *Miracles* was so keen to affirm the corporeality of resurrection, has simply offered a dream world.[133] It was a danger that he was aware of himself. As he tried to explain:

---

[130] Ibid. p.162.

[131] *Letters to Malcolm*, p. 115 (Letter 22).

[132] Ibid.

[133] Ibid. p. 117. Cf. *Miracles*, p. 162. It is significant that the Catechism adopts Tertullian's adage, 'The flesh is the hinge of salvation.' As it says: 'We believe in God who is creator of the flesh; we believe in the Word made flesh in order to redeem the flesh; we believe in the resurrection of the flesh, the fulfilment of both the creation and the redemption of the flesh.' See *Catechism of Catholic Church*, p. 1015. Cf. Tertullian, *De resurrectione*, 8, 2. Lewis adopts this Tertullian line in *Mere Christianity*, with his robust defence of corporeality. See *Mere Christianity*, p. 81.

At present we tend to think of the soul as somehow
'inside' the body. But the glorified body of the resurrection as I conceive it – the sensuous life raised from its
death – will be inside the soul. As God is not inside space
but space is in God.[134]

The world of our present experience, Lewis argued – and here
I think it is important to distinguish his use of the word 'experience' from his understanding of objective reality – is
dependent upon sense perception and cognition. Matter enters
the realm of our experience only through our perceiving it or
our understanding it. This, Lewis termed, 'becoming soul'. At
our resurrection that matter which has 'become soul' will be
raised and glorified.

Arguably Lewis' explanation raises more problems than it
solves. What does Lewis mean by matter becoming soul? And
isn't his assertion, 'Through the sense-bodies of the redeemed
the whole New Earth will arise'[135] in danger of being interpreted as the glorification of a collection of subjective human
experiences? However, what is significant here is Lewis'
genuine attempt to express an intrinsic unity of body and soul
in the resurrection. There is, he was aware, the imaginative
temptation always to consider the resurrection as nothing more
than human souls being re-vested with re-created versions
(albeit, spectacular ones) of their earthly bodies.

In other works Lewis remained on less speculative and
therefore somewhat safer ground. For example, in *Miracles* he
wrote: 'Those who attain the glorious resurrection will see the
dry bones clothed again with flesh, the fact and the myth
remarried, the literal and the metaphorical rushing
together.'[136] And, in correction of a popular misconception of
the word, 'spiritual' as meaning 'a life without space, without
history, without environment, with no sensuous elements in
it'.[137] Lewis noted:

134 *Letters to Malcolm*, pp. 115–16 (Letter 22).
135 Ibid. p. 116 (Letter 22).
136 *Miracles*, p. 170. Cf. Ezk 37:4–10.
137 *Miracles*, p. 155. In his Space Trilogy Lewis gave an example of
    such a typical misconception in the person of Jane Studdock. See
    That Hideous Strength, p. 315.

We must, indeed, believe the risen body to be extremely different from the mortal body: but the existence, in that new state, of anything that could be described as 'body' at all involves some sort of spatial relations and in the long run a whole new universe.[138]

One of his most famous analogies was in a discussion of the absence of a sex life in the new creation. Lewis was keen to assert the survival of our sexuality in the general resurrection, arguing that what may no longer be needed for the purposes of procreation may yet be retained for the purposes of glory. Comparing human sexuality to a weapon that can win victory in battle through chastity (whether this be as a celibate or in married life), Lewis observed, 'It is the beaten and the fugitives who throw away their swords. The conquerors sheathe theirs and retain them.'[139] And so Lewis imagined that a small boy, on being told of the heightened pleasures of sex, might ask if lovers eat chocolate at the same time as making love. On being told that they do not Lewis reasoned that the boy might well be left with the impression that the absence of chocolate is the main characteristic of the sexual act. 'The boy knows chocolate,' wrote Lewis; 'he does not know the positive thing that excludes it.' We are in a similar position. We have a heightened awareness of the power and pleasure of sex but we cannot imagine a greater power and pleasure – beatific vision – which would transcend it.[140]

Another well-known Lewisian analogy is that of the galloping chargers. The relation between our glorified bodies and our present earthly bodies is similar to that of 'winged, shining and world-shaking horses' and ponies given to schoolboys on which to learn to ride.

Some day we may ride bare-back, confident and rejoicing, those greater mounts ... Not that the gallop would be of any value unless it were a gallop with the King; but how

[138] *Miracles*, p. 158.
[139] Ibid. p. 169.
[140] Cf. Ibid.

else – since He has retained His own charger – should we accompany Him?[141]

One query arises here: did Lewis intend to imply that the bodies given us at the general resurrection have no more connection to our earthly bodies than a similarity of shape and breed? Interestingly, Karl Rahner once warned against eternal life being seen as simply a matter of going on after a change of horses.[142] Elsewhere we find that Lewis used more careful imagery, implying transformation rather than replacement. For example, the statue coming alive, the tin soldier being turned into flesh, an egg having to hatch before it can become a flying bird, and a house being re-built into a palace.[143]

This concept of transformation is essential to our understanding of Lewis' position on the general resurrection. Redemption, he argued, is not mere improvement but rather the transformation that is inevitable if we begin to live the life of Christ. 'Hand over the whole natural self,' wrote Lewis, and Christ 'will give you a new self instead.'[144] Again, he commented: 'The more we get what we now call "ourselves" out of the way and let Him take us over, the more truly ourselves we become.'[145] The implications of this for a theology of resurrection are expressed well in *The Great Divorce*. In one scene Lewis depicted a limping ghost carrying a red lizard on its shoulder. After some debate the ghost allows an angel to destroy the lizard which then transforms into a magnificent white stallion. The ghost, too, changes form to become an immense and golden-headed man. The man mounts his new horse and rides off into the mountains of heaven. The ensuing conversation between the narrator and MacDonald draws out the point: 'Nothing, not even the best and noblest, can go on as

---

[141] Ibid. p. 173.

[142] Cf. Karl Rahner, 'Ideas for a Theology of Death', in idem, *Theological Investigations*, Volume XIII: *Theology, Anthropology, Christology*, p. 174

[143] See *Mere Christianity*, pp. 132, 149, 164, 169, 178. Lewis borrowed the image of the house being re-built into a palace from George MacDonald.

[144] Ibid. p. 162.

[145] Ibid. p. 185.

it is now. Nothing, not even what is lowest and most bestial, will not be raised again if it submits to death.'[146] In this passage Lewis was attempting to demonstrate that all aspects of our existence will be taken up and transformed in the general resurrection, including what we might consider our more base desires. But the key idea here is death. The lizard, which represents lust, has to be put to death before it can become the stallion of true sexual desire and passion that was intended. Thus we can now understand Lewis' assertion that hell is a state of sub-humanity. Now we can see why he portrayed the damned as shadows and ghosts while the saved are magnificent and solid and full of colour. Since man is neither exclusively a body nor a soul, but an intrinsic unity of both, then a resurrection of the body is essential to any idea of transformation into true selfhood. What we now experience as self is a shadow of what awaits us. And so Lewis wrote that even the most filthy and feeblest of us could one day be made into 'a dazzling, radiant, immortal creature, pulsating all through with such energy and joy and wisdom and love.'[147] As he so wisely warned us in *The Weight of Glory:* 'It is a serious thing to live in a society of possible gods and goddesses.'[148]

---

[146] *The Great Divorce,* p. 95.
[147] Ibid. p. 170.
[148] 'The Weight of Glory', p. 39.

Chapter 2

C. S. Lewis and the Eschaton

In a collection of essays entitled, *Eschatological Rationality*, the German evangelical theologian Gerhard Sauter argues that the study of eschatology by post-Reformation writers originated in response to the question: have we a foundation for hope? Sauter was referring to such early seventeenth-century writers as Abraham Calov, Johann Gerhard, Johannes Himmel, Bartholomaeus Keckermann, and Georg Calixt. Despite their differences of systematic approach to the subject, Sauter points out that all were writing at a time 'when prospects were particularly gloomy, in the midst of religious wars and political and spiritual revolutions'. In a period characterised by what Sauter terms 'approaching catastrophe', these theologians, by placing eschatology in a place of prominence in their theology, gave an indirect but nonetheless clear answer to the question: can we hope?[1] Sauter notes that over the passage of time, however,

---

[1] Gerhard Sauter, *Eschatological Rationality: Theological Issues in Focus*, pp. 139–40. Interestingly, the history of theology sees a similar flowering of eschatology – at least in the western Churches – after the First World War. As Joseph Ratzinger has argued, the 'emerging crisis of European civilization' arising from the build up to and process of the First World War furnished humanity's sense of 'decline and fall' with its 'earliest tragic confirmation, undermining as it did so the then dominant theological Liberalism with is optimistic assessment of a purely cultural Christianity'. Although Mark Chapman has argued, 'The importance of eschatology after the First World War is undeniable, yet ... few commentators have looked in detail at the emergence and the significance of eschatology in the years *before* 1914.' The context both pre- and post-1914 is nevertheless undoubtedly one of 'approaching catastrophe' in

despite eschatology retaining its place in Reform theology, the reason for its study – the core question, if you like – became detached.

> The question motivating the theologians we have quoted so far – 'Why may we hope? What can we hope for in our situation?' – was steadily pushed more and more into the background by reflection on the End *(finis)* in its all-embracing sense. The relationship of humanity and the world in view of their end; end as annihilation or fulfilment; time and the world: these now came to be seen as epistemological or transcendental-philosophical questions.[2]

He concludes that eschatology can only really be meaningful – 'only begin to put down roots again' – if the core question is restored as the primary context. The primary stress for Sauter, then, is on the dynamic rather than the descriptive function of modern eschatology: what *invites* us to hope for a future beatitude given our history and present experience? The Catholic theologian Luis Ladaria has pointed out: 'In the coming of Christ, the "Last" has burst forth upon the world.' In other words, the End Time is made present now. 'The apparition of God in the world in the Jesus-event is the event of events, and stamps history with its definitive orientation.'[3] Thus Christian eschatology is no mere doctrine of the Last Things *(eschata)*, but an understanding of the implication of *the* Last Thing (the *Eschaton*) – Christ himself – as he impinges upon all time and every aspect of being. But Sauter's question still arises: why do we hope? How can we interpret our history, present experi-

---

the sense of the prevailing liberal Christian theology's inability to speak to the arising human situation. See Mark Chapman, *The Coming Crisis: The Impact of Eschatology on Theology in Edwardian England*, p. 11 and Joseph Ratzinger, *Eschatology: Death and Eternal Life*, p. 3.

[2] G. Sauter, *Eschatological Rationality*, p. 141.

[3] Luis Ladaria, 'Eschatology', in *Dictionary of Fundamental Theology*, p. 273.

ences, and the whole of reality in a new way because of the Christ-event?

In this chapter I aim to examine this eschatological dynamic in the writings of C. S. Lewis. I will present what I believe to be Lewis' understanding of the relationship of humanity and the world in view of its end; whether he saw the *Eschaton* as annihilation or fulfilment; and what he considered to be the eschatological implications for time and being. Sauter's criticism is that these concepts become merely epistemological or philosophical speculations, divorced from the core question of Christian faith. In Lewis' work, however, that core question is ever present. What he termed the 'dialectic of Desire'[4] had led him along a journey to faith which, once accepted and only then, allowed him to work out the eschatological implications of Christian hope. This journey from atheism through Idealism to theism and then into Christianity had confronted him 'with a God who is acting to judge and redeem,' as Gerhard Sauter puts it.[5] Lewis himself commented in *Surprised by Joy:* 'Every step I had taken, from the Absolute to "Spirit" and from "Spirit" to "God", had been a step towards the more concrete, the more imminent, the more compulsive.'[6]

An Eschatology of Desire

In *Mere Christianity*, Lewis observed that most people find it difficult to conceive of heaven beyond the idea of a grand reunion of friends and loved ones. One of the reasons for this, he concluded, is that our sights are too easily set upon this world. But another, perhaps more important reason, is that we fail to recognise the desire for heaven in our lives for what it really is. If we did learn to look into the depths of our longings, he went on, we would soon realise that what we do actually want is something ultimately unobtainable in this world.[7] Lewis

---

4   *Pilgrim's Regress,* p. xv.
5   Cf. G. Sauter, *Eschatological Rationality,* p. 140.
6   *Surprised by Joy,* p. 184.
7   Cf. *Mere Christianity,* pp. 111–12.

saw this heavenly yearning in the human capacity for romantic longing, whether it be for a first love, another country, or even – as in his own case – the learning about some new subject that captivates the soul.[8] What Lewis was referring to here was an idea that he was to develop in his later writing as the concept of *Sehnsucht*. Corbin Scott Carnell, tracing this theme throughout the Lewisian corpus, has defined it as an attitude characterised by 'a sense of separation from what is desired, a ceaseless longing which always points beyond'.[9] Lewis himself explained it in terms of unsatisfiable desire.[10] For a long time Lewis misunderstood the true nature of this desire. Often he confused the 'stab of Joy' which accompanied the experience of *Sehnsucht* with the proper goal of such a longing. 'I smuggled in the assumption that what I wanted was a "thrill", a state of my own mind,' Lewis noted.[11] Similarly, he mistook the object of his desire to be whatever was provoking its immediate cause at a particular time. So, as a child, his interest in Norse mythology, which had been one of the initial causes of his awakening to *Sehnsucht*, soon began to turn itself into a more scholarly concern. And, while Lewis came to know his way around the 'Eddaic cosmos' and 'who ran up and down it', so too it gradually began to dawn on him that this was something altogether different from the original sense of yearning that 'Northernness' had sparked off in him. Yet even when this realisation might have led Lewis to conclude that the object of *Sehnsucht* was not Norse mythology at all but rather something 'further away, more external, less subjective', still he believed that it was merely 'a mood or state within' which might be aroused by any number of experiences.[12] Gradually he came to realise that Joy is not a thing to be possessed but always 'a desire for something longer ago or further away or still "about to be"', and he even wondered whether perhaps 'all pleasures

---

[8] Cf. Ibid. p. 112.
[9] Corbin Scott Carnell, *Bright Shadow of Reality: Spiritual Longing in C. S. Lewis*, p. 27.
[10] Cf. *Surprised by Joy*, p. 12.
[11] Ibid. p. 130.
[12] Ibid. pp. 128–31.

are not substitutes for Joy'.[13] Eventually, with his conversion, Lewis came to understand the true function of *Sehnsucht*. 'To tell the truth,' he confided at the end of *Surprised by Joy*, 'the subject has lost nearly all its interest for me since I became a Christian.' He went on:

> It was valuable only as a pointer to something other and outer. While that other was in doubt, the pointer natu-rally loomed large in my thoughts ... But when we have found the road and are passing signposts every few miles, we shall not stop and stare ... 'We would be at Jerusalem'.[14]

Sehnsucht *and Eschatology*

What C. S. Lewis eventually came to realise was that the long-ings he experienced could be understood as a means by which he was being awakened to his call to eternal glory. Theologically speaking, we might say that he was positing *Sehnsucht* as a function of future eschatology: the desire for a promised future beatitude. For example, in *The Pilgrim's Regress*, Lewis observed that if one pursued the experience of *Sehnsucht* conscientiously and with due diligence, eventually one would be forced to come to the conclusion that the object causing such longing and desire must be realised only outside 'our present mode of subjective and spatio-temporal experi-ence'.[15] It has to be said that this approach is something akin to Augustine's 'restless heart'[16] and perhaps even more to

[13] Ibid. pp. 59, 132. See also C. S. Lewis, *They Stand Together: The Letters of C. S. Lewis to Arthur Greeves (1914–1963)*, p. 355.

[14] *Surprised by Joy*, p. 185.

[15] *Pilgrim's Regress,* pp. xiv–xv.

[16] Cf. St Augustine, *Confessions*, I, p. i. Zachary Hayes comments: 'For Augustine, the whole of life appeared to be a search for the mystery of God ... No matter how much we may be filled with created goods, the dynamism of the human heart impels us beyond them to the mystery of God.' See Hayes, *Visions of a Future*, p. 71.

Rahner's 'supernatural existential'.[17] Arguably this concept of *Sehnsucht* lies behind the Lewisian motif of 'another country' or 'home country'. In *Mere Christianity* Lewis noted, 'If I find in myself a desire which no experience of this world can satisfy, the most probable explanation is that I was made for another world.'[18] However, it seems to me that the Lewisian appreciation of *Sehnsucht* is more complex than this. In *The Problem of Pain*, Lewis argued that throughout life 'an unattainable ecstasy' hovers 'just beyond the grasp' of our consciousness. 'The day is coming,' he said, 'when you will wake to find, beyond all hope, that you have attained it.'[19] He explained this idea with the help of a metaphor:

> The world is like a picture with a golden background, and we the figures in that picture. Until you step off the plane of the picture into the large dimensions of death you cannot see the gold. But we have reminders of it. To change our metaphor, the blackout is not quite complete. There are chinks. At times the daily scene looks big with its secret.[20]

This is not merely, then, the promise of some future beatitude but rather a vision of a beatitude which impinges upon us in

---

[17] Cf. Karl Rahner, 'Concerning the Relationship Between Nature and Grace', in idem, *Theological Investigations*, Volume I: *God, Christ, Mary, and Grace*, pp. 297–317. George Vass comments of Rahner's theory of the supernatural existential: 'The supernatural existential is now understood *not* as a theoretical postulate in defence of gratuitous grace, but as a mode of human transcendentality; and that, secondly, it is now regarded as a conscious (yet not *gewußt!*), that is, a somehow experienced, orientation of man towards grace and glory. It has left its merely theoretical status in order to become an experience, if not of grace in its full sense, then at least of a felt correspondence between man's a priori tendency and God's gracious action.' George Vass, *The Mystery of Man and the Foundations of a Theological System, Understanding Karl Rahner: Understanding Karl Rahner*, Volume 2, p. 75.

[18] *Mere Christianity*, p. 113.

[19] Ibid. p. 112.

[20] Ibid. p. 123.

the here and now. Lewis has demonstrated a move away from a purely future-orientated eschatology. In *Surprised by Joy* we have a practical and personal example of what Lewis meant. In recording his reaction to a first reading of George MacDonald's *Phantastes*, Lewis referred to a bright shadow coming from the book and altering his hitherto held perception of reality.[21] As he described it:

> It was as though the voice which had called to me from the world's end were now speaking at my side ... If it had once eluded me by its distance, it now eluded me by proximity – something too near to see, to plain to be understood, on this side of knowledge.[22]

What I think Lewis was touching upon here was *Sehnsucht* as a function of what we would technically identify as proleptic eschatology. He had experienced a sense of displacement caused by living in the 'now but not yet' of the End Time. Or rather, as Lewis himself might have put it, he had reacted to living 'amid all the anomalies, inconveniences, hopes, and excitements of a house that is being rebuilt'.[23]

In *Surprised by Joy* Lewis defined the term *Sehnsucht* as a type of longing, characteristic of the Blue Flower motif of Romantic literature.[24] Corbin Scott Carnell explains this motif as a compulsive quest or 'pursuit of the unobtainable' which causes a certain amount of pleasure in the pursuit itself but ultimately a sense of sadness due to the unattainable nature of what is desired.[25] Interestingly, Carnell has argued: 'Wherever we find the Romantic attitude in its most intense form, we may very well find *Sehnsucht*.'[26] And the Romantic tradition, he believes,

---

[21] Cf. *Surprised by Joy*, p. 140.

[22] Ibid. p. 139.

[23] *Miracles*, p. 164.

[24] *Surprised by Joy*, p. 4.

[25] Cf. Corbin Scott Carnell, *Bright Shadow of Reality*, pp. 21–2. Lewis' reference to the 'Blue Flower' comes from the name given this particular Romantic motif. Carnell traces its origins to the search for the *Blaue Blume* in German literature and to the *Längtans Blåa Blomma* (the Blue Flower of Longing) of Scandinavian ballads dating from the Middle Ages.

[26] Ibid. p. 27.

is marked by what he refers to as 'an unusually vigorous reaction to the world'.

> This reaction may reflect acceptance or rejection of one's environment but it must be intense. It is here that the common denominator, a sense of aspiration and longing for the infinite, comes in. When the reaction is an exuberant 'Yea' to environment, we have the Romantic's traditional love of nature and sense of oneness with it. When the reaction is a vehement 'Nay', we have tales of the land of faerie, dreams of better times in the past or in the future, or an attempt to invest with wonder the everyday and the commonplace.[27]

In Lewis, I think, we find both a 'Yea' and a 'Nay' to this world: we encounter in the Lewisian corpus both a traditional love of (and sense of unity with) nature and, at the same time, a dream and hope of a better nature, an even greater unity. Indeed, to put this into the language of proleptic eschatology, we have not merely a 'Yea' and a 'Nay' but rather a 'Now' and a 'Not Yet'. The most explicit example of this is in Lewis' sermon, *The Weight of Glory*, where he explored the meaning of what he referred to as lifelong nostalgia: the 'longing to be reunited with something in the universe from which we now feel cut off'.[28] Such *Sehnsucht* is not some self-induced neurosis or, as Feuerbach and Freud would have it, some kind of wish fulfilment, but at the very heart of our reality as contingent, finite human beings, Lewis argued. Using the example of beauty, he argued that we don't want merely to see beauty – to observe it from a distance as something other; we yearn to be part of that beauty, 'to receive it into ourselves, to bathe in it'.[29] With this idea Lewis, arguably echoing the vision of the eschatological redemption of all creation offered by Paul in Romans. 8:18–25, has captured that sense of ambiguity that is present in prolep-

---

[27] Ibid. pp. 26–7. Cf. C. S. Lewis, 'On Three Ways of Writing for Children', in idem, *Of Other Worlds: Essays and Stories*, pp. 29–30.

[28] 'The Weight of Glory,' p. 36.

[29] Ibid. p. 37.

tic eschatology. 'At present we are on the outside of the world,' he wrote. 'Some day, God willing, we shall get *in*.'[30] At present we have glimmers of God's kingdom but one day that kingdom will come in fullness and without ambiguity.

Desire and Christian Hope

In 1944, in a sermon preached at the chapel of Mansfield College in Oxford, Lewis stated: 'We can hope only for what we desire.'[31] This is clearly an anthropological observation akin to the gospel pericopes of Luke 12:34 and Matthew 6:21: what we most deeply desire will direct our expectations and activities.[32] However, Lewis was also here deliberately making a correlation between human desire and the Christian theological virtue of hope.[33] In his 'allegorical apology', *The Pilgrim's Regress*, Lewis presented two characters, John and Vertue, who travel together through the world. John has left the land of Puritania to get away from the eastern mountains and the threat of the Landlord and is generally heading west in search of the Island. Vertue, too, is on a pilgrimage but not one with a clear destination as such. 'To travel hopefully is better than to arrive,' he explains. 'The great thing is to do one's thirty miles a day.'[34] Towards the end of their journey west Vertue falls into a bout of self-doubt about his lifestyle of self-imposed disci-

---

[30] Ibid.

[31] 'Transposition', p. 83.

[32] Cf., for example, Mt 6:21: 'Wherever your treasure is, that is where your heart will be too.'

[33] Note that in *Surprised by Joy* Lewis made a distinction between desire and appetite. See *Surprised by Joy*, pp. 52, 54–63. By 1960, with the publication of *The Four Loves*, I think Lewis had come to understand desire as an expression of fundamental human need. See *Four Loves*, p. 3. Such need is the basic disposition necessary to be able to answer the eschatological invitation of Isaiah 55:1: 'Oh, come to the water all you who are thirsty; though you have no money, come! Buy and eat; come, buy wine and milk without money, free!' Note, too, that it is the desperate desire – or need – of Jill to quench her thirst in *The Silver Chair* that forces her to encounter Aslan. See C. S. Lewis, *The Silver Chair*, pp. 22–4.

[34] *Pilgrim's Regress*, p. 31.

pline. 'I can't see that there is any other good in it except the mere fact of imposing my will on my inclinations,' he explains. 'And that seems to be good *training*, but training for what?'[35] He goes on:

> Supposing there is anything East and West. How can that give me a motive for going on? Because there is something pleasant ahead? That is a bribe. Because there is something dreadful behind? That is a threat. I meant to be a free man. I meant to choose things because I chose to choose them – not because I was paid for it.[36]

John's response to Vertue's self-doubt is simple. 'Give in,' he says. 'For once yield to desire. Have done with your choosing. *Want* something.'[37] This dialogue can, I think, be seen as the allegorical depiction of Lewis' own inner battle concerning his conversion to Christianity. In *Surprised by Joy* Lewis recounts his adoption of what he calls the New Look: 'no more pessimism ... no flirtations with any idea of the supernatural ... "always judging and acting ... with the greatest good sense"'.[38] This position is remarkably similar to Vertue's arrangement in which he self-consciously tries to follow the best possible rules he can find.[39] However, just as with Vertue's eventual decline into self-doubt and then silence, so Lewis' own experience led him to abandon his New Look. Through Owen Barfield's influence, he realised the inconsistency between his adopted philosophy and the actual experiences – both intellectual and emotional – that he had of the world around him.[40]

What Lewis posited, then, through both his allegory and his autobiography, was a central role for desire as a function by which hope can take shape in our human experience. As he noted in *The Screwtape Letters:* 'The deepest likings and

---

[35] Ibid. p. 134.
[36] Ibid.
[37] Ibid. p. 135.
[38] *Surprised by Joy,* p. 156.
[39] Cf. *Pilgrim's Regress,* p. 32.
[40] Cf. *Surprised by Joy,* p. 166.

impulses of any man are the raw material, the starting-point, with which the Enemy [i.e. God] has furnished him.'[41] It is an association we find in the teaching of the Catechism of the Catholic Church too:

> The virtue of hope responds to the aspiration to happiness which God has placed in the heart of every man; it takes up the hopes that inspire men's activities and purifies them so as to order them to the Kingdom of heaven; ... it opens up his heart in expectation of eternal beatitude.[42]

In other words, Christian hope gives direction and explicit expression to the already existing eschatological function of desire. Indeed, the Dominican theologian Anton Van der Walle has expressed it this way:

> Belief in a beyond should disturb us very much if it *did not* seem to match up with human longing. Faith can only be expressed meaningfully and responsibly as a human possibility if it corresponds with human longings, desires, needs and experiences.[43]

Lewis, however, went on to raise the question: how can Christian hope adequately satisfy human desire with its promise of beatitude, when the concept of that beatitude would seem to negate much of those desires? As he put it, our serious and theological talk of heaven is almost always articulated in a negative tone. He accepted, of course, that against such negatives theol-

---

41 *Screwtape Letters*, p. 51 (Letter 13). In *The Great Divorce* Lewis presented an encounter between one of the 'Bright People' called Dick and a ghost who had been his former liberal theologian friend on earth. In the course of their conversation, Dick realises that the ghost has become so vague and woolly in his thinking that he has dulled the true thirst of his intellectual reason. He then attempts a different tack to persuade the ghost to join him in the mountains of heaven. 'Can you, at least, still desire happiness?' Cf. *Great Divorce*, p. 42.

42 *Catechism*, n. 1818.

43 Van der Walle, *From Darkness to the Dawn*, p. 17. The italics are mine.

ogy sets one enormous, great positive: the Beatific Vision. Nevertheless, as Lewis asked himself, can the imaginative conception of the positive overshadow the impact of the negatives? Lewis' parable of the erudite limpets displayed the dangers of any *via negativa*. Here Lewis pictured a mystical limpet who catches a glimpse of man. Now this mystical limpet has its followers who already have some insight and vision of the nature of man. So although the mystical limpet records his new information using certain negatives – man has no shell, is not attached to a rock, is not surrounded by water – nevertheless, his disciples do get the right idea. Later, however, the erudite limpets come along. They lack the wisdom and understanding of the mystical limpet's original disciples and focus only on the negative. Thus, in their commentaries on the nature of man, they picture him to be a sort of amorphous jelly which exists nowhere and never takes nourishment, concluding that the highest form of being is to be 'a famished jelly in a dimensionless void'.[44] The point being made is that not only are our images and expressions of the End Time (and the use we make of them) important, but that there is indeed some degree of correlation between our human desires and their promised fulfilment, between our experience now and our hope for hereafter. As Lewis noted in his 1944 sermon: 'We feel, if we do not say, that the vision of God will come not to fulfil but to destroy our nature; this bleak fantasy often underlies our very use of words such as "holy" or "pure" or "spiritual"'.[45] And yet Christian theology assures us that grace builds upon nature, and that hope takes up our desires and aspirations, directing them towards the kingdom.[46] Lewis thus argued that there must be some correlation between our deepest human desires – for example, for life and health and well-being – and the fulfilment of Christian hope, even if – as the character John in *The Pilgrim's Regress* concludes – that correlation will in fact turn out to be more unlike than like.[47]

---

[44] Cf. *Miracles,* pp. 92–3.
[45] 'Transposition,' p. 84.
[46] For example, the medieval maxim: *gratia non destruit, sed praesupponit et perfecit naturam.* See also *Catechism,* nn. 1818, 2000–2.
[47] Cf. *Pilgrim's Regress,* p. 216. Cf. ibid. p. 200.

Desire and Moral Eschatology

This alignment of hope and desire sheds some important light, too, on how we are to understand Lewis' moral eschatology. Already I have made the point that in Lewis' thought there is an ontological connection between moral action and eschatological destiny – that the moral choices we make today determine the type of being we shall be in the End Time. As Lewis noted in *English Literature in the Sixteenth Century,* 'What really matters is not to obey moral rules but to be a creature of a certain kind. The wrong kind of creature is damned ... not for what it does but for what it is.'[48] Indeed, eschatologically speaking there is a 'realised' edge to this too since, for Lewis, human virtues are less like the rungs of a ladder which must be climbed in an ascent to a heaven *up there* (or, indeed, out there), and rather more like the scaffolding being put in place which enables heaven to be built in the here and now of daily existence.

The key to this connection between moral action and eschatological destiny in Lewis' thought is desire. 'When we *want* to be something other than the thing God wants us to be,' said Lewis in *The Problem of Pain,* 'we must be *wanting* what, in fact, will not make us happy.'[49] Sin, selfishness, immoral actions express our desire to be something other than God's creation. Virtue, moral conduct, goodness display, at the very least, the beginnings of a desire to be what God wants us to be. The purpose of moral codes, therefore, is to help order our desires so that we want what God wants, so that we allow him to perfect us and give us the happiness he wants us to have. There is here a clear eschatological dynamic: in moral activity our desires are being so re-ordered that we *want* God to be God for us. This means a shift away from the original sin of *wanting*

---

48 *English Literature in Sixteenth Century,* p. 187. Zachary Hayes has argued: 'The quest for meaning in human life is based on the conviction that, as human beings, we are capable of knowing and loving reality, but that we do not do so from the start. We can choose to become a particular sort of person, but we are not that sort of person from the beginning.' See Hayes, *Visions of a Future,* p. 78.
49 *Problem of Pain,* p. 37. Italics are my own.

to be gods ourselves. In this sense Lewis could argue that human morality is not about what is right and what is wrong. 'We might think that God wanted simply obedience to a set of rules,' Lewis noted in *Mere Christianity*, 'whereas He really wants people of a particular sort.'[50] Moral action, then, is not about earning a promised beatitude but rather about trying to live out the implication of that promise in the here and now. 'Not doing these things in order to be saved,' as Lewis put it, 'but because He has begun to save you already.'[51]

The advantage of this close positioning of morals and eschatology – indeed so close that I have referred to Lewis' moral eschatology – is that it enables him to suggest that moral conduct is not the end of life. In *Letters to Malcolm* Lewis argued: 'There is no morality in Heaven. The angels never knew (from within) the meaning of the word *ought*, and the blessed dead have long since gladly forgotten it.'[52] I suppose we are back to our moral scaffolding. Once the building of heaven is complete what is the use of that scaffolding? In an essay on the novels of Charles Williams, Lewis noted: 'Morality exists to be transcended. We act from duty in the hope that someday we shall do the same acts freely and delightfully.'[53] Interestingly, the Catechism states:

> The theological virtues are the foundation of Christian moral activity; they animate it and give it its special character. They inform and give life to all the moral virtues ... They are the pledge of the presence and action of the Holy Spirit in the faculties of the human being. [54]

---

[50] *Mere Christianity*, p. 66.
[51] Ibid. p. 123.
[52] *Letters to Malcolm*, p. 110 (Letter 21). This idea is given dramatic presentation in *The Silver Chair*. King Caspian, having died and now present in Aslan's country, asks Aslan if his desire to have just one glimpse of the children's world is wrong. Aslan replies that once you have died you can no longer desire wrong things. See *Silver Chair*, p. 189.
[53] C. S. Lewis, *Of This and Other Worlds*, p. 40.
[54] *Catechism*, n. 1813.

The use of the term 'pledge' is what is significant here. The New Testament sense of the word (as found, for example, in Ephesians 1:13–14; 2 Corinthians 1:22, and 2 Corinthians 5:5) is of a pledge as a first instalment with more to follow; a guarantee of what is to come. But, of course, once we are given the full amount, the initial down payment no longer holds our attention. So in heaven the theological virtues, and the moral virtues they direct and inform, will no longer be so significant in the sense that what they promise will have been given. Michael Scanlon has noted that, according to classical theology, we can say that whilst love remains, faith gives way to vision and hope to possession. 'Once God, the highest good and 'most difficult to attain' (St Thomas), is possessed securely in eternal bliss, there is nothing more to hope for.' [55] But, here and now, those virtues have an eschatological dynamic in that they not only point to the End Time but so direct and focus our desire that the End Time can begin to become a reality in our lives. We can say, perhaps, that moral virtues are like the steps that teach us a cosmic dance. Once we have learnt that dance (indeed, once we are dancing for all eternity) we will not be focusing on those initial steps even if we will be dancing infinite variations upon them: we would rather be looking to the Lord of the Dance.[56] As Jürgen Moltmann has put it much more technically: 'Ethical existence is gathered up and perfected in the aesthetical existence of doxology.'[57]

[55] Cf. Michael Scanlon, 'Hope', in *New Dictionary of Theology*, p. 493. Cf. St Thomas, *Summa Theologiae*, II-II, pp. 18, 2.
[56] Lewis used the image of dance in a number of his works. Cf. *Perelandra*, pp. 214–19, *Letters to Malcolm*, pp. 89–90 (Letter 17), *Problem of Pain*, pp. 65, 127. In *Mere Christianity* Lewis explained the inner life of the Trinity with the notion of dance and argued that the purpose of becoming a Christian is to share in this divine life. Cf. *Mere Christianity*, pp. 146–7.
[57] J. Moltmann, *The Coming of God*, p. 324. Moltmann explains this position by arguing that since the glorification of God, which is our salvation and ultimate purpose, means 'to love God for his own sake, and to enjoy God as he is in himself', then 'All moral purposes are excluded from the glorification of God, as is every economic utility. The praise of God has no purpose and no utility – if it had, God would not be praised for his own sake. It is simply meaningful in itself. The glorification of God has this in common with the child's self-forgetting delight in its game.' Ibid. p. 323.

The Implications of an Eschatological Dynamic

In his posthumous publication on prayer Lewis wrote to his fictional friend, Malcolm: 'We can't – or I can't – hear the song of a bird simply as a sound. Its meaning or message ("That's a bird") comes with it inevitably.'[58] Lewis was explaining here the idea of glory. He was attempting to show that any pleasure could become a channel of adoration. He didn't mean, simply, in the sense of giving thanks for moments of truth or goodness or beauty and the like. Rather, he argued, they may enable us to become lost in adoration of the God who sends us such moments. As he explained: 'There need be no question of thanks or praise as a separate event, something done after-wards. To experience the tiny theophany is itself to adore.'[59] This idea, then, has eschatological connotations because, as Lewis pointed out, 'This heavenly fruit is instantly redolent of the orchard where it grew. This sweet air whispers of the country from whence it blows.' Such pleasures – such perceived shafts of glory – speak not only of the divine presence but also of its promise. As Lewis put it: 'It is a message. We know we are being touched by a finger of that right hand at which there are pleasures for evermore.'[60] Interestingly, Lewis drew no distinction as to which pleasures might be vehicles for God's glory. 'No pleasure would be too ordinary,' he argued, 'or too usual for such reception; from the first taste of the air when I look out of the window ... down to one's soft slippers at bedtime.'[61]

---

[58] *Letters to Malcolm*, p. 86 (Letter 17).
[59] Ibid. Earlier in the same text Lewis had noted that we tend not to experience such theophanies because we reject what God offers us in the expectation of something other. Cf. ibid. p. 24. This idea is given dramatic form in the discussion between the Green Lady and Ransom in *Perelandra* concerning a heart 'which clung to the good it had first thought of and turned the good which was given it into no good'. Cf. *Perelandra*, pp. 68–9, and 83.
[60] *Letters to Malcolm*, p. 86 (Letter 17).
[61] Ibid. p. 87 (Letter 17). Cf. J. Moltmann, *The Coming of God*, p. 323; St Augustine, *De Doctrina Christiana*, I, p. 12: 'But since human beings, assimilated as they are to this world because of their desire to enjoy the created order instead of its actual creator ... did not recognise it, the evangelist said, "and the world did not recognise it.";

However, Lewis also suggested that the discipline of discerning such divine glory and its inherent promise itself points to our future destiny. Noting that one could, if one practised, hear simply a roar and not the roaring of the wind, Lewis went on to explain:

> We shall not be able to adore God on the highest occasions if we have learned no habit of doing so on the lowest. At best, our faith and reason will tell us that He is adorable, but we shall not have *found* Him so, not have 'tasted and seen'.[62]

All of this, of course, points to a Lewisian worldview that saw finite reality as opening out into the infinite – what Moltmann would call an 'open system'.[63] Indeed, one of the premises of Lewis' apologetic work on miracles was precisely the acceptance of different levels of being divergent upon each other. Whereas our philosophical – indeed, our metaphysical – preconceptions often limit us to thinking either of merely 'a reality with one floor' or of 'a reality with two floors', the truth is perhaps far more likely to be 'a reality like a skyscraper with several floors'.[64] It is, perhaps, no coincidence that Lewis' fiction was littered with the interaction of different worlds and different beings, or that science fiction and faerie were his more usual genres. The Narnia Chronicles and the Space Trilogy both present a vision of interacting worlds and differ-

---

Ibid., I, p. 5: 'The things which are to be enjoyed, then, are the Father and the Son and the Holy Spirit, and the Trinity comprised by them, which is a kind of single, supreme thing, shared by all who enjoy it – if indeed it is a thing and not the cause of all things, and if indeed it is a cause.'

[62] *Letters to Malcolm*, pp. 87–8 (Letter 17).

[63] Moltmann has argued: 'If we proceed from the idea of continuous creation, it immediately becomes clear that the unremitting creative presence of God in creation makes of that creation this double world of heaven and earth. A world which has been created by God, and which continues to be created every moment, is bound to be a world *open to God*.' See Jürgen Moltmann, *God in Creation: An Ecological Doctrine of Creation*, pp. 162–3.

[64] *Miracles*, p. 163.

ent types of rational being. In *The Magician's Nephew,* for example, Digory likens the Wood between the Worlds – a sort of in-between place – to the tunnel of attics that run throughout certain types of English terrace housing and from which access can, at least potentially, be gained into any one of the houses in the row.[65] Similarly, in the first two books of the Space Trilogy, Ransom travels to both Mars and Venus and discovers new forms of rational creatures – the *hrossa, pfifltriggi,* and *séroni* – and a new form of being altogether: the *eldila.*[66] Indeed, the title of the first book, *Out of the Silent Planet,* tells of the major theme of the whole Trilogy: the cosmic attempt to save a world that has turned in on itself – and thereby shut out the normal celestial interaction – through sin.

More important, however, than this interaction of worlds and beings in Lewis' fantasy and science fiction is his depiction of those worlds opening up to their true reality and potential. In the final instalment of the Space Trilogy, Lewis used the idea of Logres – King Arthur's mythical kingdom – to suggest that within the world there is an inner reality occasionally breaking through which points to the world's true intended nature. Lynn Summer has explained Logres as a Remnant – a small band of good people fighting against evil in the form of bureaucracy – but I think Lewis was referring to a much deeper reality than that.[67] As Dr Dimble, a character in the novel, explains in the following narrative:

'Britain is always haunted by something we may call Logres. Haven't you noticed that we are two countries? After every Arthur, a Mordred; behind every Milton, a Cromwell: a nation of poets, a nation of shopkeepers: the home of Sidney – and of Cecil Rhodes.'[68]

He goes on:

---

[65] Cf. C. S. Lewis, *The Magician's Nephew,* pp. 36–7.
[66] Cf. C. S. Lewis, *Out of the Silent Planet,* pp. 68, 76, and *Perelandra,* pp. 9–11, 18–20.
[67] Cf. Lynn Summer, 'King Arthur', in Jeffrey Schultz and John West, *Readers' Encyclopedia,* p. 87.
[68] *That Hideous Strength,* pp. 368–9.

'The whole work of healing Tellus [i.e. earth] depends on nursing that little spark, on incarnating that ghost. ... When Logres really dominates Britain ... why, then it will be spring.'[69]

A similar concept is introduced at the end of the Narnia series. In *The Last Battle*, having entered through the stable door and watched the final dying moments of Narnia, the children discover themselves to be in a Narnia more real and more beautiful than the Narnia outside the stable door – a 'world within a world', as Lucy puts it.[70] Discovering, too, that there is another England nearby and that all these worlds are surrounded by Aslan's own country, Mr Tumnus feels compelled to explain to Lucy:

> You are now looking at the England within England, the real England just as this is the real Narnia. And in that inner England no good thing is destroyed.[71]

Aslan, a little later, sums up what has happened: the children have died. They have passed from the 'Shadowlands' into full reality. What is significant about these eschatological fantasies is that present experience – finite being – is characterised by the *Eschaton*. Narnia and England relate to the inner Narnia and inner England as types to archetype, as shadows to reality. But there is more to it even than that. There is, Lewis believed, an ontological interconnection between them, an analogy of being. As he wrote in *Letters to Malcolm:*

> The hills and valleys of Heaven will be to those you now experience not as a copy is to an original, nor as a substitute to the genuine article, but as the flower to the root, or the diamond to the coal.[72]

---

[69] Ibid. pp. 370–1.
[70] *Last Battle*, p. 169.
[71] Ibid. p. 170.
[72] *Letters to Malcolm*, p. 117 (Letter 22). Cf. 'Transposition', p. 84.

One of the implications of this theology is that our experiences here and now must always in some respect point to the End Time; that finite reality will necessarily be characterised in some sense by absolute being. In *Miracles* Lewis pointed to one such characterisation. Our biological sonship, he argued, is merely 'a diagrammatic representation on the flat' of that divine Sonship which exists at the heart of the Trinity.[73] Similarly our experiences of earthly love are like 'rivulets to the Fountain' of that divine love which is at the centre of God himself.[74] Even our sexuality, Lewis believed, should in some way be seen as connected to and analogous with 'that creative joy which in Him is unceasing and irresistible'.[75] And, in his commentary on the *Arthuriad,* he speculated on another possible way in which the here and now might point to the hereafter. Arguing that any sense of greatness in the finite realm can only ever be akin to 'a kind of make believe or fancy-dress ball' – whether it be the 'official greatness' of kings or judges, or even the 'real greatness' of people such as Shakespeare and Erasmus – Lewis concluded:

> If we are some day to come where saints cast down their golden crowns we must here be content to assume for ourselves and to honour in others crowns of paper and tinsel, most worthy of tender laughter but not of hostile contempt.[76]

Eschatology and Kenosis

In *Miracles* Lewis referred to a pattern of death and rebirth which he believed ran throughout creation: a key principle of descent and reascent. 'It is the pattern of all vegetable life,' he observed. 'It must belittle itself into something hard, small and deathlike, it must fall into the ground: thence the new life

---

[73] *Miracles,* p. 95.
[74] *Four Loves,* p. 133.
[75] *Miracles,* p. 95.
[76] C. S. Lewis, 'Williams and the Arthuriad', in C. S. Lewis and Charles Williams, *Taliessin through Logres, The Region of the Summer Stars, Arthurian Torso,* p. 329.

reascends ... So it is also in our moral and emotional life.'[77]
John's Gospel, of course, refers to this process in a similar
way: 'Unless a wheat grain falls into the earth and dies, it
remains only a single grain; but if it dies it yields a rich
harvest. Anyone who loves his life loses it; anyone who hates
his life in this world will keep it for eternal life' (John
12:24–25). And the Synoptic Gospels, too, pick up on this
paradoxical interconnection between death and new life:
'Anyone who wants to save his life will lose it; but anyone who
loses his life for my sake, and for the sake of the gospel, will
save it. What gain, then, is it for anyone to win the whole
world and forfeit his life?' (Mark 8:35–36).[78] Lewis also saw
the death and rebirth pattern in pagan nature religions, especially in corn-king celebrations in which the god being
worshipped is effectively a personification of the harvest. The
archetype of this pattern, he believed, was to be found in the
doctrine of the incarnation. Lewis dismissed the notion that
such a doctrine is merely a derivative form of corn-king
mythology on two grounds. Firstly, unlike the pagan myths,
the Christian belief is based upon an historical figure who can
be actually identified and dated to some extent. Secondly, the
biblical data gives the impression that the disciples of the Early
Church have no knowledge of any corn-king mythology and
that it seems strange that the major religion of a God who dies
and rises again surfaces from within Judaism, from 'precisely
among the people to whom, and to whom alone almost, the
whole circle of ideas that belong to the "dying God" was
foreign'. Thus Lewis argued that the death and rebirth
pattern is a priori in God. It is present in nature because it
was there first in God. It is to be found in pagan mythology
and celebration because such mythology springs from nature.
'The doctrine of the Incarnation,' he concluded, 'puts this
principle even more emphatically at the centre ... All the
instances of it which I have mentioned turn out to be but the
transposition of the Divine theme into a minor key. I am not
now referring simply to the Crucifixion and Resurrection of

---

[77] *Miracles,* pp. 117–18.
[78] Cf. Mt 10:39, 16:25–6; Lk 9:24–5, 17:33.

Christ. The total pattern, of which they are only the turning point, is the real Death and Rebirth.' [79]

In order to understand what Lewis meant by real Death and Rebirth, I think we have to introduce the idea of kenosis. In St Paul's letter to the Philippians we find the root for such a concept. Paul, quoting from what is generally accepted to be an early Christian hymn, states of Christ Jesus: 'Who, being in the form of God, did not count equality with God something to be grasped. But he emptied himself, taking the form of a slave, becoming as human beings are' (Philippians 2:6–7). Rather than propound any sort of a kenotic Christology that suggests the incarnation involved the Second Person of the Trinity in some way giving up his divinity, or certain divine attributes – and thereby undermine the Nicene formula of *homoousios*[80] – Christian tradition has generally understood kenosis to mean that Christ was fully divine but nevertheless 'emptied himself of the glory that is his by nature'.[81] One may speak of a double kenosis – the incarnation and the crucifixion being separate acts of self-emptying (although the Philippians canticle uses the phrase, 'he humbled himself', rather than, 'he emptied himself') – or, as I think Lewis saw it, of a single kenosis. In the latter view the crucifixion is perceived as an integral part and inevitable outcome of the one kenotic act of incarnation – i.e. the lowest point, if you like, of Christ's self-emptying. Thus Christ's death and resurrection are the turning point of this wider movement of death and rebirth. The self-emptying of the Son, then, in the incarnation marks the descent, or 'real Death', of Lewis' pattern, which is completed in the physical death of Jesus of Nazareth. The resurrection of Christ and his ascension into heaven mark the movement of reascent, while

---

[79] Cf. *Miracles*, pp. 118–21.

[80] I.e. Jesus Christ is 'one in being' (*homoousios*) with the Father. Note that the Council of Chalcedon (451) re-affirmed this expression and extended it to state that Jesus Christ is 'truly God and truly man', and therefore 'one in being (*homoousios*) with the Father as to divinity' and 'one in being (*homoousios*) with us as to the humanity'. See Neuner and Dupuis, *The Christian Faith*, pp. 7, 614.

[81] 'Kenosis', in J. Komonchak, M. Collins and D. Lane, *Dictionary of Theology*, pp. 556.

Christ's parousia and the completion of the new heavens and a new earth complete the reascending and bring about a 'Rebirth'.

This discernment of descent and reascent, of course, is not unique to Lewis. John's Gospel presents the process quite clearly. In John 1:1 the Gospel states: 'In the beginning was the Word: the Word was with God and the Word was God.' Then John 1:14 goes on: 'The Word became flesh, he lived among us, and we saw his glory.' In John. 14:2b–3 Jesus prepares his Apostles for his coming passion and resurrection: 'I am going now to prepare a place for you, and after I have gone and prepared you a place, I shall return to take you to myself.' And in John 16:28 the pattern is made explicit: 'I came from the Father and have come into the world and now I am leaving the world to go to the Father.' What is significant about the Lewisian position, however, is that he saw this death and rebirth pattern – this kenotic model – written into the whole of creation, almost like nature's key signature. 'The principle runs through all life from top to bottom,' he argued in *Mere Christianity*.[82] Even the experience of *Sehnsucht* fits the pattern. 'Always it has summoned you out of yourself,' Lewis said in *The Problem of Pain*. 'And if you will not go out of yourself to follow it, if you sit down to brood on the desire and attempt to cherish it, the desire itself will evade you.' [83]

There is a real danger, of course, of reading these texts – and indeed the biblical data from which they arise – purely in terms of personal piety. The concept of dying to self, of self-surrender, is wisely and oft-quoted by writers of spirituality and mysticism. G. K. Chesterton, for example, once wrote:

> The true key of Christian mysticism is not so much self-surrender as self-forgetfulness, which we all fall into in the presence of a splendid sunrise or a little child, and which is to our highest nature as natural as singing to a bird.[84]

---

[82] *Mere Christianity*, p. 187.
[83] *The Problem of Pain*, pp. 123–4.
[84] A book review by G. K. Chesterton, originally published in *Daily News*, 30 August 1901. Cf. *The Chesterton Review*, XXVI (2000), p. 7.

Lewis, too, referred to the idea of self-forgetfulness in similar terms: 'The real test of being in the presence of God,' he wrote is that you 'forget about yourself altogether.'[85] However, Lewis' kenotic theme goes far beyond this sort of exhortation to true humility. In a paper read to the Socratic Club in 1946 Lewis argued that if God can be known, it will only be by divine revelation. And, looking to where such revelation is generally claimed, he asserted that there is to be found a common element: 'The theme of sacrifice, of mystical communion through the shed of blood, of death and rebirth.' It is, he believed, the core of all messages, pagan and even pre-pagan. Christianity, he wrote, rests not 'upon some selection of certain supposedly "higher" elements in our nature, but on the shattering and rebuilding, the death and re-birth, of that nature in every part'. In other words, this death and rebirth pattern is directed specifically to the eschaton: 'Neither Greek nor Jew nor barbarian, but a new creation.'[86]

Jürgen Moltmann, in his argument for an eschatological doctrine of creation, similarly uses a death and rebirth pattern in his development of the concept of kenosis. The Christian doctrine of *creatio ex nihilo*, he argues, while ensuring that creation is understood as distinct from God himself and therefore not an emanation, implies an *operatio Dei extra*. However, to be able to assert at the same time both an omnipotent and omnipresent God and an act *extra Deum* assumes an act of divine self-humiliation. As the Lutheran theologian says:

> In order to create a world 'outside' himself, the infinite God must have made room beforehand for a finitude in himself. It is only a withdrawal by God into himself that can free the space into which God can act creatively. The *nihil* for his *creatio ex nihilo* only comes into being because – and in so far as – the omnipotent and omnipresent God withdraws his presence and restricts his power.[87]

[85] *Mere Christianity*, p. 103. See also *Screwtape Letters*, p. 54 (Letter 14).
[86] 'Religion without Dogma?' pp. 100–1.
[87] Jürgen Moltmann, *God in Creation*, pp. 86–7.

Such self-limitation 'is the pre-supposition that makes creation possible'. It is the inward act and logically prior movement of kenosis that allows for the ecstatic, outward act of creation itself. For Moltmann this has tremendous eschatological implications. Firstly it allows him to understand the presence of evil and sin in a new light. 'The *nihil* in which God creates his creation,' Moltmann argues, 'is God-forsakenness, hell, absolute death.' He continues:

> It is against the threat of this that he [God] maintains his creation in life. Admittedly the *nihil* only acquires this menacing character through the self-isolation of created beings to which we give the name of sin and godlessness. Creation is therefore threatened, not merely by its own non-being, but also by the non-being of God its creator – that is to say, by Nothingness itself. The character of the negative that threatens it goes beyond creation itself. This is what constitutes its demonic power. Nothingness contradicts, not merely creation but God too, since he is creation's Creator.[88]

There is an inbuilt tension within creation to move towards either Nothingness or God – it cannot simply be neutral. This echoes the thoughts of Dr Dimble in Lewis' fiction, *That Hideous Strength*. 'Have you ever noticed,' he asks, 'that the universe, and every little bit of the universe, is always hardening and narrowing and coming to a point?' As he explains, 'The possibilities of even apparent neutrality are always diminishing.'[89] Secondly, Moltmann sees the 'primordial space' of Nothingness 'which [God] himself conceded through his initial self-limitation' overcome in the death and resurrection of Christ. 'By yielding up the Son to death in Godforsakenness on the cross, and by surrendering him to hell, the eternal God enters the Nothingness out of which he had created the world.' Moltmann goes on:

---

[88] Ibid., pp. 87–8.
[89] *That Hideous Strength*, p. 283.

By entering into the Godforsakenness of sin and death (which is Nothingness), God overcomes it and makes it part of his eternal life.[90]

This has eschatological connotations since, by entering Nothingness and filling it with absolute being, there is now no possibility of death. The end of the world, far from being the *annihilatio mundi* of what Moltmann calls Gnosticism's 'vulgar error', is now the eschatological hope of *transformatio mundi:*

> Even 'the end of the world' can set no limits to the God who created the world out of nothing, the God who in the Son exposed his own self to annihilating Nothingness on the cross, in order to gather that Nothingness into his eternal being ... Anyone who believes in the God who created being out of nothing, also believes in the God who gives life to the dead. This means that he hopes for the new creation of heaven and earth. His faith makes him prepared to withstand annihilation, even when there is nothing left to hope for, humanly speaking. His hope in God commits him to faithfulness to the earth.[91]

Moltmann understands this 'self-restricting love' of the creator as 'the beginning of that self-emptying of God which Philippians 2 sees as the divine mystery of the Messiah'.[92] In other words, as Lewis noted, the crucifixion and death of Christ is understood as the turning point of a wider pattern of descent and reascent that will bring about the new creation. Interestingly, Lewis too seemed to imply that the act of creation was itself an act of divine kenosis. In his essay concerning intercessory prayer, Lewis commented upon the tension implicit in the idea of contingent creatures being granted free will by a God of omnipotence. It must involve, he believed, an act of abdication on the part of God, since in granting us free will he necessarily relinquishes something of his power over

---

[90] Jürgen Moltmann, *God in Creation*, p. 91.
[91] Ibid. p. 93.
[92] Ibid. p. 88.

us.[93] Elsewhere he noted that perhaps we should speak not only of a Tragic Redeemer but also of a Tragic Creator.'[94] The implication, here, is of a kenotic model at the heart of the perichoretic relationship of the divine Persons of the Trinity: the ecstatic exercise of divine love consists in not only a continual outpouring but also an eternal surrender and self-abdication – at least in the Person of the Son. Perhaps more significantly, Lewis believed this model to be mirrored throughout existence. 'For in self-giving, if anywhere,' he asserted, 'we touch a rhythm not only of all creation but of all being.' Thus our ultimate union with God can be described as 'almost by definition, a continual self-abandonment – an opening, an unveiling, a surrender, of itself.'[95] And thus Lewis was to follow George MacDonald in understanding the self-emptying of Christ in the crucifixion as not merely the ultimate expression of that self-emptying of the Son in the act of incarnation, but also as a revelation of the kenotic activity which is at the heart of the Trinity.

> For the Eternal Word also gives Himself in sacrifice; and that not only on Calvary. For when He was crucified He 'did that in the wild weather of His outlying provinces which He had done at home in glory and gladness'.[96]

This position echoes the theology of Karl Barth, who argued that Revelation 5:12's image of a sacrificed lamb at the centre of the heavenly liturgy is given to remind us that sacrifice and self-surrender lies at the heart of the divine identity. Christ is 'the Lamb slain from the foundation of the world,' he says and Christ crucified the truest image of the invisible God that we can have.[97] Moltmann, commenting on this position, observes: 'If the central foundation of our knowledge of the Trinity is the

---

[93] Cf. C. S. Lewis, 'The Efficacy of Prayer', in *The World's Last Night*, p. 9.
[94] Cf. *Letters to Malcolm*, p. 88 (Letter 17).
[95] *The Problem of Pain*, p. 126.
[96] Ibid. Lewis quoted here from George MacDonald, *Unspoken Sermons*, 3rd series, pp. 11, 12.
[97] Cf. Karl Barth, Church Dogmatics, Volume 2: pp. 123, 166.

cross, on which the Father delivered up the Son for us through the Spirit, then it is impossible to conceive of any Trinity of substance in the transcendent primal ground of this event, in which cross and self-giving are not present.'[98] Lewis went one step further and, in *The Four Loves*, spoke about Jesus the carpenter, Jesus on the road, Jesus in the crowds, Jesus in demand, Jesus jostled and abused (and so on) all as instances of that self-same divine surrender that will ultimately hand itself over for crucifixion and is the very life of the Trinity itself.[99]

In *The Problem of Pain* Lewis made reference to a 'golden apple of selfhood' which, when 'thrown among the false gods, became an apple of discord because they scrambled for it'. Of course the whole point of the game was that each player must catch the apple but then immediately pass it on. 'To be found with it in your hands is a fault: to cling to it, death.'[100] Existence, then, takes its pattern from the creator: self-surrender, self-abdication, ecstasis (in the sense of going out of oneself), kenosis. To cling to self, to try and be in full possession, is always the real lie, the ultimate self-contradiction, and the first sin. The ghosts in *The Great Divorce*, for example, can only ever become solid enough to survive heaven by surrendering themselves and their obsessions. The same message is underlined in *Till We Have Faces*. 'We want to be our own,' Orual complains to the gods. It is only by the end of her life that she realises her possessiveness stifled real life and real existence.[101] As Lewis noted in *The Problem of Pain*: 'What is outside the system of self-giving is not earth, nor nature, nor "ordinary life", but simply and solely hell.'[102]

This 'system of self-giving' as the basic pattern of reality is fleshed out well in the Narnia Chronicles. The victory of Aslan over Jadis in *The Lion, the Witch and the Wardrobe* comes about through the 'deeper magic from before the dawn of time'. As the Lion explains:

---

[98] Jürgen Moltmann, *The Trinity and the Kingdom: The Doctrine of God*, p. 160.
[99] Cf. *Four Loves,* p. 6.
[100] *The Problem of Pain*, p. 127.
[101] Cf. *Till We Have Faces,* pp. 221, 233.
[102] *The Problem of Pain,* p. 126.

If [the Witch] could have looked a little further back, into the stillness ... she would have read there a different incantation. She would have known that when a willing victim who had committed no treachery was killed in a traitor's stead, the Table would crack and Death itself would start working backwards.[103]

Lewis himself elaborated on this idea in a letter to his boyhood friend, Arthur Greeves, written in 1949:

It [is] the rule of the universe that others can do for us what we cannot do for ourselves and one can paddle every canoe *except* one's own. That is why Christ's suffering *for us* is not a mere theological dodge but the supreme case of the law that governs the whole world: and when they mocked him by saying, 'He saved others, himself he cannot save', they were really uttering, little as they know it, the ultimate law of the spiritual world.[104]

Paul Ford, in his *Companion to Narnia,* has noted that Lewis owed this principle to Charles Williams, who himself had developed a doctrine of substituted love, or co-inherence.[105] Ford believes the deeper magic 'connotes a self-sacrificing compassion' which is written into eternity, unlike the deep magic of the Witch's demand for Edmund's life, which is merely an example of natural justice.[106] To my reading, the narrative also has connotations of the patristic 'Devil's Rights' theory of atonement. This theory argued that through sin man had defied God and offered fealty to the devil. Consequently humanity was now under the devil's rule. God is unable (or, at least, unwilling) to restore man's freedom simply by an act of divine power, since this would be to go against divine justice. In the incarnation God enters into humanity. However, the

---

[103] C. S. Lewis, *The Lion, the Witch and the Wardrobe: A Story for Children,* p. 148.
[104] *They Stand Together,* p. 514 (Letter dated 2 July 1949).
[105] Cf. Charles Williams, *Descent into Hell,* chapter 6.
[106] Ford, *Companion to Narnia,* pp. 131–2.

devil does not perceive Christ's divinity and, in the crucifixion, lays claim to Christ's life. Since Christ is innocent of the devil's claims, the devil is found to have over-reached the bounds of divine justice which thereby allows God to restore humanity to his rule. In *The Lion, the Witch and the Wardrobe*, then, the deep magic written upon the Stone Table, the firestones of the Secret Hill, and on the sceptre of the Emperor-beyond-the sea refers to the demands of divine justice. Edmund, through his treachery, has willingly (although, perhaps, unwittingly) handed himself over to the power of Jadis. However, in accepting Aslan's life in place of the traitor, Jadis has over-reached her claims upon justice and has thereby lost her own protection under it (symbolised by the Stone Table breaking in half). This theory of atonement finds another fictional expression in Lewis' *Space Trilogy* where the Bent One breaks the rules of earth's siege (the 'Seventh Law') and thereby allows God and his Oyéresu to intervene directly in inter-planetary affairs.[107] Whatever the pro's and cons of such a theory, *The Lion, the Witch and the Wardrobe* demonstrates well the kenotic thinking at the heart of Lewis' theology: reality is shot through with a pattern or law (or magic, even) which takes the form of self-surrender and self-emptying, and which finds its origins 'before the dawn of time' – in other words, in God himself.

Eschatology and Protology

One of the strengths of Jürgen Moltmann's theology is his close positioning of protology to eschatology. In *God in Creation* he argues that the New Testament themes of the kingdom of God, eternal life, and glory are all ways of describing the eschatological goal of creation. We can discern in the world, he believes, the real promise of the kingdom of glory. Just as in Jesus' parables, where the hidden presence of the future of the coming kingdom is demonstrated, so the world as creation can be said to be a parable of its own future. For Moltmann, creation is eschatological in that it is itself the real promise of the

---

[107] See *That Hideous Strength*, p. 290. Cf. St Augustine, *The Trinity*, IV, pp. 3, 17.

kingdom, rather than merely a sort of theatre or staging area within which the coming kingdom is to be played out. As he notes in *Hope and Planning* the *kabod* of the Lord is already announced in his *dabar*. In other words, the glory of God is implicit in his creating activity.[108] In *The Coming of God* Moltmann argues that this implicit glory – this promise of kingdom – is made explicit in the incarnation and finds fulfilment in the 'eschatological "handing over of the kingdom" by the Son to the Father'. As he notes,

> The consummation according to John and Paul is more than the beginning: in the beginning creation – at the end the kingdom; in the beginning God in himself – at the end God all in all. In this divine eschatology God acquires through history his eternal kingdom, in which he arrives at his rest in all things, and in which all things will live eternally in him.[109]

Interestingly, in *Letters to Malcolm*, Lewis also picked up on this line from 1 Corinthians 15:28 when he commented: 'In Pantheism God is all. But the whole point of creation surely is that He was not content to be all. He intends to be "all *in* all"'.[110] Lewis once wrote, in the context of understanding the causality of miracles, 'Everything is connected with everything else: but not all things are connected by the short and straight roads we expected.'[111] The question, then, for this study is how

---

[108] Cf. Moltmann, *God in Creation*, pp. 56, 62–3 and idem, *Hope and Planning*, p. 17. Cf. 1 Co 15:28: 'When everything has been subjected to him, then the Son himself will be subjected to the One who has subjected everything to him, so that God may be all in all.' St Athanasius spoke of the unity between the original and new creations through the creative and salvific act of the Son. Cf. St Athanasius, *On the Incarnation*, I, 1, p. i: 'The renewal of creation has been wrought by the Self-same Word who made it in the beginning. There is thus no inconsistency between creation and salvation; for the One Father has employed the same Agent for both works, effecting the salvation of the world through the same Word who made it at the first.'

[109] Jürgen Moltmann, *The Coming of God*, p. 335.

[110] *Letters to Malcolm*, p. 68 (Letter 13).

[111] *Miracles*, p. 63.

did Lewis see the interconnection – or positioning – of Christian protology and eschatology?

In the Narnia Chronicles we find something of the answer. With the first of the seven children's stories, *The Magician's Nephew*, and the final book in the series, *The Last Battle* – which, incidentally were published within ten months of each other[112] – we have the protology and eschatology of Narnia respectively. Already I have mentioned the 'system of self-giving' – based on Charles Williams' doctrine of co-inherence or substituted love – in reference to Aslan's sacrifice on the Stone Table in *The Lion, the Witch and the Wardrobe*. It is a theme that resurfaces throughout the Chronicles and which, with the writing of *The Magician's Nephew* and *The Last Battle*, is widened out and used by Lewis to unify the whole of the series.[113] For example, in *The Magician's Nephew* Lewis depicted the creation of Narnia and the introduction of evil in the form of Jadis (who is later

---

[112] According to the timeline in J. Schultz and J. West, *Readers' Encyclopedia*, p. 450, *The Magician's Nephew* was published by Bodley Head on 2 May 1955 followed by *The Last Battle* on 9 March 1956. Walter Hooper, however, sheds much light on the actual writing of the two novels. As early as 14 June 1949 Roger Lancelyn Green visited Lewis and was read two chapters of a story about a boy called Digory. This has been called the *LeFay Fragment*. Hooper notes that some of its contents then found their way into other Narnia stories. However, in 1951, having completed five of the seven Narnia Chronicles, Lewis again turned his attention to writing about the beginnings of Narnia. By November of that year Roger Lancelyn Green was aware that three-quarters of the book were written, although he felt there were certain problems with a major section of it. Between the end of 1951 and the beginning of 1953 Lewis worked on *English Literature in the Sixteenth Century, Excluding Drama*, and by March 1953 had completed *The Last Battle*. It was only then that he returned to *The Magician's Nephew*, completing the text as we now have it by early 1954. See Walter Hooper, *A Companion and Guide*, pp. 403–5.

[113] For example, Paul Ford comments that this doctrine is echoed in *The Voyage of the Dawn Treader*, where a volunteer (Reepicheep) must sail to the World's End and remain there in order to release the three Narnian lords from their enchanted sleep. See Ford, *Companion to Narnia*, p. 131. Cf. C. S. Lewis, *The Voyage of the Dawn* p. 157.

known as the White Witch). 'Evil will come of that evil,' warns Aslan to the proto-Narnians, 'but it is still a long way off, and I will see to it that the worst falls upon myself.'[114] Clearly this is a reference back (speaking in the strict chronology of order of publication) to Aslan's substitution for Edmund to satisfy Jadis' bloodlust.[115] However, the process by which all this will happen – and by which all Narnia will eventually be set free from the White Witch's evil tyranny – begins with Digory's commission by Aslan to obtain a magical apple. As the story unfolds, Digory is asked to travel to a garden to the far west of Narnia and there pluck an apple which is to be planted on behalf of the inhabitants of Narnia. The tree that then grows from this planted apple not only protects the land from Jadis' presence for many hundreds of years but also itself bears fruit, one piece of which grows into a tree (this time in England) from which is made a wardrobe. It is through this wardrobe that the Pevensie children will first enter Narnia. And it is these children, together with Aslan, who defeat Jadis once and for all and who inaugurate in Narnia a golden reign of peace and prosperity. It is important to see the doctrine of co-inherence in operation here. As Aslan says, 'Adam's race has done the harm, Adam's race shall help to heal it',[116] but nevertheless the more significant factor is the dependence of Narnian salvation upon the self-giving of others: notably, the help of Digory in *The Magician's Nephew* and of Lucy, Edmund, Susan and Peter in *The Lion, the Witch and the Wardrobe*. Lewis' 'rule of the universe that others can do for us what we cannot do for ourselves and one can paddle every canoe *except* one's own' is

---

114 *Magician's Nephew*, p. 126. This is reminiscent of Karl Barth's under-standing of predestination: 'In God's eternal purpose it is God Himself who is rejected in His Son. The self-giving of God consists, the giving and sending of His Son is fulfilled, in the fact that He is rejected in order that we might not be rejected. Predestination means that for all eternity God has determined upon man's acquittal at His own cost. It means that God has ordained that in the place of the one acquitted He Himself should be perishing and abandoned and rejected – the Lamb slain from the foundation of the world.' See Karl Barth, *Church Dogmatics*, p. 167.
115 Cf. *The Lion, the Witch and the Wardrobe*, pp. 140–1.
116 *Magician's Nephew*, p. 126.

summed up well by Aslan's comments regarding the magic apples: 'The fruit always works – it must work – but it does not work happily for any who pluck it at their own will.'[117]

Rooted in this doctrine of substituted love is the wider theme of gift. It is Aslan who *gives* the initial apple to Digory – in the sense that he commands the boy to go to the garden to collect it. It is Aslan who *gives* Digory the second fruit too, to heal his mother. And note that this other fruit must in turn be *given*, if it is to work its healing power. An interesting scene in *The Last Battle* also uses the imagery of fruit and is instantly reminiscent of *The Magician's Nephew*. The major characters are all now through the stable door. Expecting to find themselves inside the thatched stable, Tirian and the others realise that they are in the open air of early summer and near a grove of fruit trees. The characters instinctively start to pick the luscious looking fruit but then pause, filled with doubt. The fruit was so beautiful, we are told, 'that each felt, "It can't be meant for me"'. It is Peter who comes to his senses and says: 'I've a feeling we've got to a country where everything is allowed.'[118] Certainly, one of the points that Lewis was making here was to reiterate his moral eschatology: to depict how 'morality exists to be transcended' and how, whereas now 'we act from duty,' someday 'we shall do the same acts freely and delightfully'.[119] However, this scene is so evocative of the fruit garden in *The Magician's Nephew* that I believe Lewis was also making a connection between his Narnian protology and his eschatology. Whereas, in the beginning, Jadis was able to climb the garden wall and steal the magic apples (even though in the long run this led to her disadvantage), in the real Narnia, the new creation, there is no possibility of stealing or appropriating what is not one's own. In heaven, *everything* is gift. If this interpretation is correct, it certainly echoes Lewis' position in *The Problem of Pain* where he noted: 'Heaven offers nothing that a mercenary soul can desire.'[120] And, as he went on: 'As to its fellow-crea-

---

[117] Ibid. p. 162.
[118] *The Last Battle*, p. 129.
[119] *Of This and Other Worlds*, p. 40.
[120] *The Problem of Pain*, p. 120.

tures, each soul, we suppose, will be eternally engaged in giving away to all the rest that which it receives.'[121]

This theme of gift is found elsewhere in the Narnia Chronicles too. For example, the presents of Father Christmas given to Peter, Susan and Lucy are all to be used in the service of others. One might argue that the White Witch's attempt to make Narnia always winter but never Christmas implies a distrust not only of joy and festivity on her part, but also of gift and giving as a whole.[122] And notice that this reaction to gift and giving would seem to be a deliberate ploy by which Lewis differentiated between his good and evil characters. The hospitality of Mr Tumnus and Mr and Mrs Beaver in *The Lion, the Witch and the Wardrobe* are in stark contrast to the cynical practicality of the White Witch in her feeding of Edmund with Turkish Delight.[123] The selfish and ungrateful natures of both Edmund and Eustace – prior to their conversions by Aslan – are offset by the selfless generosity of those around them, especially the character of Lucy.[124] Indeed, throughout the whole series the idea of Narnia as a land of gift and freedom is one

---

[121] Ibid. p. 126.

[122] Cf. *The Lion, the Witch and the Wardrobe*, pp. 42, 100. Paul Ford, commenting on this theme of winter in the Narnia series, understands it to be a 'natural metaphor for death and lifelessness'. Thus he argues Aslan's mountain, though being incredibly high, has no snow or ice cap but is portrayed as 'bathed in late spring/midsummer'. Ford points to two examples which suggests proof of such an intention on Lewis' part. In *The Grand Miracle* Lewis concluded: 'We have the power either of withstanding the spring and sinking back into the cosmic winter, or of going on into those 'high mid-summer pomps' in which our Leader, the Son of Man, already dwells, and to which He is calling us.' Similarly, in *Miracles,* Lewis noted: ' ... the Miracles of Perfecting or of Glory, the Transfiguration, the Resurrection, and the Ascension ... are the true spring, or even the summer, of the world's new year. The Captain, the forerunner, is already in May or June, though His followers on earth are still living in the frosts and east winds of Old Nature'. See Paul Ford, *Companion to Narnia*, pp. 57–8. Cf. *Essay Collection and Other Short Pieces*, p. 9 and *Miracles*, pp. 149–50.

[123] Cf. *The Lion, the Witch and the Wardrobe*, pp. 16–26, 33–43, 68–72.

[124] For example, in *The Lion, the Witch and the Wardrobe*, Edmund seems unwilling to help find Mr Tumnus and complains about a lack of food, yet when entertained and fed by the Beavers he is unable to

that is played out in the contradistinctions between Narnians and the people of Calormen (*The Horse and His Boy*), between 'Old Narnians' and the Telmarines who follow King Miraz (*Prince Caspian*), and between loyal Narnians and those treacherous creatures who sell themselves into the service of Jadis (*The Lion, the Witch and the Wardrobe*), and Rishda Tarkaan (*The Last Battle*). In *The Magician's Nephew* the foundation for this self-giving theme is made clear in Aslan's completion of Narnian creation with the words, 'Creatures, I give you yourselves. I give you forever this land of Narnia. I give you the woods, the fruits, the rivers. I give you the stars and I give you myself.'[125] This last line is significant, I think, since, in *The Last Battle*, the criterion for entry into the real Narnia is whether or not the creatures recognise Aslan. Where they do not, they disappear into his shadow and have no place in the Narnia within Narnia.[126] In other words the standard for judgement – and thereby entry into the new creation – is acceptance of the gift of Aslan himself. Note, too, that the redemption of Edmund from the power of the White Witch – and thereby the redemption of the whole of Narnia from her power – is won through the self-gift of Aslan to Jadis in place of the traitor. This is underlined with Edmund's personal restoration to the side of good with Aslan's words to the other children: 'Here is your brother – and there is no need to talk to him about what is past.' In other words, Aslan *gives* them back their brother. Thus we can say that in the Narnia Chronicles, creation, redemption, personal reconciliation, and final judgement are all presented through this theme of gift and self-giving.

Lewis used this theme elsewhere in his writing, for example

---

enjoy anything because he can't take his mind off the Witch's Turkish Delight and her promise to make him a prince. Similarly, in *The Voyage of the Dawn Treader*, Eustace spits out Lord Rynelf's spiced wine and demands 'Plumptree's Vitaminized Nerve Food' made with distilled water instead, is ungrateful when Lucy offers him a sip of her magic cordial, steals water rations, and appears oblivious to Lucy's sacrifice in sharing her own limited ration with him. Cf. *The Lion, the Witch and the Wardrobe*, pp. 58–60, 67, 82 and *Voyage of Dawn Treader*, pp. 15, 25, 60, 61.

[125] *Magician's Nephew*, p. 109.

[126] See *The Last Battle*, p. 144.

in *The Screwtape Letters*. Here the demon Screwtape writes to his nephew, Wormwood: 'The sense of ownership in general is always to be encouraged. The humans are always putting up claims to ownership which sound equally funny in Heaven and in Hell and we must keep them doing so.'[127] Later on in the same letter Screwtape outlines his belief that, ultimately, either God or Satan can only ever claim true possession.

> All the time the joke is that the word 'Mine' in its fully possessive sense cannot be uttered by a human being about anything. In the long run either Our Father [i.e. Satan] or the Enemy [i.e. God] will say 'Mine' of each thing that exists ... At present the Enemy says 'Mine' of everything on the pedantic, legalistic ground that He made it: Our Father hopes in the end to say 'Mine' of all things on the more realistic and dynamic ground of conquest.[128]

Of course, Lewis was being ironic here. While Screwtape laughs at the pointlessness of our human tendency to possess, we – as the readers – are supposed to laugh at his own naivety. God himself is eternal self-giving and as such the pattern for all reality. Hell's desire for conquest and possession is inherently futile since there can ultimately be no possession but only self-giving and self-surrender.

This leads us into a second theme which runs throughout the Narnia Chronicles and which draws Lewis' protology towards his eschatology: the inevitable victory of good. In *The Magician's Nephew*, witnessing the creative power of Aslan through his song, the evil Jadis becomes aware of a magic quite different and more powerful than her own. Lewis comments: 'She hated it. She would have smashed that whole world, or all worlds, to pieces, if it would only stop the singing.'[129] Significantly, however, this egotistical rage is unable to threaten – and indeed, is entirely at odds with – the stately

---

[127] *Screwtape Letters*, p. 83 (Letter 21).
[128] Ibid. pp. 83–4 (Letter 21).
[129] *The Magician's Nephew*, p. 95.

presence of Aslan as he brings Narnia into being. Importantly, Jadis has absolutely no impact whatsoever on the Lion. She is completely powerless against him. This is quite different from the portrayal of good and evil in *The Lion, the Witch and the Wardrobe*. In this second book of the series – although it must be remembered that in the order of writing and publication it was actually the first – the White Witch's reign appears to be unassailable and the only hope the Narnians seem to have is in some myth about two sons of Adam and two daughters of Eve one day sitting on the thrones at Cair Paravel. Even when the Pevensie children do appear in the story and the Cair Paravel prophecy looks like it might be fulfilled, there is still an air of danger and doubt as to whether the battle against evil can actually be won. This is particularly poignant in Aslan's surrender to Jadis and her cronies at the Stone Table. 'The fool!' cries the Witch. 'The fool has come.'[130] Of course this moment of sacrifice is paradoxically both evil's proudest boast and its definitive downfall. By submitting to the deep magic Aslan unleashes a deeper magic and death itself starts to work backwards.[131] This phrase should not only be applied to Aslan's return from the dead but also to the whole of Narnia. Narnian history from this point on is now no longer one of inevitable entropy, but rather a movement towards that decisive point depicted in *The Last Battle* when there are only two choices which face the various protagonists: are they for or against Aslan? In the intervening Narnia Chronicles there is still, of course, the presence and power of evil and the existence of selfish characters. For example, *The Horse and His Boy* includes the sub-plot of Rabadash's attempt to take Archenland (and eventually Narnia) by force.[132] *Prince Caspian* tells the story of the evil King Miraz's illegal rule of Narnia and of the brave resistance against him by 'Old Narnians'.[133] *The Voyage of the Dawn Treader* includes a number of adventures – such as Deathwater Island and the Dark Island – where the fate and success of the novel's

---

[130] *The Lion, the Witch and the Wardrobe*, p. 138.
[131] See ibid. p. 148.
[132] Cf. *The Horse and His Boy*, pp. 92–5.
[133] Cf. C. S. Lewis, *Prince Caspian: The Return to Narnia*, pp. 42–88.

heroes appears in doubt.[134] *The Silver Chair* narrates the imprisonment of Prince Rilian by the Green Witch.[135] And particularly in *The Last Battle* evil again appears to have gained the upper hand in Narnia. Many of its free subjects have been duped into submitting to slavery by Shift the Ape, who has dressed up Puzzle the donkey in a lion's skin and claimed Aslan is abroad. Calormen has sent troops into Narnia undetected and has taken Cair Paravel. And the very name of Aslan is muddled and confused with that of the evil demon, Tash. Eventually everything comes to a head when King Tirian calls all true Narnians to his side to fight in a battle to the death around the stable door.[136] The primary emphasis of each of these stories, however, is not so much whether good will overcome evil – this is taken (at least in the mind of the reader) for granted – but whether or not the major protagonists are faithful to Aslan. Do they believe in him? Do they trust in him? Will they give up everything for him? These are the sorts of criteria on which they will be judged because these are the ways in which they will live out and demonstrate their allegiance to good. And, as Mr. Tumnus explains in *The Last Battle*: 'No good thing is destroyed.'[137]

An important and related theme here is what Walter Hooper has referred to as the 'Euthyphro Dilemma'. This refers to a philosophical debate that arises within Plato's *Euthyphro*. As Hooper explains:

> In this dialogue between Socrates and Euthyphro the former makes a distinction fundamental in reasoning: that the good is not good because the gods approve it, but the gods approve it because it is good.[138]

The danger with arguing this position, of course, lies in 'admitting a cosmic dyarchy, or even making God Himself the mere executor of a law somehow external and antecedent to His own

---

134 Cf. *The Voyage of the Dawn Treader*, pp. 100–1, 135–45.
135 Cf. *The Silver Chair*, pp. 25, 49–52.
136 Cf. *The Last Battle*, pp. 33, 35, 87, 108, 152.
137 *The Last Battle*, p. 170.
138 Walter Hooper, *Companion and Guide*, p. 593.

being'.[139] The problem with taking the opposite stand, however, causes even more difficulties. As Lewis noted in an essay entitled, *The Poison of Subjectivism*:

> If good is to be *defined* as what God commands, then the goodness of God Himself is emptied of meaning and the commands of an omnipotent fiend would have the same claim on us as those of the 'righteous Lord.'[140]

Earlier, in *The Problem of Pain*, Lewis had raised this dilemma and adopted the stance of the sixteenth-century Anglican divine, Richard Hooker.[141] Hooker – and thus Lewis – had argued that good and evil are not delineated through some arbitrary divine decision but come from the pattern of God himself.[142] God is infinitely good and all that he creates is good. God cannot choose evil, since this would be to go not only against his creative will but more importantly to go against himself. God cannot will what in effect would be a self-contradiction. As Lewis argued: 'His omnipotence means power to do all that is intrinsically possible, not to do the intrinsically impossible. You may attribute miracles to Him, but not nonsense.'[143] And as he stated towards the end of his essay on subjectivism:

> What is the ground of all existence is not simply a law but also a begetting love, a love begotten, and the love which, being between these two, is also immanent in all those

---

[139] C. S. Lewis, 'The Poison of Subjectivism', in *Essay Collection and Other Short Pieces*, p. 663.

[140] Ibid. This stance is given dramatic depiction in *The Last Battle* with the fraudulent use of Aslan's authority to command all sorts of evil in Narnia by Shift the Ape. Ultimately the name of Aslan comes to stand for nothing more than the name of the Calormen demon, Tash. Cf. *The Last Battle*, pp. 34–6.

[141] *The Problem of Pain*, p. 80. Cf. Richard Hooker, *Laws of Ecclesiastical Polity, Books I–IV*, p. 63. See also *Reflections on the Psalms*, p. 52.

[142] See R. Hooker, *The Laws Ecclesiastical Polity*, p. 61: 'The being of God is a kind of law to His working; for that perfection which God is, giveth perfection to that He doth.'

[143] *The Problem of Pain*, p. 15.

who are caught up to share the unity of their self-caused life. God is not merely good, but goodness; goodness not merely divine, but God.[144]

This is important because it provides the ontological framework for understanding good and evil. We might even say it supplies the logical association between the declaration of Genesis concerning the initial creation – 'And indeed it was very good' (Genesis 1:31) – and the explanation of Mr Tumnus concerning the new: that nothing good can ultimately be destroyed.[145] Since goodness is not merely a moral approbation but pertains to the very nature of absolute being – and thereby of created being as originally intended – evil must ultimately be understood as a perversion of being itself. Discussing the relationship of good and evil in a letter to Arthur Greeves, Lewis noted: 'The truth is that evil is not a real *thing* at all, like God. It is simply good *spoiled*. That is why I say there can be good without evil, but no evil without good.'[146] Thus Lewis recognised a 'bad man's perdition not as a sentence imposed on him but as the mere fact of being what he is'.[147] Thus Jadis' evil reign is doomed from the outset not because Aslan is infinitely more powerful than she is – although certainly this, too, would be true – but because she herself, by choosing what is evil, has become a self-contradiction, has become utterly self-destructive. Her pursuit of power and possession in Charn leads to her use of the 'Deplorable Word', which wreaks obliteration on the very world she seeks to rule.[148] Her theft of the magical fruit from the garden in the west may give her 'unwearying strength and endless days like a goddess', but nevertheless will also prove her decisive downfall. And in the meantime, as Aslan points out, 'Length of days with an evil heart is only length of misery and already she begins to know it.'[149] In many ways Jadis is very much like the character of

---

[144] 'Poison of Subjectivism,' p. 664.
[145] Cf. *The Last Battle*, p. 170.
[146] *They Stand Together*, p. 465 (Letter dated 12 September 1933).
[147] *The Problem of Pain*, p. 100.
[148] Cf. *The Magician's Nephew*, pp. 59–60, 164.
[149] Ibid. p. 162.

Satan in Milton's *Paradise Lost*. And as Lewis commented of Milton's depiction of such an evil: 'Throughout the poem he [Satan] is engaged in sawing off the branch he is sitting on ... since a creature revolting against a creator is revolting against the source of his own powers – including even his power to revolt.'[150] So we can say that Satan in Milton's epic poem, Jadis in Lewis' Narnia Chronicles, Weston in *Perelandra*, Wither and Frost in *That Hideous Strength*, the obstinate ghosts in *The Great Divorce*, and Screwtape and Wormwood in *The Screwtape Letters* are all examples of what Lewis referred to in *The Problem of Pain* as 'successful rebels to the end'.[151]

> They certainly do not will even the first preliminary stages of that self-abandonment through which alone the soul can reach any good. They enjoy forever the horrible freedom they have demanded, and are therefore self-enslaved: just as the blessed, forever submitting to obedience, become through all eternity more and more free.[152]

In a way we are back to the kenotic pattern of reality, that heavenly law of self-giving which characterises the life of God and the whole of his creation. For, as Lewis stressed: 'When we have said that God commands things only because they are good, we must add that one of the things intrinsically good is that rational creatures should freely surrender themselves to their Creator in obedience.'[153]

The clearest and most obvious positioning of Lewisian protology and eschatology within the Narnia Chronicles, however, comes at the end of *The Last Battle* with the presentation of Narnia within Narnia. Here all that is good of the original creation is kept but the new Narnia seems bigger and more beautiful than the old. As Lewis commented:

---

[150] *Preface to Paradise Lost,* p. 96.
[151] *The Problem of Pain,* p. 104.
[152] Ibid. p. 105.
[153] Ibid. p. 80.

The new one was a deeper country: every rock and flower and blade of grass looked as if it meant more. I can't describe it any better than that.[154]

This echoes Lewis' presentation of eschatological reality in *The Great Divorce*. There he had described heaven as bigger, more colourful, more solid and weightier than anything we can imagine. Indeed, so much so that the narrator despaired of being able to portray accurately the superior quality of what he saw. In both depictions Lewis attempted to demonstrate the continuity between the finite and infinite realities and also the vast difference. The Unicorn's exclamation in *The Last Battle* sums up something of this attempt, as well as hinting at Lewis' eschatology of desire:

I have come home at last! This is my real country! I belong here. This is the land I have been looking for all my life, though I never knew it till now. The reason why we loved the old Narnia is that it sometimes looked a little like this.[155]

It is Digory, though, who provides the metaphysical explanation for such a sentiment:

It [the original Narnia] was only a shadow or a copy of the real Narnia which has always been here and always will be here: just as our world, England and all, is only a shadow or copy of something in Aslan's real world ... Of course it is different; as different as a real thing is from a shadow or as waking life is from a dream.[156]

---

154 *The Last Battle*, p. 160.
155 Ibid. p. 161. Lewis evoked a similar sentiment in *Till We Have Faces* where Psyche tried to explain to her sister Orual how the palace of the god where she now lives was similar and yet unlike the house of amber and gold that she had dreamed about in earlier days. Cf. *Till We Have Faces*, p. 81–4.
156 *The Last Battle*, pp. 159–60.

We are back, then, to the concepts of type and archetype, of shadow and reality, which I have already discussed. What is most interesting about the inner Narnia and inner England, however, is their relationship to Aslan's own country. Whereas in the old Narnia the children perceived the country to be surrounded by mountains – Archenland to the south, the Giant's hills to the north, the ice-covered mountains in the west beyond which lies the garden, and Aslan's mountain to the far east, beyond the sea – in the new creation Mr Tumnus describes the inner Narnia and inner England as 'spurs jutting out from the great mountains of Aslan'.[157] Paul Ford has interpreted this apparent discrepancy of Narnian geography as implying that Aslan's country 'is not connected with any *created* country but every *real* country is connected with it, as peninsula to mainland'.[158] Michael Murrin has demonstrated that the geometry of the real worlds 'presupposes a single high mountain, a centre point to lower mountain ranges, which radiate from it as do spokes from a the hub of a wheel'. Murrin makes the point that Aslan's country, then, acts as 'a cosmological crossroads'. It is the 'point where all the universes come together'.[159] It is interesting that neither commentator mentions the obvious reference to Old Testament eschatology. The constant refrain from the penultimate chapter of *The Last Battle* is 'further up and further in'. And in the final chapter, as the characters approach Aslan, the scene is described thus:

> And soon they found themselves all walking together – and a great, bright procession it was – up towards the mountains higher than you could see in this world even if they were there to be seen.[160]

To my reading – and I am sure that this must have been Lewis' intention – this is instantly evocative of Isaiah 2:2–3:

[157] Ibid. p. 170.
[158] Paul Ford, *Companion to Narnia,* p. 57. Italics are mine.
[159] Michael Murrin, 'The Multiple Worlds of the Narnia Stories', in *Word and Story in C. S. Lewis,* (eds) Peter Schakel and Charles Huttar, p. 236.
[160] *The Last Battle,* p. 170.

It will happen in the final days that the mountain of Yahweh's house will rise higher than the mountains and tower about the heights. Then all the nations will stream to it, and many people will come to it and say, 'Come, let us go up to the mountain of Yahweh.'

One interesting factor in Lewis' Narnian eschatology, however, is the omission of a Charn within Charn. At the end of *The Magician's Nephew*, Aslan takes Digory and Polly back to the Wood between the Worlds and shows them 'a little hollow in the grass, with a grassy bottom, warm and dry'.

'When you were last here,' said Aslan, 'that hollow was a pool, and when you jumped into it you came to the world where a dying sun shone over the ruins of Charn. There is no pool now. That world is ended, as if it had never been.'[161]

If we take this alongside the lack of an inner Charn in *The Last Battle*, and with Mr Tumnus' assertion that nothing good is destroyed, the implication must be that by the end of its time there was nothing good left in Charn whatsoever. This is important since it points to a particular interpretation of Romans 8:20–21: 'It was not for its own purposes that creation had frustration imposed upon it, but for the purposes of him who imposed it – with the intention that the whole creation itself might be freed from its slavery to corruption and brought into the same glorious freedom as the children of God.' In other words the destiny of creation is bound up in the fate of its rational inhabitants.[162] In the fictional case of Charn, sadly,

---

[161] *The Magician's Nephew*, p. 164.
[162] Lewis commented on this pericope in his essay 'Religion and Rocketry' (first published under the title, 'Will We Lose God in Outer Space?' in *The Christian Herald* in April 1958 but later included in a collection of essays called *The World's Last Night and Other Essays* under its present title). Here he speculated that the redemption of fallen rational beings from other planets (should they exist) might be caught up in our own redemption. Cf. *World's Last Night and Other Essays*, p. 88. This idea is given dramatic form in Lewis' Space Trilogy where a sort of celestial commonwealth is

those inhabitants had decisively chosen death and destruction and so allowed no 'glorious freedom' in which the world itself could share. However, if nothing now remains of Charn – if, indeed, there is no goodness left – then how can that be said to be a victory for good? The destruction of Charn suggests evil *can* thwart the eschatological goal of God's creation, even as it destroys itself in the process. I suppose it needs to be remembered here that the Narnia Chronicles are a fictional 'supposal' rather than strict allegory, and that the destruction of Charn stands merely as a warning to what can at least potentially happen if we insist on choosing self rather than self-surrender.

The close positioning of protology to eschatology is also found in Lewis' use of the concept of the 'Great Dance'. In his science fiction novel, *Perelandra*, Lewis wrote of a cosmic dance of salvation in which all worlds become embroiled.[163] Earlier, with the publication of *The Problem of Pain*, Lewis had used a similar concept of dance. There he noted that the symbol of drama or dance was a useful one to deal with the difficulties of imagining a world created good by God and then frustrated by the evil consequences of his granting us free will. 'This may raise,' he wrote, 'the ridiculous idea that the Fall took God by

---

presented in which one planet's eternal destiny is caught up in the eternal destiny of all the others. This is perhaps clearest in *Perelandra* where the salvation of the new world of Venus is ensured by Ransom's battle against the Un-man, who tries to tempt the Green Lady to disobey Maleldil and thereby commit Perelandra's first sin. Cf. *Perelandra*, pp. 61–3, 67, 74, 103–5, 112–21, 147–50, 153, 181–2, 209–12. This emphasis of the role of humanity within eschatology is noted by Zachary Hayes, when he comments: 'Four decades ago, Yves Congar spoke of the shift from a physical style to a more anthropological style of eschatology. ... The primary focus of such reflection is not on the nature of the "final things", but on the final, life-giving, fulfilling relation between God and humanity, and *through humanity*, with the world.' (Italics are mine). See Zachary Hayes, *Visions of a Future*, pp. 69–70.

[163] Cf. *Perelandra*, p. 214. Colin Duriez and David Porter have argued that Lewis developed this concept from Charles Williams' re-working of the idea of the Great Dance found in medieval cosmology. Cf. Colin Duriez and David Porter, *The Inklings Handbook: The Lives, Thought, and Writings of C. S. Lewis, J. R. R. Tolkien, Charles Williams, Owen Barfield and their Friends*, p. 114.

surprise and upset His plan.'[164] Instead, Lewis proposed the notion of a sort of cosmic dance in which 'good, descending from God, is disturbed by evil arising from the creatures, and the resulting conflict is resolved by God's own assumption of the suffering nature which evil produces'. Thus human sin is our contribution to the eternal dance in which God produces a 'second and more complex kind of good'. More clearly, perhaps, in *Perelandra* Lewis explained it thus:

> Never did He make two things the same; and never did He utter one word twice. After earths, not better earths but beasts; after beasts not better beasts, but spirits. After a falling, not a recovery but a new creation. Out of the new creation, not a third but the mode of change itself is changed for ever.[165]

With this concept Lewis was able to assert that God saw the 'crucifixion in the act of creating the first nebula' and attempted to reconcile human freedom with divine providence. He noted, of course, that the idea of the 'Great Dance' does not mean 'that if man had remained innocent God could not then have contrived an equally splendid symphonic whole – supposing that we insist on asking such questions'. Nevertheless, it did allow him to align God's creative act with his redemptive act through Christology. For, as Lewis put it in *Perelandra*, Christ is at the centre of the dance itself. Interestingly, it also admitted of the possibility of other worlds and civilisations which were unfallen but upon which the incarnation makes an impact.[166]

Apocalyptic Versus Evolutionary Eschatologies

In 1892 Johannes Weiss noted a shift in the eschatological expectation of modern day Christians from the Early Church. No longer, he argued, do we pray, 'May grace come and the

---

[164] *The Problem of Pain*, p. 65.
[165] *Perelandra*, p. 214.
[166] Cf. *The Problem of Pain*, pp. 65, 66 and *Perelandra*, p. 216.

world pass away', but rather we 'pass our lives in the joyful confidence that this world will increasingly become the show-place for a people of God'.[167] With this observation, Weiss identified an important tension in eschatological discourse: should the End Time be understood as a crude interruption[168] upon human history – in the nature of an apocalyptic end – or is it to be seen as the crowning point of an evolutionary process? As Moltmann expresses it – in an article published in 1999 – should we have an apocalyptic expectation of, or a messianic hope for, the kingdom of God?[169] Weiss also noted that a third position was possible; indeed, one that he felt was desirable:

The world will further endure, but we, as individuals, will soon leave it . . . We do not await a Kingdom of God which is to come down from heaven to earth and abolish this world, but we do hope to be gathered with the Church of Jesus Christ into the heavenly *basileia*.'[170]

Weiss was one of a number of Scripture scholars at the end of the nineteenth century who sought to re-interpret the

---

[167] Johannes Weiss, *Jesus' Proclamation of the Kingdom of God*, p. 135.

[168] Note that Moltmann dislikes the use of the term, 'interruption'. He argues: '"Interruption" is not an eschatological category. The eschatological category is conversion. An interruption certainly deranges the normal course of things and the desired goals of our own affairs, for it disrupts the notion of linear time, the causalities and homogeneous temporality of the "river of time"; but it interrupts only "for a time"; afterwards everything goes on as before, and the general run of things remains completely unchanged. But whenever the eschatological event interrupts the conjunctions of time, these are changed fundamentally. The prophets "interrupt", but not just for a moment; they call the people to conversion of the courses of time. Conversion and rebirth to a new life change time and the experience of time, for they make-present the ultimate in the penultimate, and the future of time in the midst of time.' See Jürgen Moltmann, *The Coming of God*, p. 22.

[169] Jürgen Moltmann, 'Hope and Reality: Contradiction and Correspondence: Response to Trevor Hart', in *God will be All in All: The Eschatology of Jürgen Moltmann*, p. 79.

[170] Johannes Weiss, *Jesus' Proclamation*, pp. 135–6.

eschatological dimension of Jesus' message and mission. Lewis himself believed the hesitation of modern Christians – and even 'the modern theologian' – to give the doctrine of the Second Coming the emphasis it had once enjoyed was due in part to the eschatologism – as André Feuillet calls it – of the followers of Weiss and Schweitzer and the like. But he also noted, 'The doctrine of the Second Coming is deeply uncongenial to the whole evolutionary or developmental character of modern thought.' And he went on to say:

> We have been taught to think of the world as something that grows slowly towards perfection, something that 'progresses' or 'evolves'. Christian Apocalyptic offers us no such hope. It does not even foretell (which would be more tolerable to our habits of thought) a gradual decay. It foretells a sudden, violent end imposed from without; an extinguisher popped onto the candle, a brick flung at the gramophone, a curtain rung down on the play – 'Halt!'[171]

There are, it seems, two main dangers with such an apocalyptic approach however. Of the first of these, Lewis himself was well aware. 'This doctrine has, in the past, led Christians into very great follies,' he admitted. Not least of which is the apparent difficulty people have in believing in an apocalyptic end to the world 'without trying to guess its date'.[172] Modern writers of eschatology such as Jürgen Moltmann and Karl Rahner have raised the second problem: an undue stress on 'End' in the concept of End Time. On the one hand, Rahner was critical of any false apocalyptic eschatology that attempts to provide 'an advance report of events taking place "later"' rather than

---

171 See 'The World's Last Night', pp. 93–101. André Feuillet includes Johannes Weiss, and A. Loisy alongside Albert Schweitzer as proponents of a school of thought which believed 'expectation of the imminent parousia and the end of the present world' to be the 'essential element both of the kerygma of primitive Christianity and of the authentic teaching of Jesus'. See André Feuillet, 'Eschatologism', in Karl Rahner, *Sacramentum Mundi*, Volume 2: *Contrition to Grace*, pp. 239–42.
172 Ibid. p. 106.

'concerning redeemed man as he is now'.[173] And on the other, Moltmann argued that whereas eschatology has been said to be the 'search for the "final solution" of all insoluble problems', *Christian* eschatology has nothing to do with such 'apocalyptic "final solutions" . . . for its subject is not "the end" at all. On the contrary, what it is about is the new creation of all things.'[174]

Lewis' own position, however, was not simply apocalyptic. Certainly, in *Mere Christianity*, he spoke of 'the whole natural universe melting away like a dream' in the face of God's undisguised presence as it 'comes crashing in'.[175] But equally he noted:

> People often ask when the next step in evolution – the step to something beyond man – will happen. But on the Christian view, it has happened already. In Christ a new kind of man appeared: and the new kind of life which began in Him is to be put into us.[176]

Thus Lewis used the vocabulary of both interruption and evolution. The evolutionary step he explained in terms of *Bios* and *Zoe*. 'The Spiritual life which is in God from all eternity, and which made the whole natural universe, is *Zoe*,' he argued, whereas *Bios* refers to our natural, biological life. As he elucidated his position:

> *Bios* has, to be sure, a certain shadowy or symbolic resemblance to *Zoe*: but only the sort of resemblance there is between a photo and a place, or a statue and a man. A man who changed from having *Bios* to having *Zoe* would have gone through as big a change as a statue which changed from being a carved stone to being a real man. [177]

[173] Karl Rahner, 'Eschatology,' in idem, *Sacramentum Mundi*, p. 244.
[174] Cf. Jürgen Moltmann, *The Coming of God*, pp. x–xi.
[175] *Mere Christianity*, p. 54.
[176] Ibid. p. 50.
[177] Ibid. p. 131, 132. Cf. von Rad, 'Life and Death in the Old Testament', p. 15: 'To this extent *hayyim* corresponds more to the Greek bios (inasmuch as this means not the manner in which life is led but its duration), than to the Greek zoe. Zoe corresponds rather to the Hebrew *nepes* in so far as *nepes* means the power on which life is based: it is the actual subject of living and dying.'

Then, using the Christian vocabulary of 'putting on Christ' (Cf. Galatians 3:27), being 'born again' (Cf. 1 Peter. 1:23) and Christ 'being formed in us' (Cf. Galatians 4:19), Lewis argued that Christian discipleship was actually about being turned 'permanently into a different sort of thing; into a new little Christ, a being which, in its own small way, has the same kind of life as God'.[178] In other words, evolving from *Bios* to *Zoe*, moving from being a carved statue to being flesh and blood. This 'evolutionary step', however, begins with the 'catastrophic historical event' – as Lewis put it in *The Problem of Pain* – of the incarnation.[179] As Lewis wrote in *Miracles*,

> The New Testament writers speak as if Christ's achievement in rising from the dead was the first event of its kind in the whole history of the universe. He is the 'first fruits', the 'pioneer of life'. He has forced open a door that has been locked since the death of the first man. He has met, fought, and beaten the King of Death. Everything is different because He has done so. This is the beginning of the New Creation: a new chapter in cosmic history has opened.[180]

This new chapter in cosmic history reaches its conclusion in the Second Coming of Christ. Whereas now what is new and what is old exist side by side, at the end of time only what is new will be allowed to exist. Thus the process of our transformation is begun and ended in the coming of Christ – firstly in his incarnation and secondly in the parousia. Ultimately, then, eschatology is neither apocalyptic nor evolutionary. It is, as Jürgen Moltmann has argued, an *Adventus*.[181]

An Eschatological Understanding of Time

In *Mere Christianity* Lewis noted: 'We tend to assume that the whole universe and God himself are always moving on from

[178] *Mere Christianity*, pp. 158, 159.
[179] *The Problem of Pain*, p. 11.
[180] *Miracles*, p. 153. See also 'What are We to Make of Jesus Christ?' in *God in the Dock*, p. 76.
[181] Cf. Jürgen Moltmann, *The Coming of God*, pp. 25–9.

past to future just as we do. But many learned men do not agree with that.'[182] It was Augustine who famously developed the notion of the con-creation of time for Christian metaphysics, although such an idea was certainly prevalent in Greek philosophy before him.[183] In *Timaeus* Plato had argued, 'For before the heavens came into being there were no days or nights or months or years, but he devised and brought them into being at the same time that the heavens were put together.'[184] And where Augustine defined time as the measurement of change, noting that it is 'idle to look for time before creation' since time itself began 'with the motion of creatures' and a 'creature could not move if it did not exist',[185] Aristotle had already coined the classical formulation of *numerus motus secundum prius et posterius*.[186]

Reflecting on Psalms 90:4 – 'A thousand years are to you like a yesterday which has passed like the watch of the night' – Lewis noted that the psalmist most probably meant only 'that God was everlasting, that His life was infinite in time'. However, with 2 Peter 3:8 – 'With the Lord, a day is like a thousand years, and a thousand years are like a day' – and with these pagan philosophical and subsequent Christian developments in the understanding of time, Lewis argued that the Psalm takes on a second meaning. The Christian interpretation, he believed, has taken us out of the time series altogether and introduced the notion of 'the timeless as an eternal present'[187] – what Augustine called the eternal today of God:

---

[182] *Mere Christianity*, p. 139.

[183] St Augustine, *Concerning the City of God against the Pagans*, XI, p. 6: 'The Bible says (and the Bible never lies): "In the beginning God made heaven and earth." It must be inferred that God had created nothing before that; "in the beginning" must refer to whatever he made before all his other works. Thus there can be no doubt that the world was not created *in* time but *with* time.'

[184] Plato, *Timaeus and Critias*, p. 37.

[185] St Augustine, *The Literal Meaning of Genesis: A Commentary in Twelve Books*, V, p. 12, Cf. idem, *Confessions*, XI, p. 14 and *Genesis*, VIII, pp. 39–43.

[186] I.e. 'the numbering of movement by before and after'. Cf. Aristotle, *Physics*, IV, p. xi, 219b. Cf. St Thomas, *Summa Theologiae*, I, p. 10, 1.

[187] *Reflections on the Psalms*, pp. 118–19.

hodiernus tuus aeternitas.[188] Again this idea finds its origins in the work of Plato's *Timaeus*. Here time is presented as the 'moving image of eternity'. For, of the 'Eternal Being', Plato commented:

> For we say of it that it *was* and *shall be,* but on a true reckoning we should only say *is,* reserving *was* and *shall be* for the process of change in time: for both are motions, but that which is eternally the same and unmoved can neither be becoming older or younger owing to the lapse of time, nor can it ever become so; neither can it now have *become* nor can it come to *be* in the future; nor in general can any of the attributes which becoming attached to sensible and changing things belong to it, for they are all forms of time which in its measurable cycles imitates eternity.[189]

What is interesting about Lewis' reflection on Psalms 90:4 is his speculation over what might constitute the eschatological destiny of time. As he argued:

> The Eternal may meet us in what is, by our present measurements, a day or (more likely) a minute or a second; but we have touched what is not in any way commensurable with lengths of time, whether long or short. Hence our hope finally to emerge, if not altogether from time (that might not suit our humanity) at any rate from the tyranny, the unilinear poverty, of time, to ride it not to be ridden by it, and so to cure that always aching wound ... which mere succession and mutability inflict on us, almost equally when we are happy and when we are unhappy.[190]

For this study, then, it is important to grasp not only how Lewis presented the Christian idea of God's eternal today, but also how he understood our participation in that 'today' to operate – both in our present experience and after death.

---

[188] St Augustine, *Confessions,* XI, p.13.
[189] Plato, *Timaeus,* pp. 37–8.
[190] *Reflections on the Psalms,* p. 119.

God's Time

Most of Lewis' thought concerning the notion of an eternal present is found within the context of understanding intercessory prayer and divine providence. For example, Screwtape advises his nephew, Wormwood, not to forget the '"heads I win, tails you lose" argument'. This basically entails convincing the believer that when he prays for what doesn't happen it is proof that intercessory prayer doesn't work, and when he prays for what does happen it is merely a coincidence. Misunderstanding time as an ultimate reality, argues Screwtape, humans tend to think that God 'sees some things as present, remembers others as past, and anticipates others as future'. Thus all sorts of problems arise in balancing free will, providence, and predestination. Of course, as Screwtape concludes: 'The Enemy does not *foresee* the humans making their free contributions in a future, but *sees* them doing so in His unbounded Now. And obviously to watch a man doing something is not to make him do it.'[191] This idea is perhaps better clarified in *Mere Christianity*. Lewis used the image of a line drawn on a blank page to represent the flow of time. 'If you picture Time as a straight line along which we have to travel,' he argued, 'then you must picture God as the whole page on which the line is drawn.' In other words, God stands outside or above the experience of time. What we call yesterday or tomorrow is present for him as if today. As Lewis explained: 'All the days are "Now" for Him. He does not remember you doing things yesterday; He simply sees you doing them, because, though you have lost yesterday, He has not.'[192] Thus we can say God's act of creation is truly timeless because for him there is no past in which he could have created it. God creates within the eternal now. And if his creative act is timeless he is able also to timelessly adapt to our needs in answering our prayers of intercession.

So far these metaphysical speculations have concerned God's experience of his eternal now. In *Letters to Malcolm* and in *Miracles* Lewis complemented this perspective with a discussion

---

[191] *Screwtape Letters*, p. 107 (Letter 27).
[192] *Mere Christianity*, p. 141.

of temporality from the human viewpoint. Time, he argued, may only be a mode of our perception. Due to the limitations of our finite natures we can only apprehend reality through the experience of succession. Whilst God perceives us in our eternal – and therefore, as Lewis noted, our deepest – reality, we experience ourselves (and, indeed, all reality) through the medium of succession and change.[193] In *The Great Divorce* Lewis described time as the lens through which finite creatures see something infinite. 'That thing is Freedom,' he wrote, and can only be grasped by us through successive moments in which we are aware of ourselves making choices.[194] This notion of what is sometimes called 'external' time[195] is also explained in Screwtape's comment: 'The humans live in time and experience reality successively. To experience much of it, therefore, they must experience many different things; in other words, they must experience change.'[196] Of course, this is the basic understanding of time presented by Plato and Aristotle, and taken up by St Thomas.[197] As Adolf Darlap notes, time is here understood as the extrapolation 'from the flow of the "Now" and becomes a quantifying, measuring, continuous homogenous field'. Because of this, humans are 'exposed to time and made its slave, as though to a cosmic power'.[198] What he means by this last comment is merely that the flow of time as the

---

[193] Cf. *Letters to Malcolm*, p. 106 (Letter 20) and *Miracles* p. 187.

[194] Cf. *Great Divorce* p. 115.

[195] Cf. Adolf Darlap, 'Time', in *Encyclopedia of Theology*, pp. 1716–17.

[196] *Screwtape Letters,* p. 97 (Letter 25).

[197] Cf. Plato, *Timaeus*, p. 37; Aristotle, *Physics,* IV, pp. xi, 219b. See also St Thomas, *Summa Theologiae*, I, pp. 10, 1: 'As we attain to the knowledge of simple things by way of compound things, so we must reach to the knowledge of eternity by means of time, which is nothing but the numbering of movement by "before" and "after". For since succession occurs in every moment, and one part comes after another, the fact that we reckon before and after is movement, makes us apprehend time, which is nothing else but the measurement of before and after in movement. Ibid., I, pp. 10, 2, a3: 'Eternity is nothing else but God Himself. Hence God is not called eternal, as if He were in any way measured; but the idea of measurement is there taken according to the apprehension of our mind alone.'

[198] Darlap, 'Time', p. 1716.

measurement of change is beyond our control. As Lewis put it through the mouthpiece of Screwtape, the future is not 'a promised land which favoured heroes attain', whatever we might convince ourselves, but rather 'something which everyone reaches at the rate of sixty minutes an hour, whatever he does, whoever he is'.[199]

This concept of eternity – and time as the finite perception of it – has a number of implications for eschatology. Firstly, it raises a challenge to the notion of the End Time as some kind of future age. As Moltmann explains:

> European languages generally have two possible ways of talking about what is ahead. *Futurum* means what will be; *adventus* means what is coming. The two words go together with two different conceptions of time.[200]

The eschaton belongs to the concept of *adventus* rather than *futurum;* the End Time is the age *to come,* the fullness of time, the last times, rather than a future period *in* time. Since *futurum* is an expression of the potentiality of being, it is therefore a wholly inadequate category within which to understand the ultimate reality and fullness of being that is the gift and goal of our eternal beatitude. Even our language makes the use of *futurum* somewhat senseless. The future is a category of time, yet in talking about the End Time we are dealing not with temporal realities but with eternal reality. In the eternal now of God's presence – his eternal today as Augustine put it – the notion of future has no place. Thus, as Screwtape says, 'The humans live in time but our Enemy destines them to eternity.' He goes on to

---

[199] *Screwtape Letters*, p. 100 (Letter 25).
[200] Jürgen Moltmann, *The Coming of God*, p. 25. In his earlier work, *God in Creation,* Moltmann had noted, 'If the future is understood in the sense of *futurum,* it means what *will be* out of past and present ... On the other hand, if we understand future as *adventus,* it means what is coming – what is on the way towards the present. What we describe as a "coming" event is not something that develops out of the present. It confronts the present with something new, whether it be good or evil.' See idem, *God in Creation*, p. 133.

explain that while the present moment is at least analogous for humans to the experience of the eternal now, the future is, 'of all things, the least like eternity'. It is 'the most completely temporal part of time', he says. 'Hence nearly all vices are rooted in the future. Gratitude looks to the past and love to the present; fear, avarice, lust and ambition look ahead.'[201]

This leads into our second implication. If all times are eternally present to God and if, in our deepest reality, we stand eternally before him, then what we perceive as individual moral actions taken in time are, in fact to God, not a series of successive, broken up acts at all but a definitive and eternal stance taken before our creator. As Lewis speculated in *The Problem of Pain*:

> Is it not at least possible that along some line of his multidimensional eternity he sees you forever in the nursery pulling the wings off a fly, forever toadying, lying, and lusting as a schoolboy, forever in that moment of cowardice or insolence as a subaltern?[202]

This is important because it provides another framework within which to understand Lewis' moral eschatology. From the divine perspective, judgement is not made on a lifetime of successive acts – good or bad – but on the eternal and freely chosen disposition that those acts in time represent in deepest reality. We do not simply develop into saints or degenerate into lost souls. Before the ultimate reality of God there is only a choice of two fundamental dispositions. As Lewis noted, 'There are only two kinds of people in the end: those who say to God, "Thy will be done", and those to whom God says, in the end, "*Thy* will be done".'[203]

---

[201] Cf. *Screwtape Letters*, pp. 57–8 (Letter 15).

[202] *The Problem of Pain*, p. 45.

[203] *Great Divorce*, pp. 66–7. Cf. Mt 12:30: 'Anyone who is not with me is against me, and anyone who does not gather in with me throws away.' Or put more positively, 'Anyone who is not against us is for us.' (Mk 9:40). The latter is surely the basis for Lewis' idea of the courtesy of Deep Heaven: that when our intentions are correct, God takes us to have meant better than we knew. See *That Hideous Strength*, p. 230.

Similarly, this understanding of time has implications for our perception of the incarnation and of that kenotic pattern of reality to which I referred earlier in this chapter. As Lewis noted in *Mere Christianity* concerning the incarnation: 'This human life in God is from our point of view a particular period in the history of our world ... We therefore imagine it is also a period in the history of God's own existence.'[204] In other words, we think – even if we do not say – that there was in God a *time* when the Son was not incarnate. There is a real danger of making what can be only a notional distinction between the immanent and economic Trinity into a temporal one. There is a real danger that we thereby give God a history. But, as Lewis stated: 'God has no history. He is too completely and utterly real to have one. For, of course, to have a history means losing part of your reality (because it has already slipped away into the past).'[205] Thus we cannot 'fit Christ's earthly life in Palestine into any time-relations with His life as God beyond all space and time'. This is true, of course, but has its own potential problem: the danger of losing any distinction – notional or otherwise – between the economic and immanent. Lewis was aware of this problem and wrote in a letter to Arthur Greeves:

> On the one hand something really *new* did happen at Bethlehem: not an interpretation but an *event*. God became man. On the other hand there must be a sense in which God, being outside time, is changeless and nothing ever 'happens' to Him. I think I should reply that the event at Bethlehem was a novelty, a change to the maximum extent to which any event is a novelty or change: but that *all* time and *all* events in it, if we could see them all at once and fully understand them, are a definition or diagram of what God eternally is. But that is quite different from saying that the incarnation was simply an interpretation, or a change in *our* knowledge.[206]

---

[204] *Mere Christianity*, p. 141.
[205] Ibid.
[206] *They Stand Together*, p. 505 (Letter dated 26 December 1945).

Nevertheless, despite this difficulty we can now begin to understand more clearly why Lewis saw Christ's death and resurrection as part of that larger pattern of real Death and Rebirth. We can see too why he asserted that 'in self-giving, if anywhere, we touch a rhythm not only of all creation but of all being'. [207] The eternal now of God is one complete act of self-surrender and glory, of kenosis, of self-emptying love. Finite being participates in – or at least reflects – this ultimate reality through time: successive acts of death and rebirth. The event of the incarnation, then, is eschatological in that it is the entry into the time series of the eternal. Thus the central significant acts of Christ's life – his passion, death and resurrection – are to be seen as revealing that eternal self-surrender and filial obedience that is at the heart of the Trinity. With this event we have moved on from a purely philosophical notion of time (as expressed by Plato in *Timaeus,* for example) and into the Christian concept of realised eschatology. The eternal now of God has broken into time and transfigured it.

This new temporal framework gives a basis to the Christian assertion that Christ's redemptive sacrifice affects all times – past, present and future – and not merely first century Palestine. It makes sense of the Church's solemn Easter liturgy, when the Paschal candle is marked with the sign of the cross and the assertion made of Christ: 'All time belongs to him and all ages.'[208] Of course our daily perception of this kenotic structure to reality is still understood through the mode of succession and temporality. Hence we understand God's saving work as salvation *history*. Hence we exhort ourselves and others to individual acts of self-surrender and a daily dying to self. Ultimately, however, that mode of temporal perception will be taken away – or at least qualitatively changed in some way. And then, in death, as Zachary Hayes notes, we will experience the 'final moment of a free, personal history' and the 'decisive act of human freedom' in which we can 'either accept or reject the mystery of God'. [209] It is the moment in which our deepest

---

[207] *The Problem of Pain,* p. 126.
[208] *Roman Missal,* p. 188.
[209] Zachary Hayes, 'Death', pp. 272–3.

eternal reality is made clear to us and we realise whether or not we have accepted the gift of God himself.

Time Beyond Time

In *A Grief Observed* Lewis mourned the loss of his dead wife and posed the question: 'Where is she now?' Such questioning in grief is, of course, quite common. But what Lewis meant here was that if Joy Gresham was no longer to be identified with the dead body he had seen buried, and therefore no longer in our spatio-temporal reality, where was she? He was grappling with one of the central difficulties concerning eschatological discourse: how do we comprehend the time beyond time? The fundamental problem revolves around what is sometimes called atemporalism. In other words, can we admit of temporality within eternity, or must we interpret the End Time as meaning the end *of* time? The atemporal approach, for example, argues that after death time no longer exists, since time is anyway merely our finite apprehension of God's eternal now. Thus, one might say that while the deaths of individuals are successive from our finite point of view, from the eternal viewpoint there can be no temporal distinction. It is therefore possible to argue that after individual death one encounters immediately the general resurrection. There is no 'time' in which the soul must await the resurrection of the body. This position has a number of theological advantages. Firstly, it reinforces the strongly anti-dualist bias of Christian anthropology. By not admitting of a separate temporal existence of the soul it ensures that the human person is always viewed as the unity of body and soul. Secondly, atemporalism re-emphasizes the idea of judgement and purgatory as a process and not a place. Thus it removes the danger of viewing purgatory as a sort of temporary hell. Thirdly, it has useful pastoral connotations in dealing with grief. The joy of the saved is complete in death because he or she is simultaneously caught up in the general resurrection and re-united with former loved ones in the eternal now of divine beatitude. However, atemporal eschatology also raises a number of problems. In its 1979 letter, *Recentiores episcoporum synodi*, the Sacred Congregation for the Doctrine of the Faith affirmed, 'A spiritual element survives

and subsists after death, an element endowed with consciousness and will, so that the "human self" subsists.'[210] With
atemporalism, the reason for such an assertion is no longer
clear and the significance of the separation of body and soul in
death – as a result of the Fall – is in danger of being under-
mined. Similarly, then, the language of traditional theology
and prayer for the dead would appear to be incorrect. Why
pray for the repose of someone's soul instead of praying for
someone? For, as the Congregation warned in its document:

> The Church excludes every way of thinking or speaking
> that would render meaningless or unintelligible her
> prayers, her funeral rites and the religious acts offered for
> the dead. All these are, in their substance, *loci theologici*.[211]

More important, however, are the difficulties raised by atem-
poralism with biblical language. As the International
Theological Commission pointed out in its document, *Some
Current Questions in Eschatology:*

> The New Testament's way of speaking about the souls of
> the martyrs does not seem to remove them either from all
> reality of succession or from all perception of succession
> (Cf. Revelations 6:9–11). Similarly, if time should have no
> meaning after death, not even in some way merely analo-
> gous with its terrestrial meaning, it would be difficult to
> understand why Paul used formulas referring to the future
> (*anastesontai*) in speaking about their resurrection, when
> responding to the Thessalonians who were asking about
> the fate of the dead (Cf. 1 Thessalonians 4:13–18).[212]

The Commission, then, felt that atemporalist theories rely too
heavily on an understanding of time and eternity based on
Greek philosophical thought rather than on the biblical data.

---

[210] Sacred Congrgation for the Doctrine of the Faith, 'The Reality of
Life After Death', p. 502.
[211] Ibid.
[212] International Theological Commission, 'Some Current Questions
in Eschatology', p. 218.

Furthermore, the Commission questioned whether, without some concept of time beyond time, the 'truly corporeal nature of the resurrection' can be sufficiently taken into account, since 'A true body cannot be said to exist devoid of all notion of temporality. Even the souls of the blessed, since they are in communion with Christ who has been raised in a bodily way, cannot be thought of without any connection with time.'[213]

Lewis' own position on the concept of time beyond time, given his understanding of God's eternal today as outlined above, might be assumed to tend towards the atemporal. However, with the posthumous publication of *Letters to Malcolm* in 1964, his position is made very clear. 'I certainly believe that to be God is to enjoy an infinite present, where nothing has yet passed away and nothing is still to come,' he noted, but went on: 'Does it follow that we can say the same of saints and angels? Or at any rate exactly the same?'[214] In a line echoed by the International Theological Commission years later (and already referred to above), Lewis commented:

> I feel – can you work it out for me and tell me if it is more than a feeling – that to make the life of the blessed dead strictly timeless is inconsistent with the resurrection of the body.[215]

Thus he speculated that the dead might 'experience a time which was not quite so linear as ours'. As he put it in a letter to Sheldon Vanauken: 'I'm pretty sure eternal life doesn't mean this width-less line of moments endlessly prolonged ... but getting off that line onto its plane or even the solid.'[216] Already, particularly in his children's books and science fiction, Lewis had experimented with different understandings of the operation and experience of time. The Narnian time-series, for example, operated entirely independently of our own.[217] And,

---

[213] Cf. ibid.
[214] *Letters to Malcolm,* p. 105 (Letter 20).
[215] Ibid.
[216] Sheldon Vanauken, *A Severe Mercy*, p. 205.
[217] Cf. *The Lion, the Witch and the Wardrobe*, pp. 27, 170; *Prince Caspian,* pp. 24–5, 34; *The Voyage of the Dawn Treader*, pp. 13, 19; and *The Silver Chair*, pp. 39–40.

in *Perelandra*, Ransom explains how an Oysara experiences time and duration quite differently from ourselves.

> 'You mean he has been waiting in the next room all these hours?'
> 'Not waiting. They never have that experience. You and I are conscious of waiting, because we have a body that grows tired or restless, and therefore a sense of cumulative duration. Also we can distinguish duties and spare time and therefore have a concept of leisure. It is not like that with him. He has been here all this time, but you can no more call it *waiting* that you can call the whole of his existence *waiting*. You might as well say that a tree in a wood was waiting, or the sunlight waiting on the side of a hill.'[218]

Thus in *Letters to Malcolm*, Lewis suggested that the dead might enjoy a time that had 'thickness as well as length'. As he pointed out, 'The question is not whether the dead are part of timeless reality ... the question is whether they share the divine perspective of timelessness.'[219] This is important since Lewis has here – with the idea of temporal perception – allowed a reconciliation of Greek philosophical categories and biblical language. There may well be a necessary distinction to be made in how created beings – even glorified ones – apprehend the eternal now. As Lewis noted in *The Great Divorce*: 'Ye *cannot* know eternal reality by a definition. Time itself, and all acts and events that fill Time, are the definition, and it must be lived.'[220] In other words, we apprehend reality through participating in it. It is possible, Lewis speculated, that such participation will always require some sort of experience of time.

---

[218] *Perelandra*, p. 29. See also *Dark Tower*, pp. 72–7. Here the author played with some speculative ideas on the dimensions of time, which would be experienced differently depending upon one's perspective.
[219] *Letters to Malcolm*, pp. 105, 106 (Letter 20).
[220] *Great Divorce*, p. 115.

Kairos Versus Chronos

Two concepts with strong biblical roots that help with this understanding of time beyond time are *kairos* and *chronos*. In the New Testament, *kairos* is used in reference to a suitable time, such as Paul's use of the phrase, 'the time of my favour' (2 Corinthians 6:2), to a specific and decisive event in history, for example the coming of God's kingdom (Mark 1:15), or to a future period marked out by characteristic circumstances, e.g. the end times or messianic age (e.g. Matthew 6:3; 1 Timothy 4:1). *Chronos*, on the other hand, is used simply to refer to the passing of time, from which we get the English use of 'chronology' and 'chronological'. *Kairos*, then, is time defined by event. *Chronos* is time as measurement of change or experience of succession. A simple example to elucidate these two concepts of time would be to compare the experience of becoming engrossed in a compelling and entertaining film with waiting for a kettle to boil. In the first instance we are caught up in the event that is characterising the passing of time and thus experiencing *kairos*. In the second we are awaiting the future outcome of a present activity – i.e. we await the kettle to boil so that we can make a cup of tea – and so we are engaged by *chronos:* the sense of succession and measurement of change. Such concepts, if not such terminology, are to be found in Lewis' thought. For example, towards the end of his science fiction novel, *Perelandra,* Lewis presented a discussion about the experience of time through the characters of Ransom and Tor:

'They did not wait long,' said Ransom, 'for I feel it is still early in the morning.'
'But not the same morning,' said Tor.
'We have been here long, then?' asked Ransom.
'Yes,' said Tor. 'I did not know it till now. But we have accomplished one whole circle about Arbol since we met on this mountain top.'
'A year?' said Ransom. 'A whole year? O Heavens, what may by now have happened in my own dark world! Did you know, Father, that so much time was passing?'
'I did not feel it pass,' said Tor. 'I believe the waves of time will often change for us henceforward. We are

coming to have it in our own choice whether we shall be above them and see many waves together or whether we shall reach them one by one as we used to.'[221]

They have not noticed the time pass because they were experiencing *kairos* rather than *chronos* – they were engaged in what filled the time rather than its particular measurement. By contrast Lewis presented a more negative experience in his Narnia Chronicles. In *The Magician's Nephew* both Digory and Polly experience the tedium of waiting for Uncle Andrew and the Witch, Jadis, to return to the house in London:

> So while Digory was staring out of the dining-room window, Polly was lying in bed, and both were thinking how terribly slow the time could go.[222]

Similarly, in *The Voyage of the Dawn Treader*, Lucy finds herself reading the magician's book to try and find out how to reverse the invisibility spell put on the Dufflepuds. The Chief Dufflepud had been unable to tell her whereabouts in the large book the spell might be situated and 'expected her to begin at the beginning and go on till she came to it'. But Lucy finds the whole process exasperating. 'It might take me days and weeks!' she says, noting also, 'and I feel already as if I'd been in this place for hours.'[223] In both these examples, the experience of time as *chronos* is heightened somewhat through some kind of trepidation. Digory and Polly are concerned with what Jadis and Uncle Andrew might get up to in London and wonder how and if they will ever be able to use the magic rings to get Jadis out of their world again. Lucy is filled with fear at the thought of being in the magician's house without his consent or knowledge – a fear compounded by the notion given her by the Dufflepuds that the magician is evil.

This distinction of the experience of time is an important one for eschatology, particularly if – as Lewis seemed to do – we wish

---

[221] *Perelandra*, p. 220.
[222] *The Magician's Nephew*, p. 80.
[223] *The Voyage of the Dawn Treader,* p. 117.

to admit of some experience of time beyond time. Thus when Lewis wrote that one day we might 'hope finally to emerge, if not altogether from time ... at any rate from the tyranny, the unilinear poverty, of time',[224] it could be understood in terms of experiencing time no longer as *chronos* but as *kairos*. Similarly, when in *Letters to Malcolm* he spoke of time having 'thickness as well as length' this could be understood as *kairos*. The distinction becomes even more useful when we want to promote a realised eschatology. The meeting of Old and New natures, of temporality with End Time, is given clear expression in the concept of the *kairological* experience of time transcending the chronological experience. As Lewis noted of prayer:

> The attempt is not to escape from space and time and from my creaturely situation as a subject facing objects ... The situation itself is, at every moment, a possible theophany. Here is the holy ground: the Bush is burning now.[225]

In experiencing time as *kairos* we are fully engaged in the present moment, which as Lewis argued in *The Screwtape Letters* is the nearest situation we can admit to sharing in the eternal now of God.[226]

Another interesting aspect of this *kairological* interpretation of time is the sense it makes of the experience of *Sehnsucht*. As Lewis described this act of longing, *Sehnsucht* involves both a reminiscence of something past and a longing for something future which become an engaging experience which characterises the present. I am not sure we could say *Sehnsucht*, as such, was strictly an experience of *kairos* but it does point to the decisive definition of time as ultimately being about what fills it. It expresses a longing for the End Time when reminiscence of things lost and longing for things to come will give way to the overwhelming experience of things – I should say, the Last Thing – given in the eternal present.

---

[224] *Reflections on the Psalms*, p. 119.
[225] *Letters to Malcolm*, p. 78 (Letter 15).
[226] See *Screwtape Letters*, p. 57 (Letter 15).

Chapter 3

Developing a Worldview

In his Oxford Kaiser Lectures, given between the 23 and 25 May 2000, the American psychiatrist Armand Nicholi contrasted what he termed the 'conflicting worldviews of Sigmund Freud and C. S. Lewis'.[1] Noting that Freud had defined a worldview as 'an intellectual construction which solves all the problems of our existence uniformly on the basis of one over-riding hypothesis', Nicholi commented: 'We all possess a worldview whether we like it or not. We either assume existence a matter of chance or we presume an intelligence beyond what we see.' As professor of psychiatry at Harvard Medical School, Nicholi's interest in the Lewisian worldview focused largely on its shift from a materialist position – and, in that sense, one not dissimilar to Freud's – to a deeply held supernaturalist position. With such a shift came a change in both character and conduct. By his conversion Lewis moved, Nicholi observed, 'from wary introvert to a personable, outgoing extrovert with scores of friends and colleagues'. In this chapter I also aim to examine Lewis' worldview and the important alteration in outlook that his conversion to Christianity conferred. I made the point in my introductory chapter that Lewis was neither a professional theologian nor a formal eschatologist as such. Nevertheless, the examination of his work undertaken so far has demonstrated, firstly, the prominence and pervasiveness of eschatology to the Lewisian corpus and, secondly, how coherent that eschatology is when tested. For someone who described himself as a layman and an

---

[1] Armand Nicholi, *The Conflicting Worldviews of Sigmund Freud and C. S. Lewis.*

amateur, Lewis came extraordinarily close to presenting a systematic position. What may be helpful, then, is to explore in some detail how the Lewisian worldview informed and fed his eschatology. Indeed, how it was essentially an eschatological worldview.

Determining Influences

One of Lewis' most heartfelt prejudices about literary criticism and an issue that haunted him throughout his academic career finds perhaps its purest expression in an exchange with the Milton scholar, E. M. W. Tillyard, which was later published as *The Personal Heresy: A Controversy*. Bruce Edwards has pointed out that Lewis' formulation of his position was forged over a long time, having first surfaced in a presentation he made as an undergraduate to the Oxford literary society, the Martlets, in 1924. 'Six years later,' notes Edwards, 'Lewis addressed the Martlets once again, this time as a don and not as a student, having fully conceptualised the malady he believed plagued contemporary criticism.'[2] This malady – at least in debate with Tillyard – concerned the latter's premise that 'all poetry is about the poet's state of mind' and that to read Milton's work correctly one must read it as an 'expression of Milton's personality'. Lewis opposed such a position by arguing that the point of criticism is not to 'reconstruct the poet's psyche between the lines of the poem nor to deconstruct the poem as concealed biography; rather it is to help the reader see with ever greater clarity the world depicted in and through the poem that the poet has intentionally composed'.[3] Lewis had somewhat simplified Tillyard's position by suggesting that his criticism called upon merely trivial details about a poet's life to explain a particular poem. Defending himself Tillyard argued that what he had meant by 'the poet's state of mind' included, in fact, the whole social and historical context out of which the poet spoke

---

[2] Bruce L. Edwards, 'The Personal Heresy: A Controversy', in Schultz and West, *Readers' Encyclopedia*, p. 318.
[3] Ibid. Cf. C. S. Lewis and E. M. W. Tillyard, *The Personal Heresy: A Controversy*, p. 17 and C. S. Lewis, *An Experiment in Criticism*, p. 121.

and of how he reflected his own particular era.[4] Edwards has commented that Lewis' stance in this debate reflected his deeper concern with the growth of subjectivism and relativism.

> In subject matter and focus, *The Personal Heresy* does exemplify what would become Lewis' consistent themes in all of his post-conversion nonfiction work, championing as it does the cogency of the doctrine of objective value, opposing the relativistic mindset ascendant in Western culture, and directing his readers' attention to the concreteness of a real world that cannot be wished away.[5]

Bearing this renowned dispute in mind, then, it is with some hesitation that I embark upon an examination of the determining influences in Lewis' life. Chad Walsh, writing in 1949 in a commentary on Lewis' work thus far, said: 'I am inclined to share Lewis' own belief that one should study a writer's books rather than his personality.'[6] Nevertheless, the construction of any worldview does not spring out of thin air and it would seem irresponsible not to study in more detail the formation of Lewis' *Weltanschauung*, particularly given his own candour in recognising and acknowledging his influences as given, for example, in his autobiography *Surprised by Joy*. Lewis himself once said: 'Reading between the lines is inevitable, but we must practise it with great caution or we may find mares' nests.'[7] It is, therefore, with great caution that I proceed.

Personal Influences

In his introduction to the posthumous publication of C. S. Lewis' diary, kept more or less assiduously between 1922 and

---

4 Cf. Bruce Edwards. 'The Personal Heresy', p. 319. See Tillyard's counter argument in *Personal Heresy*, p. 139: 'The poet is also an historian, in that he can express (and this can be expressed only by artistic means) what his contemporaries felt about certain events and ideas, and what it felt like to be alive just then.'

5 Edwards, 'The Personal Heresy', p. 319.

6 Chad Walsh, *C. S. Lewis: Apostle to the Skeptics*, p. 10.

7 *Experiment in Criticism*, p. 119.

1927, Walter Hooper comments of the complex relationship between Lewis and Janie Moore:

> The nature of their intimacy, its duration, and the circumstances under which it ended are largely unknown to us ... Life is more richly-textured – or as Lewis would put it, 'thicker' – than we expect it to be. None of us is either this or that; rather we and all the 'ordinary' people we meet and know are many things at once, full of shading and nuance.[8]

Hooper makes a vital point applicable to all relationships in general and one which I would like to take as a proviso to this section of my study. It is surely impossible to comprehend the full influence we have on one another, let alone to make such comprehension an exact science as a detached observer. My aim here is not biography and I make no pretence at listing the full number of Lewis' more influential associates. Rather, I aim to note some of the key people whom Lewis himself acknowledged as being of influence and to see if it is possible to say in what way – if any – they may have contributed to the formulation of his eschatological worldview.

In the area of his intellectual development I believe there to be three significant figures, each of whom made a unique impact upon C. S. Lewis: William T. Kirkpatrick, Owen Barfield, and Charles Williams. Kirkpatrick, or the 'Great Knock' as he was nicknamed by the Lewis family, had tutored not only both the Lewis boys – Jack and his brother Warnie (the former for Oxford and the latter for entry into Sandhurst) – at his home in Bookham, Surrey, but also, when previously headmaster of Lurgan College, Co. Armagh, their father Albert. On hearing the news of Kirkpatrick's death in 1921 C. S. Lewis wrote: 'It is ... but plainest fact to say that I at least owe to him in the intellectual sphere as much as one human being can owe another.'[9] Similarly, in *Surprised by Joy* Lewis

---

[8] Walter Hooper, 'Introduction' to C. S. Lewis, *All My Road Before Me: The Diary of C. S. Lewis 1922–1927*, p. 9.
[9] *Letters of C. S. Lewis*, p. 126 (Letter dated 28 March 1921).

admitted: 'My debt to him is very great, my reverence to this day undiminished.'[10] This living embodiment of nineteenth-century atheistic rationalism, as Lewis once described him, came initially as rather a surprise. The young Jack had heard from his father such accounts of his future tutor that he was left with the distinct impression that Kirkpatrick would be something of an arch-sentimentalist. Indeed, on arriving in Bookham the fifteen-year-old fully expected to encounter in the Great Knock 'a perpetual luke-warm shower bath of sentimentality'.[11] What he actually experienced was the – by now famous – confrontation with a ruthless dialectician in which the young boy's innocent attempts at polite conversation about the surrounding Surrey countryside were torn to shreds. 'Here was a man who thought not about you but about what you said,' recorded Lewis in *Surprised by Joy*.[12] A. N. Wilson, in his biography of Lewis, has doubted the authenticity of Kirkpatrick's characterisation as presented in this Lewisian account. 'From all the evidence which survives,' he argues, 'we can see that the Great Knock of *Surprised by Joy* is quite as much an imaginative projection as the Victorian sentimentalist beloved of Lewis' father.'[13] But, nevertheless, even Wilson admits, 'Some of his [Kirkpatrick's] forceful dialectic techniques got passed on to his pupil.'[14] Certainly the dialectical nature of some of Lewis' arguments – both in his writing and teaching – owes itself to William Kirkpatrick's influence. Roger Lancelyn Green and Walter Hooper noted in their biography of Lewis: 'He never outgrew the teachings of the "Great Knock" ... If a friend made a thoughtless remark or a loose generality in conversation, Lewis would boom out, "I challenge that" and the foils of logic would be clashing in a moment.'[15]

---

10 *Surprised by Joy, p.* 114.
11 Ibid. p. 103.
12 Ibid. p. 106.
13 A. N. Wilson, *C. S. Lewis: A Biography*, p. 39.
14 Ibid. p. 42.
15 Roger Lancelyn Green and Walter Hooper, *C. S. Lewis: A Biography,* p. 153. Chad Walsh, commenting on Lewis' impact upon American students of the 1960s, observed: 'Lewis seems too theoretical and abstract. They find in his books very little to do

And Humphrey Carpenter similarly observed of Lewis' tutorials given at Magdalen College:

> When teaching, he turned for a model to the method of his old tutor Kirkpatrick ... This frightened all but the toughest-minded students. A few managed to fight back and even win a point – which was just what Lewis wanted them to do – but the majority were cowed by the force of his dialectic and went away abashed.[16]

In addition to dialectic Lewis also gained from the Great Knock a wide-ranging knowledge of the Classics, which was to be taken up in his Oxford undergraduate career. Homer, Demosthenes, Cicero, Lucretius, Catullus, Tacitus, Herodotus, Virgil, Euripides, Sophocles, and Aeschylus: all of these were studied at Bookham, alongside French, Italian, and even some degree of German literature. And so, during the period between 1914 and his going up to Oxford in 1917, Lewis experienced an intellectual challenge combined with the freedom and encouragement to read widely. Wilson quotes from one of Kirkpatrick's reports to Albert Lewis on the ability of his son: 'It is the maturity and originality of his literary judgements which is so unusual and surprising.'[17] And Lewis' brother Warnie noted in his memoir, published as a preface to a collection of Jack's letters:

> The stimulation of a sharp and vigorous mind, the romantic beauty which the Surrey countryside then possessed, the ordered security of Jack's life, his freedom to read widely and gratuitously – these factors combined to develop his particular gifts and determine his future.[18]

---

with political and social questions ... I think they also find him too much of a rationalist and Thomist for their tastes.' See Chad Walsh, 'Impact on America', in *Light on C. S. Lewis*, ed. Jocelyn Gibb, p. 115.

[16] Humphrey Carpenter, *The Inklings: C. S. Lewis, J. R. R. Tolkien, Charles Williams and their Friends*, p. 58.

[17] A. N. Wilson, *C. S. Lewis*, p. 41.

[18] W. H. Lewis, 'Memoir', in *Letters of C. S. Lewis*, pp. 25–6.

The legacy of William Kirkpatrick's impact upon the young C. S. Lewis, then, was the development of a strongly analytical mind, the encouragement of an appetite for dialectic, and the provision of knowledge of a vast scope of literature coming from many different periods, genres, and languages.

The second major person of influence in Lewis' intellectual sphere was his friend from their undergraduate days, Owen Barfield. In his diary entry for Sunday 9 July 1922 Lewis recorded: 'Barfield towers above us all.'[19] Indeed Humphrey Carpenter has commented of their friendship: '[Lewis] regarded Barfield as in every way an intellectual equal and in some respects superior to himself.'[20] In *Surprised by Joy* Lewis paid tribute to Barfield, describing him as a type of every man's 'Second Friend'. The 'First Friend' – in Lewis' case being Arthur Greeves – is like an *alter ego*. The 'Second' is more of an 'anti-self'. As Lewis described it, he is 'the man who disagrees with you about everything', someone who shares the same interests but 'has approached them all at a different angle'.[21] A. N. Wilson has indicated of the early years of their friendship:

> Lewis was to say that Barfield changed him a good deal more than he did Barfield, and this was probably true. The thing they disagreed about most forcefully was religion, Barfield being set on the course which was to lead him to embrace theosophy, and Lewis at this stage still being an ardent atheist.[22]

The debate that this growing divergence of religious belief provoked was referred to by Lewis in *Surprised by Joy* as the 'Great War', and was to be one of the turning points of his life. And whilst Barfield never converted Lewis to anthroposophism nevertheless, their ongoing intellectual debate affected his thought in at least two important ways. The first of these was

---

[19] *All My Road Before Me*, p. 67.
[20] Humphrey Carpenter, *The Inklings*, p. 33.
[21] *Surprised by Joy*, p. 155.
[22] A. N. Wilson, *C. S. Lewis*, p. 64.

what Lewis came to call chronological snobbery: in other words, a type of intellectual faddism in which the latest assumptions are uncritically accepted in place of those held by a previous generation. The second, more significantly perhaps, was to demonstrate an inconsistency in Lewis' own thinking. Until that time he had adopted a realist position, very much the intellectual child of Kirkpatrick's atheistic rationalism. Nevertheless, Barfield argued that whilst professing such trenchant realism Lewis had also unwittingly adopted a role for the imaginative faculty that was more akin to an idealist or theistic position. Whereas Lewis might have *claimed* that imaginative vision cannot be invoked as a source of certainty or truth, Barfield argued that he *lived* quite differently. As Carpenter puts it, 'Barfield ... did his best to convince Lewis that imagination and aesthetic experience did lead, if not automatically to objective truth, then at least to a better understanding of the world.'[23] The result of this was that Lewis eventually gave up realism.

In addition to his being instrumental in Lewis' shift towards idealism – a shift that would eventually lead him into theism and from there into Christianity – Owen Barfield was also significantly influential in the development of Lewis' understanding of the workings of language and myth. Having gained a First in English whilst at Wadham College, Oxford, Barfield stayed up to take a B.Litt., the thesis of which was later published in 1928 as a short book entitled, *Poetic Diction*. Howard Nemerov, in his foreword to a relatively recent American edition of this book, comments that there are 'two main ways of taking poetic diction as a subject of study'. The first is as a technical matter, the realm of working poets. But with the second he notes:

> The question of poetic diction becomes ... nothing less than the question of primary perception, or imagination itself, of how thought ever emerged (if it did) out of a world of things.[24]

---

[23] Humphrey Carpenter, *The Inklings*, p. 37. Cf. *Surprised by Joy*, p. 161.
[24] Howard Nemerov, 'Foreword' to Owen Barfield, *Poetic Diction: A Study in Meaning*, pp. 2–3.

The aim of Barfield's thesis – and subsequently of his book – was to explore the nature of poetry and why it had the ability to 'arouse aesthetic imagination'.[25] As Humphrey Carpenter succinctly explains:

> Barfield examined the history of words, and came to the conclusion that mythology, far from being (as the philologist Max Müller called it) 'a disease of language', is closely associated with the very origin of all speech and literature.[26]

With his theory of 'ancient semantic unity', Barfield argued that whereas now words may have both a literal referent and a metaphorical meaning – for example, the Greek word *pneuma* having the literal referents 'wind' and 'breath', and the metaphorical application 'spirit' to mean 'the principle of life within man or animal' – originally there was a time in early language when such division was impossible. *Pneuma* initially meant neither 'wind' nor 'breath' – or even 'the principle of life within man or animal' – but had its own 'peculiar meaning, which has since, in the course of the evolution of consciousness, crystallized into the three meanings specified'.[27] Thus, as Lyle H. Smith concludes:

---

[25] Cf. Owen Barfield, *Poetic Diction*, pp. 41–2.

[26] Humphrey Carpenter, *The Inklings*, p. 41.

[27] Cf. Barfield, *Poetic Diction*, pp. 80–1. Bede Griffiths commented that in his book Barfield 'had discovered by the study of words ... one of the most profound secrets not only of the growth of language, but also of the evolution of man and the universe ... Thus language progresses from symbols that are deep and rich and manifold in meaning to words that are precise and clear and prosaic but lacking the poetic quality of early speech. This threw a flood of light for me on human evolution. We do not progress from a simple materialistic view of life to a mere spiritual understanding, but from a rich, complex, global experience of life to a more rational, analytical understanding, in other words from poetry to prose.' See Bede Griffiths, 'The Adventure of Faith', in Jocelyn Gibb, *Light on C. S. Lewis*, pp. 13–14. I believe that Lewis himself was attempting to explore this idea in his science fiction novel, *Out of the Silent Planet*, published in 1938, some ten years after the original publication of Barfield's thesis.

Owen Barfield challenged the claim of philosophy and science to metaphor-free language by demonstrating that all language is radically metaphorical.[28]

Lewis himself noted of Barfield's thinking: 'Much of the thought which he afterwards put into *Poetic Diction* had already become mine before that important little book appeared. It would be strange if it had not.'[29] It is to this thought that I shall return in more detail in the next chapter.

The final figure of influence upon C. S. Lewis' intellectual formation to be considered is Charles Williams. Lewis first came across Williams' thought in 1936 when, upon listening to his friend, Neville Coghill's, forceful appreciation of the novel, *The Place of the Lion*, he decided to borrow the book and see for himself what all the fuss was about. At about the same time Lewis had submitted the manuscript of his first major academic piece of writing (which would later bear the title, *The Allegory of Love*) to the Oxford University Press for publication. By coincidence the proofs of that manuscript were handed to one Charles Williams, who was then working for the Press and was based in their London office. As Humphrey Carpenter recounts:

Williams had no sooner finished reading the book and had written a paragraph praising it than he heard from Milford [his senior at the OUP] that Lewis had been saying complimentary things about *The Place of the Lion*. A day later he received a letter from Lewis saying that he thought the novel remarkable.[30]

After a brief exchange of letters the two men agreed to meet up in London and continued to do so periodically until Williams' removal (with the rest of his London office) to Oxford at the start of the Second World War. With this move, and Williams' regular attendance at meetings of the Inklings now possible, his influence over Lewis began to be asserted. A. N. Wilson notes of

---

[28] Lyle H. Smith, 'C. S. Lewis and the Making of Metaphor', in Peter Schakel and Charles Huttar, *Word and Story*, p. 12.
[29] *Surprised by Joy*, p. 155.
[30] Humphrey Carpenter, *The Inklings*, p. 99.

Williams: 'He had real charm, which made canny figures such as Tolkien distrust him. Lewis was bowled over by him, and was anxious that as many people as possible should have the benefit of his wisdom.'[31] One of the results of this 'anxiety' was that Lewis managed to get Williams a series of lectures to be given at Oxford University on the subject of Milton. While these lectures were generally regarded as a great success, Humphrey Carpenter has argued, 'On no one was the effect of the lectures more marked than on Lewis himself.'[32] Like his open acknowledgement of debt to his tutor William Kirkpatrick in *Surprised by Joy*, Lewis was equally candid about his discipleship of Charles Williams. As Erik Routley wrote in James Como's *C. S. Lewis at the Breakfast Table*: 'Lewis always said he owed everything to Charles Williams. In a sense he mediated Charles Williams to ordinary people.'[33] In a letter to Arthur Greeves, Lewis described his mentor as about as ugly as a chimpanzee but, when speaking, so animated that he resembled an angel.[34] When Williams died in 1945, aged just fifty-eight, Lewis said of

---

[31] A. N. Wilson, *C. S. Lewis*, p. 170. Interestingly, Humphrey Carpenter is more forthright in what lay behind Tolkien's distrust of Williams: 'From the beginning of their acquaintance Tolkien was to some extent suspicious of Williams. This was understandable, for while Williams and Lewis had got to know each other by admiring each other's books Tolkien simply had Williams thrust upon him. The first thing he knew about Williams was Lewis declaring that he had made the acquaintance of a most marvellous person, and that he (Tolkien) would undoubtedly love Williams as soon as he met him. The most generous-hearted person would have been a little suspicious of this, and Tolkien responded by becoming faintly jealous.' Carpenter, *The Inklings*, p. 120. Roger Lancelyn Green and Walter Hooper record a letter from J. R. R. Tolkien to Dick Plotz dated 12 September 1965: 'I knew Charles Williams only as a friend of C. S. L ... We like one another and enjoyed talking (mostly in jest) but we had nothing to say to one another at deeper (or higher) levels.' Green and Hooper observe that Charles Williams' admittance to the circle of Inklings eventually led to 'some cooling on Tolkien's part'. See Green and Hooper, *C. S. Lewis*, p. 172.

[32] Humphrey Carpenter, *The Inklings*, p. 181.

[33] Erik Routley, 'A Prophet', in *C. S. Lewis at the Breakfast Table and other Reminiscences*, ed. James Como, p. 35.

[34] Cf. *They Stand Together*, pp. 500–1 (Letter dated 30 January 1944).

him: 'When the idea of death and the idea of Williams met in my mind, it was the idea of death that changed.'[35]

A. N. Wilson has assessed Williams' intellectual strength as deriving from the ability to hold a number of contradictory ideas in harmony. 'For example, he was able to reconcile membership of the Church of England (rather High) with belonging to such occult groups as the Order of the Golden Dawn.'[36] It was probably this capacity that led to the Catholic (and more theologically conservative) Tolkien to say of Williams' writing: 'I had read or heard a good deal of his work but found it wholly alien, and sometimes very distasteful, occasionally ridiculous.' He even once, in an unguarded moment, referred to Williams as a 'witch doctor'.[37] Certainly Williams' novels could be a heady mix of intense thriller and occult supernaturalism as well as impressive learning. But, as Charles Hefling has said:

> They can convince the reader as perhaps nothing else could that what they depict is objectively real – that the routine stream of sights and sounds which meets us every day runs deeper than we suppose, and that an intangible dimension exists in, with, and under every moment of our experience ... People who knew him personally observed the same coexistence of the mundane and the otherworldly in Williams himself.[38]

[35] C. S. Lewis, 'Preface', to *Essays Presented to Charles Williams*, ed. idem, p. xiv.

[36] A. N. Wilson, *C. S. Lewis*, p. 148. Humphrey Carpenter notes: 'There does not seem to have been anything in Waite's "temple" of the Golden Dawn which was opposed to Christianity ... Waite himself discouraged the Order of the Golden Dawn from practising "Magia", the renaissance term for white magic, and certainly he was opposed to any meddling in "Goetia" or black magic ... So, though he [Williams] soon outgrew the Golden Dawn and left the Order (the date of this is not known), the symbolism and the knowledge of the occult that he had acquired during his membership remained valuable to him, not least because in its extreme form black magic was the polar opposite of Christianity; and his mind was always drawn to an awareness of the opposite pole of any argument or belief.' Humphrey Carpenter, *The Inklings*, p. 83.

[37] Cf. Humphrey Carpenter, *The Inklings*, p. 121.

[38] Charles Helfing, 'The Pattern of the Glory', in *Charles Williams, Essential Writings in Spirituality and Theology*, ed. Charles Hefling, p. 4.

T. S. Eliot commented of the extraordinary diversity of genre in Williams' writing (he wrote almost forty books including theology, poetry, history and literary criticism as well as fiction) that 'what he had to say was beyond his resources, and probably beyond the resources of language, to say once for all through any one medium of expression'.[39] Of Williams' specific influence on Lewis' own work there may be any number of particular examples, such as the debt Lewis owed for his preface to Milton's *Paradise Lost*, or the Arthurian themes woven into his Space Trilogy, or even A. N. Wilson's suggestion that Lewis' choice of Aslan in the Narnia Chronicles was influenced by his reading of *The Place of the Lion*.[40] Interestingly, Walter Hooper records a conversation with Lewis in which the latter replied to a question about 'the vogue for tracing the "influence" of Williams' in his work:

> I have never been consciously influenced by Williams, never believed that I was in any way imitating him. On the other hand, there may have been a great deal of unconscious influence going on.[41]

What is perhaps more important than speculation about specific examples of influence is the more general, two-pronged impact of Williams' thought upon C. S. Lewis: an impact, I believe, that struck at his appreciation of the Platonic theory of Forms, and at his understanding of the relationship between the natural and the supernatural. Of the first of these, Williams' novel, *The Place of the Lion*, is a good example. Lewis summarised the story in his letter to Greeves, saying:

---

[39] T. S. Eliot, 'Introduction', to Charles Williams, *All Hallows Eve*, p. xi.
[40] Cf. A. N. Wilson, *C. S. Lewis*, p. 150. Interestingly, Brian Horne argues, 'I have no doubt that Williams illuminated and enriched Lewis' life to a degree and in a way that is incalculable ... But the question of influence in Lewis' work is problematic. If we look for evidence of Williams' ideas changing and shaping Lewis' own in any substantial way, we shall look in vain ... But the influence is there, elusive and tantalising.' Brian Horne, 'A Peculiar Debt: The Influence of Charles Williams on C. S. Lewis', in *Rumours of Heaven: Essays in Celebration of C. S. Lewis*, ed. Andrew Walker and James Patrick, p. 86.
[41] Cf. Roger Lancelyn Green and Walter Hooper, *C. S. Lewis*, p. 218.

It is based on the Platonic theory of the other world in
which the archtypes of all earthly qualities exist: and in
the novel, owing to a bit of machinery which doesn't
matter, these archtypes start sucking our world back.[42]

Certainly Lewis was fully cognizant of the Platonic use of archetype and ectype prior to meeting Charles Williams, but it was
with Williams' influence that an idea took seed: Lewis began to
see how imaginatively one could develop such concepts to say
something about both this world and the world to come. The
fantastical application of typology used in Williams' novels –
particularly *The Place of the Lion* – was eventually to find a more
reasoned and rigorous employment in the presentation of
Lewisian eschatology, for example, as found in *The Last Battle,
The Weight of Glory* and *Transposition*. The second prong of
Williams' impact was perhaps even more significant: the
opening up to Lewis – again, imaginatively – of the dynamic
interplay between the natural and supernatural. E. Martin
Browne, a contemporary of Williams, said of him:

I have never met any human being in whom the divisions
between body and spirit, natural and supernatural,
temporal and eternal were so non-existent, nor any writer
who so consistently took their non-existence for
granted.[43]

T. S. Eliot similarly noted: 'To him the supernatural was
perfectly natural, and the natural was also supernatural.'[44]
And, as A. N. Wilson comments: 'Williams ... had an almost
matter-of-fact awareness of the other world. Angels – or "angel-
icals" as he would have preferred to call them in his strange
idiolect – were as real to him as omnibuses or mortgage repay-
ments.'[45] This vision of the natural world suffused with
elements of the supernatural comes strongly into Lewis' own

[42] *They Stand Together*, p. 479 (Letter dated 26 February 1936).
[43] E. Martin Browne, *Two in One*, p. 101.
[44] T. S. Eliot, 'Introduction', p. xiv.
[45] A. N. Wilson, *C. S. Lewis*, p. 149.

fictional writing. The Narnia Chronicles, for example, portray not only a world alive (Narnia) with the supernatural and fantastical but also an interplay of worlds, each with the potential to open out into the others. The Space Trilogy, similarly, uses rich imagery to tell of a universe pregnant with the supernatural if only we could perceive it. The emptiness of space becomes the experience of deep heaven for Ransom on his traumatic journey to Mars.[46] Thomas Howard, commenting on *Out of the Silent Planet*, argues:

> We will have misunderstood Lewis' interests ... if we think that the locale of those interests is anywhere other than the real, palpable stuff of our human life here on this planet.[47]

In *That Hideous Strength* Lewis portrayed the mundane petty politics of a university as being at the centre of nothing less than a cosmic and supernatural battle.[48] Interestingly, it can be argued that Lewis' favourite novel – although sadly, perhaps, his least successful – dealt precisely with this concept of the perception of the supernatural within the natural. *Till We Have Faces* chronicles the journey of Orual to a deeper understanding of self, religion, and reality. The story ends with Orual perceiving in a new light the deep truths of the ancient and rather barbaric cult of Ungit. In this novel Lewis had taken the Cupid and Psyche myth – first found in *Metamorphoses* by Lucius Apuleius Platonicus – and re-written it with a number of adaptations. One of these adaptations was to make Psyche's palace invisible to mortal eyes. This change introduced what Lewis called a 'more ambivalent motive' for the central character, and allowed the tale to take on an examination not only of human jealousy but of how such human traits – like jealousy,

---

[46] Cf. *Out of the Silent Planet*, pp. 40, 154.

[47] Thomas Howard, *C. S. Lewis, Man of Letters: A Reading of his Fiction*, p. 79.

[48] Indeed, Roger Lancelyn Green and Walter Hooper have noted that *That Hideous Strength* 'has been described as a Charles Williams novel written by C. S. Lewis'. See Green and Hooper, *C. S. Lewis*, p. 205.

possessiveness, and so on – can distort one's view of reality: how, when we insist on clinging to and clutching at the purely natural, we miss what is ultimately supernatural. This, of course, is deeply eschatological. Lewis had adopted Williams' poetic worldview – of city pavements suddenly melting away to reveal the 'firmer under-stone' of the eternal City of God, for example. But whereas for Williams 'the conventional distinction between the natural and supernatural' was blurred – and Carpenter comments that as 'the years passed he came to feel that no barrier really existed between the two states'[49] – for Lewis the distinction was more orthodox and remained. The 'home country' idea found in Lewis' writings is not merely a question of our personal perception in the here and now. Rather Lewis proposed that our present experiences can hint at a deeper reality, but that crucially that deeper reality itself can only be revealed to us fully at the end of time. As Orual put it: 'How can [the gods] meet us face to face until we have faces?'[50]

Undoubtedly there are other people of influence who will have played some part in Lewis' intellectual formation. In *Surprised by Joy*, for example, Lewis ranked his schoolmaster 'Smewgy' from Malvern College alongside Kirkpatrick.[51] Similarly, E. F. Carritt, his philosophy tutor from his Oxford undergraduate days, must have played an important role. There were his friends too: Arthur Greeves, A. K. Hamilton, A. C. Harwood, Neville Coghill, Hugo Dyson, and J. R. R. Tolkien – all of these were significant in some way, the latter four being the catalysts for his conversion to Christianity. But since their influence is well attested to – not least by Lewis himself in his autobiography – it is perhaps unnecessary to go into further detail. The three I have examined – Williams, Barfield, and Kirkpatrick – are significant in that they represent three important strands of Lewisian eschatology: a deeply held supernaturalist worldview, an epistemology in which imagination as well as reason has a part to play, and a logical

---

[49] Cf. Humphrey Carpenter, *The Inklings*, p. 85.
[50] *Till We Have Faces*, p. 223.
[51] Cf. *Surprised by Joy*, p. 114. Smewgy's real name was Harry Wakelyn Smith.

and dialectical tendency which lends itself not only to the apologetic literary style, but also to general clarity and keen observation. Eric Routley suggested that Lewis mediated Charles Williams, but Lewis did more than merely mediate.[52] C. S. Lewis combined aspects of Williams' own worldview together with the fruit borne of Kirkpatrick's tutoring and the intellectual stimulus provided by the 'Great War' with Owen Barfield. He also supplied his own Christian orthodoxy – for, at times, Williams veered towards the occult or even anthroposophy[53] – and his vast knowledge of literature and myth. Added together these ingredients made a sure recipe from which Lewis was able to produce the sort of eschatology that I have already demonstrated.

Literary Influences

C. S. Lewis was notoriously well read and his own work drew upon an impressive array of literary sources. In addition, then, to the key figures of personal influence that I have mentioned above there are also a number of major literary texts that will have borne some impact upon the development of Lewis' worldview; these, too, need to be examined. Anyone who has

[52] Eric Routley, 'A Prophet', p. 35.
[53] Humphrey Carpenter notes 'Owen Barfield feels he might have found some common philosophical or theological ground with Charles Williams if he had ever had the chance to talk at length with him. But they never found the opportunity for a lengthy conversation. He recalls that at their first meeting, Williams, not knowing that Barfield was a disciple of Steiner, opened the conversation by saying: "I have just been talking to someone who told me I was an Anthroposophist." Elsewhere Carpenter records Lewis' own reaction to some of Williams' thinking: "He [Charles Williams] is largely a self-educated man, labouring under an almost oriental richness of imagination ("Clotted glory from Charles" as Dyson called it) which could be saved from turning silly or even vulgar in print only by a severe early discipline which he never had.' Carpenter then comments: 'Lewis was surely thinking of his own "severe early discipline" under Kirkpatrick.' Lewis also wrote of Williams: 'He has an undisciplined mind and sometimes admits into his theology ideas whose proper place is in his romances.' Cf. Carpenter, *The Inklings*, p. 115–16, 155, n.1.

dipped into Lewis' diary, or looked at any of his published letters, or read *Surprised by Joy* will know that the scholar himself noted the enormous number of influential works of literature that affected his thinking.[54] As with the previous section – where I aimed to draw upon only three of a number of possible key influences – here, too, I propose to limit my study to what I believe to be the most significant texts in contributing towards Lewisian eschatology.

The first writers to be considered are Milton and Dante. Of the former Humphrey Carpenter has suggested:

> Since his conversion, [Lewis'] own orthodox and super-naturalist Christian faith had already inclined him to accept the theology of *Paradise Lost* almost in its entirety, and to dismiss as irrelevant the reservations held by many modern critics of the poem.[55]

Certainly in his *A Preface to Paradise Lost* Lewis warned his readers, 'I myself am a Christian, and that some (by no means all) of the things which the atheist reader must "try to feel as if he believed" I actually, in cold prose, do believe.'[56] I have already shown how Lewis drew upon Milton's poetry to understand the parasitical nature of evil, the reality of judgement and damnation as self-imposed, and the concept of morality as something to be 'swallowed up' at the end of time. A. N. Wilson has noted that in Milton's poetry, with its 'stories of great temptation, of interplanetary flights, wrestlings with the power of good and evil, Lewis found something which had already engaged his own pen, and would continue to do so'.[57] It is clear, too, how *Paradise Lost* was an influential text upon the young atheistic mind of C. S. Lewis. In an early letter to Greeves concerning the epic poem, Lewis wrote: 'Don't you

[54] Paul Ford has produced a short but useful article concerning these works. See Paul Ford, 'Books of Influence', in Schultz and West, *Readers' Encyclopedia*, pp. 102–4.
[55] Humphry Carpenter, *The Inklings*, pp. 180–1.
[56] *Preface to Paradise Lost*, p. 65.
[57] A. N. Wilson, *C. S. Lewis*, pp. 173–4.

love all the descriptions of Hell?'[58] And later, in *Surprised by Joy*, Lewis acknowledged that Milton had been one of a number of writers – alongside MacDonald, Chesterton, Johnson, and Spenser – whom initially he thought good despite their Christianity, but later realised appealed to him precisely because of their Christian content.[59] Significantly, in later life, Lewis was to come to appreciate fully the work of Milton's poetry as expressive of Christian myth.[60]

If Milton, then, for Lewis was a prime example of the possible interconnection between Christian creed and Christian myth, Dante was to remind him of the vital importance of appropriate imagery in the marriage of these two genres. In *Letters to Malcolm* Lewis compared the Low Church tendency to be 'too cosily at ease with Sion' with the impact upon Dante of meeting the Apostles in his arrival in *Paradiso*: 'They affected him like mountains.'[61] Dante used a poetic image to capture what he saw to be a fundamental truth: the saints in glory are overwhelmingly greater than ourselves here and now. Lewis was to use the same idea in his own attempt at describing paradise, *The Great Divorce*. In each work what is significant is the way imagery is used to underpin a credal position or particular worldview. Dante's description of paradise and the saints is not mere accident. As Lewis noted in his work, *The Discarded Image*: 'Nothing about literature can be more essential than the language it uses ... it implies an outlook, reveals a mental activity.'[62] What *The Divine Comedy* revealed to Lewis was the

---

58   *They Stand Together*, p. 184 (Letter dated 20 May 1917). Walter Hooper and Roger Lancelyn Green quote from a diary extract for Thursday 5 March 1908, in which Lewis wrote: 'Miss Harper comes, lessons. Dinner ... I am carpentring at a sword. I read "Paradise Lost", reflections there-on.' Lewis was aged nine at this stage. See Green and Hooper, *C. S. Lewis*, p. 7.

59   Cf. *Surprised by Joy*, p. 166.

60   See *Letters of C. S. Lewis*, p. 503 (Letter dated 21 March 1962).

61   *Letters to Malcolm*, p. 11 (Letter 2). Cf. Dante Alighieri, *The Divine Comedy, Paradiso*, XXV, pp. 37–9: 'The second fire offered me this comfort;/ at which my eyes were lifted to the mountains/ whose weight of light before had kept me bent.'

62   C. S. Lewis, *The Discarded Image: An Introduction to Medieval and Renaissance Literature*, p. 6.

ordered nature of the medieval mind and a powerful ability to relate detailed imagination. Interestingly, much of Lewis' own fictional writing followed a similar style. His Space Trilogy – *Perelandra* in particular – is clearly so comprehensive in its description that the reader can be in no doubt whatsoever as to what the writer was imagining. The Narnia Chronicles, likewise, are rich in observational detail. Perhaps this is no surprise for an author who claimed his writing began with seeing pictures.[63] What both Milton and Dante gave to Lewis was a magnificent example of how poetic imagery – when done well – was the best vehicle for communicating religious belief.[64] As he argued in a letter to his brother Warnie: 'Religion and poetry are about the only language in modern Europe – if you can regard them as 'languages' – which still have traces of the dream in them, still have something to say.'[65]

Whereas Milton and Dante provided Lewis with what he perceived to be an orthodox framework from which to write his own versions of Christian mythology, the writings of William Morris and George MacDonald enabled him to see his experience of *Sehnsucht* as a pointer to another world. In a letter to Arthur Greeves, dated 22 September 1931, Lewis wrote: 'It only needs a page or two of Morris to sting you wide awake into uncontrollable longing.'[66] A few years later, in 1937, Lewis addressed the Martlets and argued:

> Morris, like a true Pagan, does not tell us (because he does not think he knows) the ultimate significance of those moments in which we cannot help reaching out for

---

[63] See C. S. Lewis 'It All Began with a Picture', in *Of Other Worlds*, p. 42.

[64] A. N. Wilson has commented: 'There have been plenty of good writers who were also Christians. Plenty of Christians have tried their hand at putting their beliefs into prose or poetry, usually with calamitous aesthetic results. There have been very few with the gift of Dante or John Milton, who have written at their very best when being most Christian. It was to this great tradition, though as a self-confessedly very junior follower, that Lewis quite easily and naturally belonged.' See Wilson, *C. S. Lewis*, p. 156.

[65] *Letters of C. S. Lewis*, p. 296 (Letter dated 17 January 1932).

[66] Ibid. p. 287 (Letter dated 22 September 1931).

something beyond the visible world and so discovering 'at what unmeasured price Man sets his life'. He neither seeks to justify them like a Christian nor to repress them like a materialist. He simply presents the tension.[67]

However, it was George MacDonald who ultimately made sense of this tension for C. S. Lewis. 'The MacDonald conception of death,' he confided to Greeves in 1931, 'is really the answer to Morris: but I don't think I should have understood it without going through Morris ... He shows you *just how far* you can go without knowing God.'[68] On reading MacDonald's *Phantastes*, whilst as a boy on a train journey returning to Bookham, Lewis found 'all that had already charmed [him] in Malory, Spenser, Morris and Yeats'. But, as he recorded in *Surprised by Joy*: 'In another sense all was changed. I did not yet know (and I was long in learning) the name of the new quality ... It was Holiness.'[69] Whereas Morris had enkindled within Lewis an imaginative longing – and thereby a frustration with a purely this-worldly existence – MacDonald had taken up that imaginative longing (or, as Lewis put it, baptised his imagination)[70] and gradually opened up for him the possibility that

---

[67] C. S. Lewis, 'William Morris', in idem, *Selected Literary Essays*, p. 225.

[68] *They Stand Together*, p. 422 (Letter dated 22 September 1931).

[69] *Surprised by Joy*, p. 139. In a letter to Sister Penelope, Lewis commented: 'I think your task of finding suitable fiction for the convalescents must be interesting. Do you know George MacDonald's fantasies for grown-ups (his tales for children you probably already know): *Phantastes & Lilith* I found endlessly attractive, and full of what I felt to be holiness before I really knew that it was.' *Letters of C. S. Lewis*, p. 322 (Letter dated 9 July 1939). Elsewhere Lewis wrote: 'I have never concealed the fact that I regarded him [MacDonald] as my master; indeed I fancy I have never written a book in which I did not quote from him ... It must be thirty years ago that I bought – almost unwillingly, for I had looked at the volume on that bookstall and rejected it on a dozen previous occasions – the Everyman edition of *Phantastes*. A few hours later I knew I had crossed a great frontier.' See C. S. Lewis, 'Preface', to *George MacDonald, An Anthology: 365 Readings*, p. xxxvii.

[70] *Surprised by Joy*, p. 140.

what it pointed to was a promised, other-worldly fulfilment. Thus Morris and MacDonald together provided a literary cata- lyst, if you like, for Lewis to adopt – and then adapt – the Miltonian and Dantean worldviews.

MacDonald also influenced Lewis in his appreciation of the literary form of fantasy. That fantasy, faerie, and science fiction (and for the latter, David Lindsay's *Voyage to Arcturus* was also influential) were all forms that appealed to Lewis the reader and the writer is no surprise. They allowed him – perhaps more than any straight 'realistic' fiction could – to capture and make explicit a sense of otherness, a hint of the supernatural. The company of Tolkien and Williams needs to be considered here too. All three were interested in mythology and attempted to reproduce it in their writings. Each undoubtedly had an influence upon the others. For, as Hefling notes, each wrote fantasy, each shared the conviction that the story form was often the best literary vehicle with which to convey a point, and each reflected in their fiction a Christian worldview. But nevertheless, and despite their common interests and influences, Hefling suggests:

> The comparison only goes so far. Lewis never seems to leave the lecturer's podium; writing fiction is a species of teaching. Tolkien is just the opposite in that narrative, for him, needs no further purpose. Telling a story is an end in itself ... Williams does not fit either mold. Certainly his stories, like Lewis', are *about* something, other than them- selves; but they are not about Christianity in the sense that they translate Christian tenets into imaginative prose.[71]

In Lewis' work, then, there is something altogether Chestertonian: even in his fiction he remained an apologist.[72]

---

[71]   Hefling, 'The Pattern of Glory', pp. 2–3.
[72]   Aidan Mackey has commented: '[G. K. Chesterton and C. S. Lewis] each had a fierce intellectual honesty and a taste for chivalrous and good-humoured – though entirely serious – battle for truth through controversy and debate.' Similarly he noted, 'The years which sepa- rated the lives of these two Christian warriors are irrelevant. They stood, and stand, shoulder to shoulder, each ... bearing arms as volunteers in the service of the same Captain.' See Aidan Mackey, 'The Christian Influence of G. K. Chesterton on C. S. Lewis', in A. Walker and J. H. Patrick, *Rumours of Heaven*, pp. 81, 82.

A number of commentators have highlighted the similarities of Lewis and Chesterton's apologetics: their ruthless logic, their humour, their tendency to *reductio ad absurdum* in argument.[73] Some point to a direct literary influence of G. K. Chesterton upon Lewis, citing the admission by Lewis himself of the impact that Chesterton's *The Everlasting Man* made upon him in early life, and the number of Chesterton's works that were to be found in Lewis' personal library collection.[74] John L. Wright has even gone so far as to say that whereas George Mac-Donald's *Phantastes* baptised Lewis' imagination, Chesterton 'in a certain sense helped to baptise' his intellect.[75] Personally I think this somewhat over-states the case. Lewis was affected and influenced by Chesterton, certainly, but, as James Patrick notes, 'Between the use of reason made by Chesterton and that made by Lewis, there were significant differences.'[76] Chesterton may have had a brilliance and originality much like John Henry Newman, but 'Lewis's mind was, on the other hand, synthetic and historical'.[77]

> He [Lewis] was gifted with the ability to bring under the unifying pattern of reason a broad range of historical evidence and to present convincingly the principles involved.[78]

[73] Cf. Gisbert Kranza, 'Affinities in Lewis and Chesterton', in *The Chesterton Review, C. S. Lewis Special Issue*, pp. 323–9.

[74] Cf. C. S. Lewis, 'Cross-examination', in *Essay Collection*, pp. 551–3, and *Surprised by Joy*, pp. 147–8. See also Iain Benson, 'The Influence of the Writings of G. K. Chesterton on C. S. Lewis: the Textual Part', in *The Chesterton Review*, pp. 357–67. Benson catalogues the copies of Chesterton's books that were found in Lewis' library when it was housed at Wroxton Hall near Banbury, compiled in 1985 and prior to their removal to the Marion E. Wade collection at Wheaton College in Illinois. He also provides a list of Lewis' writings that contain references to G. K. Chesterton.

[75] John L. Wright, 'Goodness in Chesterton and Lewis', in *The Chesterton Review*, p. 345.

[76] James Patrick, 'Reason in Chesterton and Lewis', in *The Chesterton Review*, p. 353.

[77] Ibid. p. 354.

[78] Ibid.

There is a sense, then, throughout Lewis' writing, of his attempting to *present* the reader with a ready-made worldview, a sense which is just not found – or at least not as strongly – in the works of J. R. R. Tolkien and Charles Williams.[79]

Owen Barfield once distinguished three elements to Lewis' character, referring to the 'imaginative Lewis', the 'religious Lewis', and the 'logical Lewis'.[80] Already, with only the few determining influences that I have here outlined, we can see those strands being formed. Both Barfield and (later) the Lewis scholar, Peter Schakel, have argued that C. S. Lewis kept – until relatively late in life – a separation between the imaginative and logical spheres. 'However deep Lewis's devotion to imagination,' argues Schakel, 'he was unable to commit himself fully to its efficacy and relied on the intellect to convey his central ideas, even in his imaginative fiction.'[81] Whilst I believe this to be true – and it is perhaps, a sign of the legacy of William T. Kirkpatrick's rationalism – nevertheless I don't feel it to be a weakness. In both the development and presentation of his eschatological worldview Lewis employed reason and imagination. It is, perhaps, precisely because reason – and the

---

79 Brian Horne has made the point: 'When it came to expounding the Christian faith, Lewis, as Austin Farrer remarked, "was apologist from temper, conviction and from modesty". It was part of Lewis' nature to be combative (not aggressive), to want to argue and debate, and in the process of that debate to reach conclusions … The approach of Williams was quite different. There were, of course, occasions when he felt the need to answer specific questions, but usually when it came to theology he was a "theologian" pure and simple. The delight lay in the art of speculation, not in argumentation."' See Brian Horne, 'A Peculiar Debt', p. 87. A former student, John Wain, notes of Lewis: 'He had a naturally rhetorical streak in him that made it a pleasure to cultivate the arts of winning people's attention and assent. Lewis's father was a lawyer, and the first thing that strikes one on opening any of Lewis's books is that he is always persuading, always arguing a case.' See John Wain, 'A Great Clerke', in J. Como, *C. S. Lewis at the Breakfast Table*, p. 69.

80 Cf. Owen Barfield, 'Lewis, Truth, and Imagination', in *Owen Barfield on C. S. Lewis*, ed. G. B. Tennyson, pp. 94–5.

81 Peter Schakel, *Imagination and the Arts in C. S. Lewis: Journeying to Narnia and Other Worlds*, p. x.

'logical Lewis' – played the more prominent role that this worldview stands up to theological scrutiny: and why it cannot be easily dismissed as merely a loose collection of 'arbitrary imaginative representations'.[82]

Identifying a Tradition

Unquestionably one of the consequences of Lewis' wide reading was the vast overview of historical, literary, philosophical and theological trends that he absorbed and was then able to employ in his own thought. James Como has noted that for some, '[Lewis] was the best-read man of his generation, one who read everything and remembered everything he read.'[83] A particular and striking characteristic of much of his academic writing is the breadth and scope of his knowledge. For example, as J. A. W. Bennett has said of Lewis' *English Literature in the Sixteenth Century*:

> Several pages ... remind us that for many years he taught political theory, and so knew his Hobbes as well as his Hooker, his Machiavelli as well as his More.[84]

It is important to remember that prior to his election as English tutor and fellow of Magdalen in 1925 Lewis had held out for a philosophical post in Oxford. He had even spent the second half of 1924 and the first half of the following year standing in for E. F. Carritt as a temporary philosophy tutor at

---

82 Cf. SCDF, 'The Reality of Life After Death', p. 502. Interestingly, Austin Farrer once commented: 'Someone wrote to me yesterday that Lewis was a split personality because the imaginative and the rationalistic held so curious a balance in his mind; and he himself tells us how his imaginative development raced away in boyhood and was afterwards called to order by logic.' But Farrer concluded that it was 'this feeling intellect, this intellectual imagination that made the strength of his [C. S. Lewis'] writings'. Cf. Austin Farrer, 'In His Image', in Como, *C. S. Lewis at the Breakfast Table*, p. 243.

83 J. Como, *C. S. Lewis at the Breakfast Table*, p. xxiii.

84 J. A. W. Bennett, 'Grete Clerk', in J. Gibb, *Light on C. S. Lewis*, p. 47.

University College. Far from being a narrow English specialist as such, Lewis had managed to carry into his literary field all that he had learnt from his background in Classics and Philosophy. Examining the Lewisian corpus, it is somewhat difficult – if not in fact altogether misleading – to speak of Lewis writing from a particular philosophical or theological tradition. He extrapolated. He was a master of pastiche. And, while there are recurrent themes and associated schools from which he drew, it is best to be rather wary of simplistic labels.

Philosophical School

In both *Surprised by Joy* and *The Pilgrim's Regress* Lewis himself marked out his intellectual development through a number of schools. As he put it in his preface to the third edition of the latter, 'My own progress had been from "popular realism" to Philosophical Idealism; from Idealism to Pantheism; from Pantheism to Theism; and from Theism to Christianity.'[85] James Patrick, in *The Magdalen Metaphysicals: Idealism and Orthodoxy at Oxford 1901–1945*, has argued:

> Lewis was drawn into the milieu established at Magdalen by Smith and Webb as his own thought developed toward an appreciation for history and classical metaphysics and away from the realism of his philosophy tutor E. F. Carritt.[86]

This milieu, according to Patrick, was in a broad sense the philosophical heir to the type of nineteenth-century English

---

[85] *Pilgrim's Regress*, p. ix.

[86] James Patrick, *The Magdalen Metaphysicals: Idealism and Orthodoxy at Oxford 1901–1945*, p. xvi. J. A. Smith was a fellow of Magdalen College, Oxford and Waynflete Professor of Philosophy from 1910 until 1935. Clement Webb was fellow at Magdalen from 1889 until 1922 and then from 1938 an honorary fellow of the college until his death in 1954. Adam Fox, who was dean of divinity and a fellow of Magdalen College during Lewis' early years there, noted that Jack 'had a real reverence for J. A. [Smith]'. See Adam Fox, 'At the Breakfast Table', in J. Como, *C. S. Lewis at the Breakfast Table*, p. 93.

idealism espoused by Thomas Hill Green and John Ruskin. However, although J. A. Smith and others interpreted this inheritance 'in the light of the thought of the seventeenth-century Italian philosopher Giambattista Vico and his modern disciples Croce and Giovanni Gentile', Lewis himself was 'never a member of what he called the Italian School, and on more than one occasion expressed disapproval of Croce'.[87] Of his initial shift from atheistic realism to a form of idealism, Lewis recorded in *Surprised by Joy*:

> It is astonishing ... that I could regard this position as something quite distinct from Theism ... But there were in those days all sorts of blankets, insulators, and insurances which enabled one to get all the conveniences of Theism, without believing in God. The English Hegelians, writers like T. H. Green, Bradley, and Bosanquet (then mighty names), dealt in precisely such wares.[88]

Whereas this philosophical progression towards Christianity – the 'logical Lewis' reasoning his way towards theology – might be portrayed as an ever-onward march, Austin Farrer has made the point that Lewis' position was somewhat more complicated. In *The Problem of Pain*, for example, Farrer believed that the weaknesses of Lewis' arguments lay in his 'foible' of perceiving man 'too narrowly as a moral will' and his relation with God as 'too narrowly a moral relation'.[89] As Farrer went on:

> Man, to Lewis, is an immortal subject; pains are his moral remedies, salutary disciplines ... But this is not all the truth, nor perhaps the half of it. Pain is the sting of death, the foretaste and ultimately the experience of sheer destruction. Pain cannot be related to the will of God as an evil turned into a moral instrument.[90]

---

[87] Cf. J. Patrick, *The Magdalen Metaphysicals*, pp. xv and xxiv.
[88] *Surprised by Joy*, pp. 162–3.
[89] Austin Farrer, 'The Christian Apologist', in J. Gibb, *Light on C. S. Lewis*, p. 40.
[90] Ibid.

This 'foible' of Lewis' is to be blamed, according to Farrer, on his shift through philosophical idealism in which, as Lewis himself described it, 'The whole universe was, in the last resort, mental.'[91] Although Lewis moved away from such a position in his Christian life, he was 'still able to overlook the full involvement of the reasonable soul in a random and perishable system'.[92] If Lewis was never entirely to shake off his post-Hegelian idealism, James Patrick notes that his dabbling in what, in *Surprised by Joy*, Lewis called his 'Stoical Monism', or 'New Look', similarly had an enduring influence.[93] As Patrick says:

> Elements of the 'New Look', his monistic realism of the years 1920–1922, would persist even after he began the metaphysical pilgrimage that ended in his return to the Anglicanism he had abandoned as a schoolboy.[94]

For example, Patrick notes of Lewis' philosophy lectures given between 1924 and 1925: 'Lewis was sufficiently rooted in classical metaphysics to insist that Locke's empiricism had failed, but enough of a realist to want no more of subjective idealism.'[95] Thus the later Lewis, it seems, was neither a strict idealist nor a strict realist but, perhaps, something in between. As Patrick puts it: 'It was in Lewis' works that the quest for unity in its inescapable combination with Christianity passed out of the academy and into the lives of ordinary folk. In his works metaphysics lived; history found significant unity; and reason joined imagination.'[96]

Two areas important to Lewis' eschatological thought that deserve some further philosophical comment here are his understanding of *Sehnsucht* and his use of Platonic idealism. Of *Sehnsucht*, James Patrick asserts:

91 *Surprised by Joy*, p. 162.
92 A. Farrer, 'The Christian Apologist', p. 41.
93 *Surprised by Joy*, p. 159.
94 J. Patrick, *The Magdalen Metaphysicals*, p. 109.
95 Ibid. p. 116.
96 Ibid. p. 131.

Lewis' estimate of the importance of joy was not unique. Ruskin was describing the same experience when he wrote of his youthful 'perception of sanctity in the whole of nature, from the slightest to the vastest; an instinctive awe mixed with delight; an indefinable thrill . . . '[97]

Importantly, then, the idealism of Ruskin provided Lewis with a philosophical framework within which to make sense of his aesthetic and imaginative experiences – precisely the experiences Barfield was attacking him on during their 'Great War' in an effort to show up the untenable nature of Lewis' realist position. With the breakdown of his early 1920s 'New Look' and his insertion into the prevailing idealism of Magdalen College in 1925, Lewis was to build upon Ruskin's view of 'instinctive awe' and produce, in *The Pilgrim's Regress*, for example, a defence of what he called 'Romanticism' which 'had about it an intelligibility, like Coleridge's primary imagination, directing those who sought it not toward the daemonic irrationality of Nietzsche but toward Reason'.[98] In other words, in Ruskin and his followers Lewis found a way of marrying his imaginative faculty (and most importantly his experience of *Sehnsucht*) with his rationalist, 'Kirkian' tendencies; a marriage he had hitherto been unable to undertake. Of the use of Platonism I have already pointed to Charles Williams' influence – at least at an imaginative level – in the application of the Platonic theory of Forms. In the Narnia Chronicles and in his sermon on the theory of transposition Lewis employed the ideas of archetype and ectype to demonstrate both a continuity and a newness concerning the age to come. In *The Last Battle* Digory exclaims of the Narnia within Narnia: 'Of course it is different; as different as a real thing is from a shadow or as waking life is from a dream . . . It's all in Plato, all in Plato: bless me, what *do* they teach them at these schools!'[99] Paul Ford has commented that Lewis was giving here 'a broad hint as to a major theme that underlies the Chronicles'. And he goes on to say:

---

[97] Ibid. p. 111.
[98] Ibid.
[99] *The Last Battle*, p. 159–60.

In addition to some obvious uses of Platonic thought and imagery at various key points of the tales, there is an almost continuous Platonic undercurrent which is often hardly noticeable.[100]

In *Transposition* Lewis constructed a fable of a woman who gives birth to a son whilst imprisoned in a dungeon and who tries to explain to that son, as he grows older, the reality of the outside world. This fable is, of course, a re-working of Plato's cave.[101] The question here, then, is not so much did Lewis employ Platonism: he evidently did. Rather, was Lewis a Platonist? Gregory Wolfe, in his assessment of the use of language and myth in Lewis' Space Trilogy, has argued:

> The tension between [Lewis'] Platonism and sacramentalism is a source of some confusion and uncertainty in the trilogy ... To be sure, Lewis did increasingly move away from a cruder form of Platonic idealism ... But Platonism was a persistent mental habit with Lewis ... [102]

Interestingly, despite this 'persistent mental habit', Lewis was well aware of the weaknesses – especially for Christianity – of the Platonic position. In a letter to Bede Griffiths written in 1940, Lewis noted: 'I fear Plato thought the concrete flesh and grass bad and have no doubt he was wrong.'[103] My own assessment of the Lewisian corpus leads me to accept that Lewis was indeed heavily influenced by a Christianised Platonism, in the school of St Augustine and Boethius, but not that he was a Platonist as such. We are back to Lewis' extrapolation: his plucking from different sources to articulate best his Christian worldview.[104]

---

[100] P. Ford, *Companion to Narnia*, p. 316.

[101] Cf. Plato, *The Republic*, VII, p. vii, pp. 514–5.

[102] Cf. Gregory Wolfe, 'Essential Speech: Language and Myth in the Ransom Trilogy', in P. Schakel and C. Huttar, *Word and Story*, p. 74.

[103] *Letters of C. S. Lewis*, p. 335 (Letter dated 17 January 1940).

[104] A good example of this extrapolation from any number of philosophical sources – and the consequent difficulties it causes for appropriating Lewis to a particular school – is given in Corbin Scott Carnell's summation of the Lewisian position. See

John Bremer has noted that between 1920 and 1940 the philosophical fashions of Oxford changed radically and the 'old Hegelian and subjective idealism of Lewis's days as a student – the school of Thomas Hill Green – gradually came to be considered outmoded'.[105] With the advent of Logical Positivism and linguistic analysis, then, and with his own move away from philosophical endeavour into literary history, it is no surprise that Lewis should have found himself, as Austin Farrer later put it, to be not 'quite at home in what we may call our post-positivist era'.[106] Indeed, Bremer asserts that Lewis 'seems to have made no serious effort to keep up with these developments' and that by 'so limiting his study, Lewis perhaps did himself a disservice'.[107] Humphrey Carpenter equally notes:

> By the 1940s Lewis was simply behind the times as a philosopher. He still argued along the lines taken by the post-Hegelians who had been fashionable in his under-graduate days; but among Oxford philosophers it was now as if Hegel and his disciples had never been.[108]

Certainly Lewis paid for such neglect in his celebrated debate at the Socratic Club in 1948 with the Cambridge philosopher and Catholic, Elizabeth Anscombe. Bede Griffiths recalled Lewis as admitting that Anscombe had 'completely demolished

---

Carnell, *Bright Shadow of Reality*, p. 71. Cf. also Walsh, *Apostle to the Skeptics*, p. 138. In a letter to Corbin Scott Carnell dated 10 December 1958, Lewis wrote: 'As I perhaps said before, a great many people think I'm being Thomist where I'm really being Aristotelian ... I am certainly not anti-Thomist. He is one of the great philosophers. On points at issue between Christian Platonism and Christian Aristotelianism I have not got a clean line.' Letters of C. S. Lewis to Corbin Scott Carnell held at the Bodleian Library, Oxford (MS. Facs. c. 48).

105 John Bremer, 'Philosophy', in J. Schultz and J. West, *Readers' Encyclopedia*, p. 320.
106 A. Farrer, 'The Christian Apologist', p. 30.
107 Cf. J. Bremer, 'Philosophy', p. 320.
108 H. Carpenter, *The Inklings*, p. 216.

his argument' for the existence of God during this debate.[109]
And Carpenter comments that although Lewis' 'most fervent
supporters felt she [Anscombe] had not demonstrated her
point successfully', nevertheless 'many who were at the meeting
thought that a conclusive blow had been struck against one of
[Lewis'] most fundamental arguments'.[110] It is perhaps Walter
Hooper who pinpoints the philosophical shift that faced Lewis
during this period:

> The new trend in philosophy at Oxford and Cambridge
> was to break away from theology and devote itself to the
> study of language. Philosophy was no longer metaphysics,
> but logical analysis, and, to reduce the Socratic's problem
> into the simplest form possible, the question now was not
> 'Does God exist?' but 'What do we mean by the word,
> "God"?'[111]

By this stage, however, Lewis was no longer a working philosopher. Certainly he used philosophy in his writing, particularly
in his apologetics – and as Humphrey Carpenter observes, one
of the effects of the shock of the Anscombe debate was that
Lewis 'wrote no further books of Christian apologetics for ten
years, apart from a collection of sermons'[112] – but, as John

---

[109] Cf. Bede Griffiths, 'The Adventure of Faith', p. 21: '[Lewis'] arguments for the existence of God were challenged by Elizabeth
Anscombe, a Catholic, who was a logical positivist. I remember
Lewis saying to me that she had completely demolished his argument and remarking that he thought, as she was a Catholic, she
might have least have provided an alternative argument ... Lewis
was certainly disturbed by this but, of course, it did not affect his
faith. He had no illusion about the relation of philosophy to faith.'
This issue as to whether or not Lewis was defeated by Anscombe
has been debated almost ever since their meeting at the Socratic
Club. Walter Hooper has said to me that Anscombe did not attack
Lewis' arguments for God as such but his specific argument
concerning causality as put forward in chapter three of *Miracles*.
[110] H. Carpenter, *The Inklings*, p. 217. The debate can be followed in the
minutes of the meeting found in the *Socratic Digest*, IV, pp. 7–15.
[111] Walter Hooper, 'Oxford's Bonny Fighter', in J. Como, *C. S. Lewis
at the Breakfast Table*, p. 168.
[112] H. Carpenter, *The Inklings*, p. 217.

Bremer argues, 'Perhaps the best summation is that Lewis was a philosophical writer, not a writer of philosophy.'[113] Lewis said of himself, upon taking up the English fellowship at Magdalen and thereby abandoning professional philosophy, 'I have come to think that if I had the mind, I have not the brain and nerves for a life of pure philosophy.'[114] If, by the 1940s, Oxford philosophy had seen a break away from theology and metaphysics towards linguistics, Lewis himself had already made a similar but converse break. As Farrer put it:

> Philosophy is an ever-shifting, never-ending public discussion, and a man who drops out of the game drops out of philosophy. But theological belief is not a philosophical position, it is the exercise of a relation with the most solidly real of all beings.[115]

With his conversion to Christianity, Lewis' primary concern was no longer with epistemological or metaphysical positions but with his relationship with God. Undoubtedly this relationship had philosophical implications for him but Lewis had made the break. He had moved towards theology just as contemporary philosophy was moving away from it.

Theological School

Richard Ladborough, one of Lewis' close friends from his Cambridge days, recalls: '[Lewis] was orthodox in belief but seemed to have little sense of the Church.'[116] Such a sentiment is certainly borne out by a reading of his works. Lewis tended in his writing, at times, to present a rather ahistorical and personal Christianity. Bede Griffiths noted that Lewis had 'very little sense of the Church as a living organism, growing by stages through the centuries, as Newman portrayed it in his

---

[113] J. Bremer 'Philosophy', p. 321.
[114] *Letters of C. S. Lewis*, p. 212 (Letter dated 14 August 1925).
[115] A. Farrer, 'The Christian Apologist', p. 31.
[116] Richard Ladborough, 'In Cambridge', in J. Como, *C. S. Lewis at the Breakfast Table*, p. 103.

Development of Christian Doctrine.[117] Interestingly, too, Charles Wrong remembers a conversation with Lewis in which Wrong observed, 'Charles Williams struck me as a man for whom the question of religious denomination appeared almost irrelevant.' 'Yes,' Lewis replied, 'but I think that's true of *all* good Christians.'[118] This apparent non-denominationalism is compounded in Lewis' writings because of his deliberate decision to expound what he called 'mere Christianity', what Lewis elsewhere explained as, 'The belief that has been common to nearly all Christians at all times.'[119] Needless to say, Lewis *was* denominational and his faith *was* the faith of a tradition and communal experience. Lewis was a practising Anglican: 'A very ordinary layman of the Church of England, not especially "high", nor especially "low", nor especially anything else,' as he once described himself.[120] Some commentators have argued

---

[117] Bede Griffiths, 'The Adventure of Faith', p. 21. Griffiths went on to say: 'In fact I remember him saying to me once that he thought Charles Kingsley had the better of the argument with Newman, which produced the *Apologia*. This is surely a surprising judgement and shows how fundamentally unsympathetic he was to the Catholic outlook.'

[118] Charles Wrong, 'A Chance Meeting', in J. Como, *C. S. Lewis at the Breakfast Table*, p. 110. Interestingly, James Patrick has noted of the major differences between C. S. Lewis and G. K. Chesterton: 'For Lewis, philosophy produced more knowledge than the Bloomsbury philosophers could comfortably bear, but not so much as to drive one to the uncomfortable certainties of Maritain. Christianity was a hall, off which denominational rooms opened. For Chesterton, it was a vast building with a porch, perhaps many porches, yet conversion meant leaving the porch and entering the one Church.' See J. Patrick, 'Reason in Chesterton and Lewis', p. 354.

[119] *Mere Christianity*, p. vi. Interestingly, the Catholic writer, John Willis, argues that the basis for Lewis' 'mere Christianity' is the *via media* of the Anglican tradition itself. He is critical of this basis for, he asserts, 'from the Catholic vantage point' such a *via media* does not exist at all. 'The very topics he [Lewis] attempted to avoid – Pope, Magisterium, sacraments – are essential ingredients to the theological whole.' See John Willis, *Pleasures Forevermore: the Theology of C. S. Lewis*, p. xx. Personally, I am not convinced that Lewis' 'mere Christianity' can be so easily equated with any Anglican notion of a *via media*.

[120] Ibid.

that Lewis never really shook off the Ulster Protestantism of his youth. J. R. R. Tolkien once noted:

> It was not for some time that I realized that there was more in the title *Pilgrim's Regress* than I had understood (or the author either, maybe). Lewis would regress. He would not re-enter Christianity by a new door, but by the old one: at least in the sense that in taking it up again he would also take up, or reawaken, the prejudices so sedulously planted in boyhood. He would become again a Northern Ireland protestant.[121]

It seems to me, however, that what is most striking about Lewis' Christian writing is precisely its lack of any sense of tradition in the technical sense of the word, that is, of something being handed on. Lewis' position is one that has been rationally worked out rather than received. Bede Griffiths expressed surprise that Lewis showed very little interest in the Fathers of the Church. 'With his wide classical culture one would have expected him to be naturally attracted to the Greek and Latin Fathers,' Griffiths recalled, 'but apart from mention of St Augustine's *Confessions* I don't remember his ever referring to one of the Fathers.'[122] Although a former student, Luke Rigby, has recounted Lewis making 'indirect references that showed a deep knowledge of the works of medieval theologians, notably St Thomas Aquinas and Duns Scotus',[123] Griffiths asserted that Lewis 'was most unsympathetic to the revival of Thomism' and that he didn't find 'St Thomas himself very attractive (though, of course, he appreciated the Thomist elements in the poetry of Dante)'.[124] Certainly Lewis had a working knowledge of St Thomas' *Summa Theologiae*, since he said himself that he had used it to provide a background to teaching the literature of that period.[125] And this is perhaps

---

[121] See H. Carpenter, *The Inklings*, p. 50.
[122] Bede Griffiths, 'The Adventure of Faith', p. 21.
[123] Luke Rigby, 'A Solid Man', in J. Como, *C. S. Lewis at the Breakfast Table*, p. 40.
[124] Bede Griffiths, 'The Adventure of Faith', p. 21.
[125] Cf. Corbin Scott Carnell, *Bright Shadow of Reality*, pp. 70–1. Chad

the point: Lewis' knowledge of his sources – and he clearly admired and drew upon the works of Augustine, Athanasius, Richard Hooker, William Tyndale, Thomas Traherne, and John Bunyan amongst others – came from their use as literary texts rather than as theological ones.[126] Furthermore, as Corbin Scott Carnell points out, since Lewis tended to draw upon older literary sources, 'He had less to say to those caught up in the Existential theology of his time.' Nevertheless, such a tendency had its advantages too: Lewis was able to aim at 'the simplicity and clearness of Augustine or Hooker, untrammeled by the deliberate ambiguities of some contemporary theologians'.[127]

Walsh has also noted this use of St Thomas 'as a convenient reference work' and argued that Lewis may 'have indirectly absorbed a good deal of Aquinas via Dante'. Chad Walsh, *Apostle to the Skeptics*, p. 138.

[126] In his introduction to Sr Penelope's translation of *De Incarnatione*, Lewis noted: 'I myself was first led into reading the Christian classics, almost accidentally, as a result of my English studies. Some, such as Hooker, Herbert, Traherne, Taylor and Bunyan, I read because they are themselves great English writers; others, such as Boethius, St Augustine, Thomas Aquinas, and Dante, because they were "influences". George MacDonald I had found for myself at the age of sixteen and never wavered in my allegiance.' See C. S. Lewis, 'Introduction', to *On the Incarnation*, p. 6. Chad Walsh has noted: 'Among the theologians (in addition to MacDonald) he [Lewis] has been especially attracted to St Augustine, St Athanasius (whose battle against the Arian heresy was strikingly similar to Lewis' war on Modernist Christianity), and Hooker (especially the earlier writings).' Walsh, *Apostle to the Skeptics*, p.138.

[127] Cf. Corbin Scott Carnell, *Bright Shadow of Reality*, pp. 68–9. William Luther White has commented: 'Dr Hugh R. Macintosh notes in *Types of Modern Theology* that typically German theology "is prone to advance in a zigzag manner, tacking from one extreme to another, enveloping all in a fierce spirit of party, equipping each new school with the penetrating power of a one-sided fervour as well as with the practically effective slogan which calls men round to a newly erected banner". C. S. Lewis would have agreed with Dr Macintosh, I think, that a less exciting arena produces a theology of far sounder judgement. Lewis was no theological extremist of any variety. He deliberately avoided identifying himself with current schools of theological debate. It is possible, therefore, that the partisans of

Austin Farrer once described Lewis' theological approach as being 'the standard answer of the time – Biblical Revelation read through Rudolf Otto's spectacles: a world haunted by the supernatural, a conscience haunted by the moral absolute, a history haunted by the divine claim of Christ'.[128] Carnell, too, has noted this influence of Otto's thought, particularly from his book *The Idea of the Holy* in which the central theme concerns the numinous – feelings of awe, humility, fascination, and so on, in the face of holiness: a non-rational awareness, or even awakening, in the presence of something altogether Other.[129] However, Carnell also argues that Lewis' understanding of his primary experience of the numinous – his experience of *Sehnsucht* – owes much to the medieval tradition and in particular to Augustine.[130] In his examination of *eros* as a means of grace Carnell comments:

There are many good things to be enjoyed in this life, among them beauty, friendship, and love, but they are never quite what we anticipate nor quite what we remember. We are beckoned on continually toward that which will satisfy our hearts. This may sound like only a paraphrase of Augustine's 'We are restless till we rest in Thee.' But Lewis says somewhat more, with more careful analy-

---

various camps will find his thought suspect. But it is also probable that his theological contribution will prove more lasting than those of most theological faddists in the current decade.' See William Luther White, *The Images of Man in C. S. Lewis*, p. 212.

[128] A. Farrer, 'The Christian Apologist', p. 34.

[129] See Corbin Scott Carnell, *Bright Shadow of Reality*, p. 69. Cf. Rudolf Otto, *The Idea of the Holy: An Enquiry into the Non-rational Factor in the Idea of the Divine and its Relation to the Rational*, pp. 9–11. Here Otto noted that what he called the 'creature-feeling' of dependence 'is itself a first subjective concomitant and effect of another feeling-element, which casts it like a shadow, but which in itself indubitably has immediate and primary reference to an object outside the self'. John Harvey notes: 'It is Otto's purpose to emphasize that this [i.e. the numinous] is an objective reality, not merely a subjective feeling in the mind.' See John Harvey, 'Translator's Preface', to R. Otto, *The Idea of the Holy*, p. xvi.

[130] Ibid. p. 148.

sis. He is arguing that God is present in every good but is not to be identified with that good.[131]

Austin Farrer argued that Lewis was somewhat unsure of his theology on this point; that the diffidence with which he asked, 'Do we ever fully desire anything *but* heaven?' in *The Problem of Pain* could be explained partially on the grounds of his not knowing how common an experience he was tapping into, and partially because he was still as yet undecided as to whether such romantic yearning indicated an 'appetite for heaven' or 'the ultimate refinement of covetousness'.[132] If there is such hesitancy in Lewis' understanding of longing in his early apologetic work, it is dispelled in later thought and Paul Ford is correct when he suggests,

> [Lewis'] own deepest experiences are recognizably one with the Platonic-Augustinian 'ascent of the soul' in which the human heart, incited by the limited goods and beauties of creation, discovers within itself a restless, piercing desire for the unlimited source of all reality and perfection.[133]

Ian Boyd has argued that C. S. Lewis 'emphasises the collapse of human happiness and the experience of human failure and of self-deception as essential parts of our journey to God'.[134]

> For him, grace is most likely to work through failure, through disillusionment, and even through the experience of sin: his journey to God is Augustinian. Life on earth is a life in the shadowlands.[135]

---

[131] Corbin Scott Carnell, 'C. S. Lewis on Eros as a means of Grace', in *Imagination and the Spirit: Essays in Literature and the Christian Faith Presented to Clyde S. Kilby*, p. 349.

[132] Cf. A. Farrer, 'The Christian Apologist', pp. 39–40.

[133] Paul Ford, *Companion to Narnia*, p. 316.

[134] Ian Boyd, 'Chesterton and C. S. Lewis', in *The Chesterton Review*, XVII, p. 308.

[135] Ibid.

This echoes what Janine Goffar has called Lewis' 'pessimism'. I think, however, that a careful nuance has to be stressed here. As Goffar admits: 'Lewis loved life immensely, yet he retained a sober awareness of its dangers and sufferings.' She goes on, 'His hearty relish of life was precisely *because* he realised its potential for pain and horror, and therefore he more fully cherished all its loveliness, as one might treasure a rose garden on prison grounds.'[136] For Lewis – as for St Augustine – this 'pessimism' might otherwise be called a realistic optimism: a view of the world that doesn't seek to underplay the sufferings of everyday life and the trials and tribulations of sin and temptation but one that looks to grace. If we do live now in the shadowlands – and, indeed, Lewis used the phrase – it is because we are awaiting in hope for the dawn of a bright and eternal new day.[137]

⁘⁙⁘

Arguably Chad Walsh summed up Lewis' theological position when he said: 'A careful reading of Lewis' books leaves the conviction that he is squarely in the middle of the Christian tradition.'[138] And John Willis was accurate in his assessment that Lewis' theology is 'almost never original; he does not

---

[136] Janine Goffar, *The C. S. Lewis Index: A Comprehensive Guide to Lewis's Writings and Ideas*, p. xi.

[137] Cf. *The Last Battle*, p. 171 and *Weight of Glory*, pp. 35–7. It is interesting to note that Zachary Hayes has commented: 'For many of our contemporaries, the word "hope" is associated with a sort of romantic inability to see and to deal with the pain and tragedy of human experience. If the biblical tradition of Abraham is seen as a paradigm of hope, it is clear that the sort of hope suggested here is far removed from such naiveté. Biblical hope does not emerge out of a sense that all life is light and clear. On the contrary, Abraham's hope emerges out of some great ambiguity.' See Hayes, *Visions of Future*, p. 22.

[138] Chad Walsh, *Apostle to the Skeptics*, p. 75. Indeed, commenting on his diverse reading of theologians such as Hooker, Herbert, Traherne, Taylor, Law, Augustine, Aquinas, and MacDonald, Lewis noted: 'The divisions of Christianity are undeniable and are by some of these writers most fiercely expressed. But if any man is tempted to think – as one might be tempted who read only

intend it to be'. What is original, Willis contends, 'is his style of writing, his clearness of expression, his lucidity of thought, his illustrations, metaphors, analogies, and most of all his charming winsomeness'.[139] Kathleen Raine has commented of C. S. Lewis both: 'To meet him was to know that here was a man of great learning, continuously kindled into life by imagination,' and: 'What was best of all in his immense learning was that it had an orientation.'[140] It is this latter statement, I think, that can be the key to understanding Lewis' thought and work. Towards the end of *The Pilgrim's Regress* the character John, having been converted to Christianity, returns through the land to his home of Puritania. However on this journey – on this 'regression' – things look very different to the way they had before. 'Courage,' John is urged, upon being disconcerted by this change in perception, 'you are seeing the land as it really is.' In case we had missed the point, Lewis later added a subtitle to the chapter: 'John now first sees the real shape of the world we live in – How we walk on a knife-edge between Heaven and Hell.'[141] He was suggesting, as Clyde Kilby has commented, 'That the Christian view puts everything else in a new perspective.'[142] Corbin Scott Carnell has noted: 'In Lewis we sometimes think we are listening to an argument, but . . . we are in fact being presented with a vision.'[143] It is the development of this vision that has been at the heart of our discussion in this chapter. Lewis himself once wrote, in his debate with E. M. W. Tillyard, 'The poet is not a man who asks me to look at

---

contemporaries – that "Christianity" is a word of so many meanings that it means nothing at all, he can learn beyond all doubt, by stepping out of his own century, that this is not so. Measured against the ages, "mere Christianity" turns out to be no insipid interdenominational transparency, but something positive, self-consistent, and inexhaustible.' See 'Introduction', to *On the Incarnation*, p. 6.

[139] John Willis, *Pleasures Forevermore*, p. xix.
[140] Cf. Kathleen Raine, 'From a Poet', in J. Gibb, *Light on C. S. Lewis*, p. 102–5.
[141] *Pilgrim's Regress*, p. 221.
[142] Clyde Kilby, *The Christian World of C. S. Lewis*, p. 35.
[143] Corbin Scott Carnell, *Bright Shadow of Reality*, p. 60.

him; he is a man who says, "Look at that" and points.'[144]
Ultimately Lewis was neither a philosopher nor a theologian
but a Christian poet. His real power 'was not in proof', as
Austin Farrer has said, 'it was depiction'.[145] And in the
Lewisian corpus what is depicted is an eschatological
Weltanschauung. Sometimes this worldview is illustrated
through reasoned logic; sometimes it is portrayed through
vivid imagination. Often it is presented through both.
Interestingly, it seems, the *Weltanschauung* of the 'religious
Lewis' – to use again Barfield's threefold distinction – only
emerged once the 'logical Lewis' and the 'imaginative Lewis'
had somehow been reconciled. It is to this reconciliation – this
somewhat unequal marriage of reason and imagination in C. S.
Lewis – that I want to turn in the next chapter.

---

[144] *Personal Heresy*, p. 11.
[145] A. Farrer, 'In His Image', p. 243.

Chapter 4

Metaphysics and Metaphor

In his book, *Heaven: A Traveller's Guide to the Undiscovered Country*, the English Catholic journalist and broadcaster Peter Stanford comments:

> In our secular age heaven has become something of a by-word for a wide-spread sense of powerlessness and bemusement when faced with death, a word and a metaphor stripped of any directly denominational religious significance but retaining the dream of a place that is both 'other' and full of consolation.[1]

Having presented a broad-sweeping overview of Christianity's (and, to some extent, other major world religions') various descriptions of heaven, Stanford suggests that modern, secular society tends to draw largely upon the imagery of the life to come rather than its doctrine. In other words, heaven – at least at the popular level – is detached from its place in eschatological theology and becomes a vague symbol of hope in the face of death and human melancholy. Faced with the terminally ill, with an horrific road accident, with the tragic death of a child, with whichever of the myriad forms of human suffering and mortality that may present themselves, secular society finds itself reaching for a concept of heaven that will console it through a promise of a future and eternal panacea. It does not, generally, concern itself with those related (Christian) eschatological concepts of the real meaning of death, judgement,

[1] Peter Stanford, *Heaven: A Traveller's Guide to the Undiscovered Country*, pp. 331–2.

purgatory, hell, general resurrection, and the parousia. Stanford contrasts this secular and imaginative use of the heaven-concept – which he admits is largely the representation of the afterlife as some sort of a reunion with loved ones – with what he sees to be a growing trend in Christian theology: the avoidance of any and all imaginative representation of the heavenly realm. John Paul II, he claims, in the first twenty-one years of his pontificate 'had not deigned to mention heaven publicly at all' until in July 1999, in St Peter's Square, he announced:

> The heaven in which we will find ourselves is neither an abstraction nor a physical place among the clouds ... [It is rather] a living and personal relationship with the Holy Trinity ... close communion and full intimacy with God ... Heaven is a blessed community of those who remained faithful to Jesus Christ in their lifetimes, and are now at one with His glory.[2]

Similarly, Stanford argues that the Catechism is sketchy about the subject of paradise preferring merely to state: 'Heaven is the ultimate end and the fulfilment of the deepest human longings, the state of supreme, definitive happiness.'[3] Anglicanism fares little better under Stanford's assessment. He notes a BBC poll, taken in December 1999, which reported that around forty per cent of Anglican clergy had admitted that they did not believe in heaven as a physical place.

> Questioned about the findings, an embarrassed Bishop of Oxford, Richard Harries, tried to put a good gloss on what was being presented as yet more evidence of a

---

[2] Ibid. p. 299.
[3] Ibid. p. 300. Cf. *Catechism*, n. 1024. Actually Stanford is somewhat selective in what he quotes. For example, he ignores n. 1027 which states: 'This mystery of blessed communion with God and all who are in Christ is beyond all understanding and description. Scripture speaks of it in images: life, light, peace, wedding feast, wine of the kingdom, the Father's house, the heavenly Jerusalem, paradise: "no eye has seen, no ear heard, nor the heart of man conceived, what God has prepared for those who love him."' See *Catechism*, n. 1027.

Church that scarcely believed in God. He spoke of a 'symbolic realism' that was neither literal truth nor poetic myth, but something in between about which he was less than precise. To be fair, his position sounded remarkably similar to that of Pope John Paul II.[4]

Leaving aside for the moment Stanford's journalistic tendency to over-simplification, the point he makes has some validity. Modern Christian eschatology has increasingly moved towards a theocentric and apophatic approach to heaven whilst popular spirituality seems to clamour more and more for an anthropocentric and cataphatic one. And, as Stanford concludes, 'If Christianity has given up talking about heaven, others are still using the bank of imagery it built up to good effect.'[5]

It seems to me that what Stanford diagnoses as the modern malaise – heavenly metaphor divided from its metaphysical referent – and what modern day Christianity appears to want to avoid – paucity of image in the first place – are overcome in C. S. Lewis. Significantly, in *A Grief Observed*, Lewis was critical of any notion of heaven as a celestial cure-all. 'Talk to me about the truth of religion,' he wrote, 'and I'll listen gladly. Talk to me about the duty of religion and I'll listen submissively. But don't come talking to me about the consolations of religion or I shall suspect that you don't understand.'[6] For Lewis, the concept of heaven wasn't merely a metaphor for human impotency in the face of death, nor for our aspirations of a better world. For Lewis, heaven was the 'by-word' for ultimate reality. This is the metaphysic that underpinned his popular use of metaphor. And it is to this union of metaphysics and metaphor that I now want to turn.

Imagination and Reason

To begin, it is necessary to explore how C. S. Lewis employed both metaphysics and metaphor in his epistemology; in other

---

[4] P. Stanford, *Heaven*, p. 301.
[5] Ibid. p. 332.
[6] *A Grief Observed*, p. 23.

words, what role did each play in the Lewisian theory of knowledge. This leads us, initially, to an examination of the relationship between reason and imagination in Lewis' thought: what might be called a 'morganatic' marriage in which Reason undoubtedly wears the trousers. 'Reason is our starting point,' wrote Lewis in *Miracles*, for 'if the value of our reasoning is in doubt, you cannot try to establish it by reasoning.'[7] With this application of the law of non-contradiction,[8] Lewis attempted to strike a blow against scepticism. If 'a proof that there are no proofs is nonsensical', Lewis went on, 'so is a proof that there are proofs.'[9] In other words, either one accepts the possibility of truth and its apprehension through reason or one doesn't, but there is no middle ground. Of course throughout the history of philosophy there has been much middle ground and, indeed, it was precisely this middle ground that Lewis debated with Elizabeth Anscombe at the Socratic Club in 1948. But a year earlier, with the publication of *Miracles*, Lewis had attacked this too by arguing that it was no good adopting a limited use of reason such as might be called applied or practical, which 'enables us to set a bone and build a bridge and make a Sputnik',[10] whilst at the same time refuting the 'high pretensions of reason' such as 'when we fly off into speculation and try to get general views of "reality"' and so on. We just don't live like that, believed Lewis. There may be 'no more theology, no more ontology, no more metaphysics' under this system, but equally there could be no more generalisations of any kind.

In my opinion, Lewis' epistemology was largely Augustinian. In *Miracles* he propounded his position thus: 'The human mind in the act of knowing is illuminated by the Divine reason. It is set free, in the measure required, from the huge nexus of non-rational causation; free from this to be determined by the truth known.'[11] This sits neatly alongside what Augustine said in *De Magistro* 12.40:

[7] *Miracles*, p. 21.
[8] E.g. as expressed by Aristotle's dictum: 'Nothing can both be and not be at the same time in the same respect.'
[9] *Miracles*, p. 21.
[10] Ibid.
[11] Ibid. p. 22–3.

When we deal with things that we perceive by the mind, namely by the intellect and reason, we're speaking of things that we look upon immediately in the inner light of Truth, in virtue of which the so-called inner man is illuminated and rejoices.[12]

Of course, caution is always required when considering Augustine's doctrine of divine illumination. As Mark Jordan has commented, it is all too easy to ascribe to Augustine 'discrete doctrines ... usually without the dialectical nuances he would have considered indispensable'.[13] Etienne Gilson, one of the Catholic historians of philosophy actually favoured by C. S. Lewis,[14] argued that although divine illumination is 'rightly considered ... a distinctive feature of [Augustine's] philosophy', nevertheless it is to be understood in metaphorical terms. The act by which the mind comes to know truth, according to Gilson's interpretation of Augustine, is comparable to the act by which the eye sees a body. God is to our minds as the sun is to our sight. Thus, 'As the sun is the source of light, so God is the source of truth.'[15] Gilson went on to observe:

---

[12] St Augustine, *Against the Academicians and The Teacher*, pp. 140–1. In his introduction Peter King comments: 'The test of truth is inside, Augustine argues. What gets conveyed from one person to another are at best putative knowledge-claims that each recipient judges for himself. In items perceived by the senses, we have knowledge when the sensible object itself is present to us. In items perceived by the mind, we look upon these "immediately in the inner light of Truth" and know them.' See ibid. p. xix. In *Against the Academicians*, 3.17.37 Augustine noted: 'For my purposes, it's enough that Plato perceived that there are two worlds: an intelligible world where truth itself resides, and this sensible world that we obviously sense by sight and touch. The former is the true world, the latter only truthlike and made to its image. Consequently, truth about the former world is refined and brightened (so to speak) in the soul that knows itself.' See ibid. p. 87. Cf. also St Augustine, *Soliliquia*, 1.1.3 and 1.6.12.

[13] Mark Jordan, 'Augustine', in *The Cambridge Dictionary of Philosophy*, p. 61.

[14] See *Letters of C. S. Lewis*, p. 311 (Letter dated 7 June 1934).

[15] Etienne Gilson, *The Christian Philosophy of St. Augustine*, p. 77.

The intellectual mind which Augustine assigns to man as his own and which is, therefore, created, can be called a natural light, if we may be allowed to use a phrase which Augustine does not employ but which does no violence to his thought. The result of divine illumination is not, normally at least, a supernatural illumination; on the contrary, to be the receptive subject of divine illumination belongs by definition to the nature of the human intellect. There is here no fusion with the supernatural order nor emanation therefrom.[16]

Similarly, Lewis did not argue for an epistemology dependent upon moments of divine illumination in the sense of supernatural or mystical insights. Rather, the ultimate truth of God allows us to perceive, and determines how we might do so, the fundamental truths of nature. As Lewis said in *Miracles*,

To call the act of knowing – the act, not of remembering that something was so in the past, but of 'seeing' that it must be so always and in any possible world – to call this act 'supernatural', is some violence to our ordinary linguistic usage. But of course we do not mean by this that it is spooky, or sensational, or even (in any religious sense) 'spiritual'. We mean only that it 'won't fit in'; that such an act, to be what it claims to be – and if it is not, all our thinking is discredited – cannot be merely the exhibition at a particular place and time of that total, and largely mindless, system of events called 'Nature'. It must break sufficiently free from that universal chain in order to be determined by what knows it.[17]

This position, like that of St Augustine, implies a metaphysical worldview: underlying the truths apprehended through human reason must be an ultimate truth – God himself – to guarantee them. And thus, as Lewis argued it, 'Reason is given before Nature and on reason our concept of Nature depends.

---

[16] Ibid. p. 79.
[17] *Miracles*, p. 23.

Our acts of inference are prior to our picture of Nature almost as the telephone is prior to the friend's voice we hear by it.'[18] I believe, then, that Lewis would have agreed with the Jesuit, Gerald McCool, when he wrote: 'By his nature, not only is man a rational animal, he is a metaphysical animal. Human reason is transcendent.'[19]

Lewis' position also belonged to what Wilbur Urban called the 'high evaluation of language'.[20] Briefly put, Urban argued that the major turning points in Western history have all been marked by philosophical debate concerning the nature of language. A 'high evaluation' of language tends to accept a belief in universals and connects a word closely with the thing it designates whereas a 'low evaluation' tends to detach the word from the thing, taking a somewhat more nominalist stance.[21] The Lewis scholar, Doris Myers, has pointed to the end of the First World War as being just such a turning point and indeed a time when 'the old battle between the high and low evaluations of language was fought out anew'. She goes on:

---

[18] Ibid.

[19] Gerald McCool, *From Unity to Pluralism: The Internal Evolution of Thomism*, p. 192.

[20] Cf. Wilbur Urban, *Language and Reality: The Philosophy of Language and the Principles of Symbolism*, p. 23: 'It may be taken for granted, I suppose, that the notion of a traditional philosophy, of a *philosophia perennis,* in the sense of the Greco-Christian tradition, is more and more being accepted as a true description of the story of Western philosophy ... I suppose that it would also be agreed that this same tradition is based upon a high evaluation of language; on a doctrine of reason which identifies it, in some degree at least, with the Word, the *Logos.* Bergson is certainly not far wrong when he tells us that this entire tradition is based upon a trust in language. This high evaluation of language is the underlying assumption of all periods of rationalism and is uniformly accompanied by some belief in the reality of universals, since the very naming of anything immediately universalises it in some sense and to some degree.'

[21] Cf. Doris Myers, *C. S. Lewis in Context*, p. 1. Cf. W. Urban, *Language and Reality,* pp. 23–4. Urban defined nominalism in this context as a 'disbelief in the reality of the universal' which thus undermines the validity of naming and communication, and leads ultimately to scepticism and relativism.

C. S. Lewis was involved in this struggle. In the process of reaching an informed, intellectually based decision to embrace Christianity, he had to decide how to evaluate language.[22]

As Urban has identified, one of the significant differences between the 'high' and 'low' schools was the acceptance or rejection of universals; that is, as David Knowles describes it, 'Of the degree of reality and significance attributable to the mental perception of a similarity between groups of individual beings.'[23] Briefly put the problem is this: if, when I perceive two individual roses, I can identify each as a rose, am I implying that they are the same *thing*? To do so would be to assert there is only one rose before me and yet I have perceived two individual *things* that I identify as 'rose'. If I accept a belief in universals – and belong to what Urban called the 'high evaluation' of language school – then I assert (as D. J. B. Hawkins puts it) 'that [that] which is really rose [is] itself something apart from particular roses and belonging to a different order of being'.[24] In other words, the universal is something real and distinct from the particular. On the other hand, if I take the nominalist position – and thus belong to Urban's 'low evaluation' school – I find myself rejecting the reality of universals, believing them to be merely intellectual concepts which enable thought and speech. As Knowles explains it:

> [For the nominalist] the universal is something purely intra-mental, the concomitant of the intuitional realization of the individual thing. A given thing, a dog or rose, evokes in the human mind a mental 'sign' (*signum naturale*) which is the same in all men, as is a laugh or a cry; each race of men then gives to this sign a verbal sign or term in its own language which we attach to our mental image and which recalls that image to our mind.[25]

[22] D. Myers, *C. S. Lewis in Context*, p. 1.
[23] David Knowles, *The Evolution of Medieval Thought*, p. 98.
[24] D. J. B. Hawkins, *A Sketch of Medieval Philosophy*, p. 35.
[25] David Knowles, *Evolution of Medieval Thought*, p. 294. Jeffrey Burton Russell describes nominalism thus: 'Nominalism, the dominant

Lewis, it seems, identified himself with a realist position quite early on in his thinking. In a letter written to Owen Barfield during their 'Great War' – that running battle of ideas that continued between the two friends from Barfield's conversion to anthroposophy in 1923 until around the time of Lewis' conversion to Christianity in 1931 – Lewis observed: 'Of course a universal is what it is whether we are so lucky to see it or not. The green common to many leaves is a universal whether or not I see why it must be common or not.'[26]

The issue is complicated further, however, by the broad range of interpretations from those who hold that universals are real. An ultra-realist position, as held by Plato, argues that the universals are real and to be found in the realm of the Ideas or Forms, quite distinct from the intellectual process or the particular thing in itself.[27] A modified form of this ultra-

---

intellectual trend [of the late Middles Ages and Reformation] was based on the rejection of the Platonic, idealistic belief – known as *realism* – that abstract ideas have an intrinsic reality over and above the reality of individuals ... We know that Socrates and Plato are both human, Ockham observed, by direct experience and intuition. We do not need to refer to an abstract quality "humanity" to know this. People could tell a man from a finback whale before Plato invented realism. We have no evidence that "humanity" exists, only individual humans; no evidence that "finback whaleness" exists, only individual finback whales. Knowledge of abstract qualities is therefore a creation of human beings rather than a reflection of the external world itself.' Jeffrey Burton Russell, *The Prince of Darkness: Radical Evil and the Power of Good in History*, p. 157.

[26] 'Great War' correspondence of C. S. Lewis and Owen Barfield held at the Bodleian Library, Oxford (MS. Facs. c. 54), p. 54.

[27] Etienne Gilson argued that Plato himself did not address the issue of existence as such in his theory of Ideas. 'Since sensible things are but images of Ideas, Ideas themselves are bound to make up another world, the intelligible world,' Gilson noted. But earlier he had argued: 'To say that such realities exist is most confusing, because the only existence we can imagine is that of sensible things. Now, if Ideas *are*, in what sense can they be said *to be?* ... If we are here vainly looking to Plato for an answer, the reason probably is that we are asking him the wrong question. He has just told us what it is for him to be, and we keep asking him what it is to exist.' Cf. Etienne Gilson, *Being and Some Philosophers*, pp. 14–15, 19. An objection to Gilson's theory, however, is that existence

realism is to be found in the epistemology of Duns Scotus who, according to Paul Haffner, held that 'the universals were real entities apart from their existence in individuals'.[28] Another realist position would be to move away from the notion of the extramental nature of universals whilst still affirming their reality. As D. W. Mertz puts it:

> Universals are retained as the abstracted, nonpredicative content of predicative, hence individuated, instances of universals. The result is a form of the classic scholastic ontology of moderate realism.[29]

This position is found in St Thomas who argued that the universals are 'virtually present in individuals, from which they are abstracted by our intellect'.[30] At first glance this moderate

---

must be presumed in Plato's concept of the Ideas if he is to answer the moral, linguistic, epistemological, ontological and political questions that he tried to address. Similarly, one might address an Aristotelian-like critique by arguing that the Ideas must exist if they are to impart existence to anything else.

28 Paul Haffner, *The Mystery of Reason*, p. 13.

29 D. W. Mertz, *Moderate Realism and Its Logic*, p. xiv. The term 'realism' in philosophy is always a confusing one as its usage has a number of distinctions. For example, Plato could be said to be a realist in the sense (as used above) that he believed the Forms were real. On the other hand, he could be said to be an idealist in the sense that the Forms are recognised only in the intellect and as such are ideas, rather than the result of direct sense perception. As Lewis observed in *An Experiment in Criticism*, 'The word *realism* has one meaning in logic, where its opposite is nominalism, and another in metaphysics, where its opposite is idealism.' *Experiment in Criticism*, p. 57.

30 Paul Haffner, *The Mystery of Reason*, p. 13. Haffner observes that this moderate realism position finds its roots in the thought of Peter Abelard who, reacting to both the 'crude nominalism of Roscelin on the one side, and to the exaggerated realism of William of Champeaux on the other', produced an epistemology which, 'while bearing some similarities to nominalism, was very similar to the moderate realism which began to take root about a half century after his death'. Haffner suggests that Abelard's difficulties with St Bernard of Clairvaux were due, in part, to the latter's tendency 'to disinherit reason in favour of contemplation

realism looks suspiciously like nominalism, asserting as it does that the universals are abstracted intellectually from the particular instance. But the key difference lies in whether such universals are considered real or not. For nominalism, they are merely signs. For moderate realists, however, there are truly universal concepts to which things correspond in reality, but in the intellect rather than to some separate universal entity. However, the universal is nonetheless real for its abstraction in the intellect. And this has important metaphysical implications, for, as Frank Farrell comments, 'The important idea here is that reality is not the child of our abilities for organising meaning and evidence gathering, but is an independent measure of how good those abilities get to be.'[31] Furthermore, as St Thomas observed, 'The intellectual soul as comprehending universals has a power extending to the infinite.'[32] The nominalist rejection of this, as the historical legacy of William of Ockham has shown, denies the transcendent quality of the human intellect, thereby leading to the divorce of faith and reason and, ultimately, the descent into epistemological scepticism.

The particular linguistic debate in which Lewis found himself is best portrayed, according to Myers, by two contrasting publications of the 1920s: C. K. Ogden and I. A. Richards' *The Meaning of Meaning*, published in 1923 and Owen

---

and ecstatic vision. If the principles "Reason aids Faith" and "Faith aids Reason" are to be taken as the inspiration of scholastic theology, Abelard was typically inclined to emphasize the former, and not lay stress on the latter. His influence on the philosophers and theologians of the thirteenth century was, however, very great. It was exercised chiefly through Peter Lombard, his pupil, and other shapers of the *Books of the Sentences*', Ibid. pp. 84–5. Frederick Copleston noted that St Thomas denied both the ultra realism of Plato and the early medievals, but 'no more than Abelard was he willing to reject Platonism lock, stock and barrel, that is to say, Platonism as developed by St Augustine'. Frederick Copleston, *A History of Philosophy*, Volume 2: *Mediaeval Philosophy: Augustine to Scotus*, p. 175.

[31] Frank Farrell, *Subjectivity, Realism, and Postmodernism – the Recovery of the World*, p. 149.

[32] St Thomas, *Summa Theologiae*, I, pp. 76, 5, a4.

Barfield's *Poetic Diction*, which came out in 1928.[33] Ogden and Richards, both working in Cambridge at the time, proposed a low evaluation of language in which the 'superstition' that 'words ... always imply things corresponding to them' needed to be resisted.[34] 'In some ways,' Ogden and Richards wrote, 'the twentieth century suffers more grievously than any previous age from the ravages of such verbal superstitions.'[35] As Myers explains their position:

> The seemingly sophisticated philosophy of the ancient Greeks is based on their misconception that language has some necessary relationship to the structure of reality. Out of this misconception they created 'the World of Beings, in which bogus entities reside'.[36]

'The persistence of the primitive linguistic outlook,' Ogden and Richards believed, 'not only throughout the whole religious world, but in the work of the profoundest thinkers, is indeed one of the most curious features of modern thought.'[37] The aim, then, of their work was to rid language of its 'bogus entities' and to do this they adopted a theory of meaning in which the association between word and object (or symbol and referent) was established gradually through common use, similar to the process 'through which the dinner bell came to have meaning for Pavlov's dogs'.[38] As Myers comments, 'This behaviorist formulation eliminates "the primitive idea that Words and Things are related by some magic bond" which leads to the use of symbols that have no referent.' Since metaphors by their very nature have more than one referent, arising when 'a speaker abstracts similarities between something physical and some

---

[33] Myers mistakenly cites Barfield's work as published in 1926.

[34] Doris Myers, *C. S. Lewis in Context*, p. 5.

[35] C. K. Ogden and I. A. Richards, *The Meaning of Meaning: A Study of the Influence of Language upon Thought and of the Science of Symbolism*, p. 47.

[36] Doris Myers, *C. S. Lewis in Context*, p. 5.

[37] C. K. Ogden and I. A. Richards, *The Meaning of Meaning*, p. 48.

[38] Doris Myers, *C. S. Lewis in Context*, 5. Cf. C. K. Ogden and I. A. Richards, *The Meaning of Meaning*, pp. 73, 82–3.

other thing', or when 'the properties of a referent within one universe of discourse are applied to another universe of discourse', their linguistic use must be confined 'only to poetic, emotional, and nonreferential discourse'. Owen Barfield, on the other hand, held a 'high evaluation of language' in which he proposed the mind as 'an active participant in the very nature of the universe'. And far from being an abstraction, or at best a colourful trope fit only for the realm of poetic diction, metaphor, he believed, was 'the source of both language and knowledge'.[39] As Barfield himself put it:

> Now my normal everyday experience, as human being, of the world around me depends entirely on what *I* bring to the sense-datum from within; and the absorption of this metaphor into my imagination has enabled me to bring more than I could before. It has created something in me, a faculty or a part of a faculty, enabling me to observe what I hitherto could not observe. This ability to recognize significant resemblances and analogies, considered as in action, I shall call *knowledge*; considered as a *state*, and apart from the effort by which it is imparted and acquired, I shall call it *wisdom*.[40]

It is significant that whilst Lewis sided with Barfield more than Ogden and Richards in himself proposing a high evaluation of language, he did not fully adopt the Barfieldian position. For Barfield (following the work of Rudolf Steiner), imagination was a way to truth. Lewis strongly resisted this anthroposophical position and in his essay, 'Bluspels and Flalansferes', stated his position:

> I am a rationalist. For me, reason is the natural organ of truth; but imagination is the organ of meaning. Imagination, producing new metaphors or revivifying old, is not the cause of truth but its condition.[41]

---

[39] Cf. Doris Myers, *C. S. Lewis in Context*, p. 5–7.
[40] Owen Barfield, *Poetic Diction*, p. 55.
[41] C. S. Lewis, 'Bluspels and Flalansferes: A Semantic Nightmare', in *Selected Literary Essays*, p. 265.

For Lewis the problem was that imagination could lead into falsehood and fantasy. Whilst analogy might enable one to perceive more clearly (although, equally, bad analogy could obscure), it had no ability to prove or refute the veracity of its referent. Lewis, then, disagreed with his friend Barfield that, in itself, imagination enabled the apprehension of truth. 'We are not talking of truth, but of meaning,' he wrote in 'Bluspels': 'meaning which is the antecedent condition of both truth and falsehood, whose antithesis is nor error but nonsense.'[42] As Lionel Adey explains, 'Imagination, Lewis maintained, does not enable us to make true statements, though we can make none without it.'[43] Demonstrating again the legacy of Kirkpatrick's dialectical rationalism, Lewis insisted that truth could only be ascertained through the logical application of reason, with which of course both Ogden and Richards would have agreed. But, unlike them, he also sided with Barfield in dismissing out of hand the notion that one could remove metaphor and simile from language and produce a purely scientific or logical language with which to reason. Whilst truth was to be apprehended through reason, it could only have meaning – only make any actual sense to the human mind – through imagination.

The Metaphorical Versus the Literal

In 'Bluspels and Flalansferes' Lewis presented his theory for a radical metaphorical understanding of language. Distinguishing between what he termed 'magistral' and 'pupillary' metaphors, Lewis went on to examine the effect on both language and knowledge of the fossilisation of such metaphors over time. The two examples that he gave serve as the title to the piece. 'Bluspels', he suggested, might be the corruption over time of a magistral metaphor used in the process of teaching Kant's understanding of categories and perception. Should Kant be faced with the question, 'How do I know that whatever

---

[42] Ibid.
[43] Lionel Adey, *C. S. Lewis: Writer, Dreamer, & Mentor*, p. 33.

comes round the corner will be blue?' he would make the supposition, 'I am wearing blue spectacles,' runs the metaphor. The importance of the magistral metaphor, for Lewis' purpose, was that it is freely chosen by the teacher to illustrate more clearly the point he wants to make. In other words, the metaphor is at the service of its user (or maker) in the understanding of truth. Flalansferes, on the other hand, represents the corruption of a pupillary metaphor – the 'Flatlanders' sphere' – which might be used, Lewis hypothesised, to convey a mathematical concept. To assist with a student's perception of the finiteness of space, Lewis proposed a mathematician might well give the example of 'a race of people who knew only two dimensions – like the Flatlanders'. Although they live on a global planet like our own, they can have no conception of the land's curvature.Thus they believe that they are living on a plane, and since that plane in any direction (of the two directions that they can perceive) appears to have no end, they conclude their land must be infinite. But to those of us who can imagine the global planet from our three dimensions it is clearly finite. And so the mathematician concludes: 'Can you not conceive that as these Flatlanders are to you, so you might be to a creature that intuited four dimensions?' Here the point Lewis wanted to impress was that in this second type of metaphor the user is very much the pupil rather than the master and that there can only be meaning if three conditions are met: firstly, that it is an appropriate metaphor – in other words, it does serve to illustrate a concept validly; secondly, that the imagery used in the metaphor is clearly understood; and finally that the user recognises that it is a metaphor.[44] Lewis' real concern, however, was with the effects of the fossilisation of these metaphors: the impact on meaning of their use in language once they have become dead. In the case of the magistral metaphor, Lewis noted, the teacher using the metaphor would still know what he meant by it. But in the case of the pupillary metaphor the effect would depend upon the pupil. In the example given, if the pupil had gone no further in his study of mathematics and had forgotten the original

[44] Cf. 'Bluspels', pp. 253–6.

meaning of the 'Flalansfere' metaphor, then he would be lack meaningful discourse whenever he used the word. The term would have become meaningless. On the other hand, if the pupil had proceeded to become a mathematician then, even though the metaphor had become corrupted into the noun 'Flalansfere', it could do no real harm. In both cases – magistral and pupillary – the issue is whether or not there is movement beyond the metaphor to the apprehension of truth. 'Where the metaphor is our only method of reaching a given idea at all, there our thinking is limited by the metaphor so long as we retain the metaphor; and when the metaphor becomes fossilized, our "thinking" is not thinking at all.'[45]

Up until this stage, at least, it seems as if Lewis would have allowed for a distinction in language between what could be considered metaphorical and what could be regarded as literal. 'We have hitherto been speaking as if we had two methods of thought open to us,' acknowledged Lewis.[46] But, of course, as he noted in *Miracles,* 'It is a serious mistake to think that metaphor is an optional thing.'[47] Taking the example of *anima,* Lewis questioned whether it was possible to overlook that word's buried metaphor and give an explanation of the soul which was not metaphorical. Referring to psychology's preference for understanding the human soul in terms of 'complexes, repressions, censors, engrams, and the like', Lewis observed the term soul which originally meant breath has simply been replaced by a variety of new words with original meanings such as 'tyings-up, shovings-back, Roman magistrates, and scratchings'.[48] Thus he concluded: 'It is abundantly clear that the freedom from a given metaphor which we admittedly enjoy in some cases is often only a freedom to choose between that metaphor and others.' To avoid talking nonsense then, to avoid being a slave to metaphors whether dead or alive, magistral or pupillary, one must use them with conscious meaning or else abandon them for a language more literal (as indeed Ogden and Richards

---

[45] Cf. ibid. pp. 257–8.
[46] Ibid. p. 261.
[47] *Miracles*, p. 75.
[48] 'Bluspels', p. 261.

had proposed). But there is no more literal language, contended Lewis.

In her commentary on Ogden and Richards' 'low evaluation' of language, Doris Myers notes:

> They do not explicitly state that their method will replace religion, but they do occasionally use salvation rhetoric, as in the assertion that their approach will 'free" us from metaphysicians and bishops and 'restore our faith" in physicists.[49]

Lewis, too, it seems was aware of the implications of such a linguistic position and in *The Abolition of Man* attempted to demonstrate these in his criticism of Alec King and Martin Ketley's book, *The Control of Language*, published in 1939. King and Ketley were two Australian schoolteachers who had attempted to apply Ogden and Richards' theory to the teaching of English at the secondary level in education. This book – later referred to in *Abolition* as 'The Green Book' by 'Gaius and Titius'[50] – was passed to Lewis for review. Myers remarks that Lewis' annotation of his review copy demonstrates the anger he must have felt at encountering such a book.

> For him [Lewis], the success of the low view of language on the university level was bad enough; its introduction into secondary schools, with the inevitable over-simplification and the greater defencelessness of the younger students, would lead to the loss of humane discourse. If carried to its logical conclusion, it would lead to the destruction of everything that makes human beings truly human.[51]

Unsurprisingly, his criticism of King and Ketley was more than simply a question of linguistic niceties. In *Abolition* Lewis was

---

[49] Doris Myers, *C. S. Lewis in Context*, p. 6.
[50] C. S. Lewis, *The Abolition of Man: Or Reflections on Education with Special Reference to the Teaching of English in the Upper Forms of Schools*, p. 1.
[51] Doris Myers, *C. S. Lewis in Context*, p. 72–3.

out to defend a whole metaphysical system. One of his major complaints was that the two Australians seemed to be encouraging students to 'devalue and suppress emotions'. As Myers notes,

> In their fear of language as a tool for control they are unable to describe the correct role of emotion in human life ... The student is advised to avoid communicating his own such feelings and to write so as to promote calm, rational, thought. In other words, the authors encourage the student to suppress his sincere excitement and write on a more superficial, cowardly level.[52]

The problem here, according to Lewis, was that 'the very possibility of a sentiment being reasonable – or even unreasonable – has been excluded from the outset'.[53] Since King and Ketley aimed to separate out what they believed to be 'value judgements' from ordinary speech, they threatened not only the meaningful use of language but also the concept of value. Perhaps 'valour and good faith and justice' can indeed be taught on purely 'rational or biological or modern grounds' and without 'appeal to objective value', argued Lewis, but nevertheless, 'without the aid of trained emotions the intellect is powerless against the animal organism'. What Lewis was really reacting to, in King and Ketley's work, was the metaphysical implications of what they proposed. Language, Lewis believed (and here he largely followed much of Barfield's thought as stated in *Poetic Diction*[54]), reflected not just our thinking but a certain reality. As he noted in 'Bluspels':

---

[52] Ibid. p. 76. Cf. Alec King and Martin Ketley, *The Control of Language: A Critical Approach to Reading and Writing*, p. 84.

[53] *Abolition*, pp. 12, 15.

[54] Cf. Owen Barfield, *Poetic Diction*, p. 86: 'Men do not *invent* those mysterious relations between separate external objects, and between objects and feelings or ideas, which it is the function of poetry to reveal. These relations exist independently, not indeed of Thought, but of any individual thinker. And according to whether the footsteps are echoed in primitive language or, later on, in the made mode of metaphors of poets, we hear them after a different fashion and for different reasons.'

I said at the outset that the truth we won by metaphor could not be greater than the truth of the metaphor itself ... If those original equations, between good and light, or evil and dark, between breath and soul and all the others, were from the beginning arbitrary and fanciful – if there is not, in fact, a kind of psycho-physical parallelism (or more) in the universe – then all our thinking is nonsensical. But we cannot, without contradiction, believe it to be nonsensical.[55]

This idea of a 'psycho-physical parallelism' was precisely what Ogden and Richards were out to attack. But, as Lewis had tried to demonstrate, we can no more strip our language of its metaphorical content than we can shut our eyes to the world around us. Acknowledging that the motivation behind the low evaluation school was probably quite noble – a reaction against the terrible and destructive propaganda of the First World War[56] – Lewis argued that their given response was utterly wrong. It would not be through stripping language of metaphor and value judgements that we would enable the masses to withstand such manipulation; rather it would be through educating them to appreciate the radically metaphorical nature of language, and instilling in them the concept of objective truth and value, that propaganda could be avoided.[57]

Underpinning this attack on the low evaluation of language is an important inter-connection in Lewis' epistemology between metaphor and metaphysics. An example from the Narnia Chronicles will serve to make the point. In *The Silver Chair* the Green Witch catches the children, Eustace and Polly, and their guide the Marshwiggle, Puddleglum, in the attempt to rescue from her underground prison the heir to the Narnian throne, Prince Rilian. To stop them from succeeding she casts a hypnotic spell which causes them to doubt all their previous experiences. Gradually she convinces them that everything they had experienced outside of her cave was a

---

[55] 'Bluspels', p. 265.
[56] Cf. A. King and M. Ketley, *The Control of Language*, pp. 61–3.
[57] Cf. *Abolition*, p. 16.

dream – a metaphorical wish-fulfilment whose referents can be found only in her world. The following excerpt makes clearer what I mean:

> You have seen lamps, and so you imagined a bigger and better lamp and called it the *sun*. You've seen cats, and now you want a bigger and better cat, and it's to be called a *lion*. Well, 'tis a pretty make-believe, ... And look how you can put nothing into your make-believe world without copying it from the real world, this world of mine, which is the only world.[58]

Gene Edward Veith has commented of this text that, in the character of the Green Witch, Lewis was satirising postmodernism and deconstructionalism. The Witch, he says, 'Like a contemporary critic, deconstructs language by showing its metaphorical complexities, then concludes that "there is no Narnia, no Overworld, no sky, no sun, no Aslan". They are all "made-up"; that is to say, in postmodernist terms, they are constructions.'[59] This may be so, but a more obvious – if not unrelated – observation would be that Lewis was satirising the kind of nineteenth-century atheistic rationalism of Feuerbach, which was to lead to the psycho-analytical critique of religion by Freud and the socio-historical critique of the same by Marx. For Feuerbach – as for Freud and Marx, although in different ways – God, heaven and religion were all projections. 'The outer world is nothing more than the *reality of a known idea*', claimed Feuerbach in *The Essence of Christianity*, 'the satisfaction of a conscious desire, the fulfilment of a wish; it is only the *removal of limits* which here oppose themselves to the realization of the idea'.[60] For Lewis, of course, the implications of this are nonsense. In an article entitled, 'Meditation in a Toolshed', he discussed the distinction between looking *at* something and

---

[58] *The Silver Chair*, pp. 143–4.

[59] Gene Edward Veith, 'A Vision, Within a Dream, Within the Truth: C. S. Lewis as Evangelist to the Postmodernists', in *C. S. Lewis, Lightbearer in the Shadowlands: the Evangelistic Vision of C. S. Lewis*, p. 371.

[60] L. Feuerbach, *The Essence of Christianity*, p. 178.

looking *along* it. For example, a young man falls in love with a young girl and finds her deeply attractive and totally absorbing. The experience of being in love is Lewis' looking *along*. The analysis of a scientist who can describe the young man's feelings for the girl entirely in terms of genetics and biology accounts for what he means by looking *at*. The problem, Lewis argued, is that those who tend to look *at* have tended to hold sway over those who look *along*; those who would dissect and analyse have been given greater credibility than those who have experienced.[61] Why not twist it the other way around, he suggested. Why not say to the rationalist who would break everything down into evolutionary survival instincts, the human body's chemistry, and societal taboos that perhaps it can be built up? 'If you will only step inside, the real things that look to you like instincts and taboos will suddenly reveal their real, transcendental nature.'[62] What Lewis was really objecting to here was a crude scientism that believed the answer to everything could be found through its critical dissection. 'We must,' he asserted, 'on the pain of idiocy, deny from the very outset that looking *at* is, by its own nature, intrinsically truer or better than looking *along*. One must look both *along* and *at* everything.'[63] This is important for understanding Lewis' position in reference to language. Language, he believed, is much more than simply a text one can deconstruct, or, in other words, look

---

[61] Cf. C. S. Lewis, 'Meditation in a Toolshed', in *Essay Collection and Other Short Pieces*, pp. 607–8.

[62] 'Meditation in a Toolshed', p. 608.

[63] 'Ibid. p. 609. In *The Pilgrim's Regress,* the character John becomes imprisoned by 'the Spirit of the Age', depicted as a stone giant, the size of a mountain, which when it gazed upon anything made it transparent. 'Consequently, when John looked round into the dungeon, he retreated from his fellow prisoners in terror, for the place seemed to be thronged with demons. A woman was seated near him, but he did not know it as a woman, because, through the face, he saw the skull and through that the brain and the passages of the nose, and the larynx, and the saliva moving in the glands and the blood in the veins.' See *Pilgrim's Regress*, p. 60. Lewis was satirising here Freudianism, Marxism and any other approach which looked *at* rather than *along* reality and in effect reduced humanity and human experience to the sum of neuroses or complexes or historical conditionings.

at. It is expressive of life and reality. As Lyle Smith has commented: 'Language itself cannot be properly understood apart from a preexisting concept of meaning.'[64] Alonso Schökel developed this idea also when he argued:

> Language is more than a conglomeration of grammatical rules – with their exceptions – and a range of vocabulary. Many other elements, idioms, turns of phrase, literary formulas, cultural clichés, must be included in any consideration of language as a social fact. These are all pre-existing material offering a set of possibilities to be actualised in the vitality of the language and employed by him who would use it freely.[65]

In *A Preface to Paradise Lost* Lewis argued a similar case when he suggested of rhetoric and poetry, 'Both these arts, in my opinion, definitely aim at doing something to an audience. And both do it by using language to control what already exists in our minds.'[66] In other words, communication is much richer than simply the signification of objects or facts. Indeed, one of the primary reasons for the existence of metaphor (in particular) is to enable the expression and understanding of truths that go beyond mere labelling in language. It allows interpretation, comparison, the recognition of resemblance and so forth: the interplay between not just words and things, but life and meaning. For Lewis metaphor is the tool that pertains to the understanding of those metaphysical truths beyond the world of immediate sense perception. We might say, then, that Lewis appears to be, epistemologically speaking, a moderate realist. In *A Preface to Paradise Lost* he laments the 'decay of Logic, resulting in an untroubled assumption that the particular is real and the universal is not'.[67] In *Miracles* he attacked the

---

[64] Lyle H. Smith, 'C. S. Lewis and the Making of Metaphor', p. 23.
[65] Luis Alonso Schökel, *The Inspired Word: Scripture in the Light of Language and Literature,* trans. Francis Martin (Montreal, Palm Publishers, 1965), p. 126.
[66] *Preface to Paradise Lost*, p. 53.
[67] Ibid. p. 55.

naturalist position – those who would claim, 'Yes. I quite agree that there is no such thing as wrong and right. I admit that no moral judgement can be "true" or "correct" and, consequently, that no one system of morality can be better or worse than another' – because of its implicit nominalism. For, if one wants to go down the nominalist route, if one wants to deny the reality of universals and thereby logically to question the existence of any transcendental verification of our claims to right and wrong, then so be it:

> But then they must stick to it; and fortunately (though inconsistently) most real Naturalists do not. A moment after they have admitted that good and evil are illusions, you will find them exhorting us to work for posterity, to educate, revolutionise, liquidate, live and die for the good of the human race.[68]

It strikes me that Lewis' epistemological realism was borne out of an abhorrence of the metaphysical implications of holding to any other position. It is almost an act of faith, much like that of Puddleglum's in *The Silver Chair*:

> Suppose we *have* only dreamed, or made up, all those things – trees and grass and sun and moon and stars and Aslan himself. Suppose we have. Then all I can say is that, in that case, the made-up things seem a good deal more important than the real ones.[69]

Paul Ford notes of this passage: 'Puddleglum's bravery, obedience, and obstinate faith in Aslan ... finally breaks the enchantment – not some sort of philosophical attainment or illumination.'[70] Lewis was applying here – I believe – the lesson he had learnt during his earlier 'Great War' with Owen Barfield. Barfield had convinced Lewis that his trenchant philosophy of the time bore little resemblance to the way he

---

[68] Cf. *Miracles*, pp. 36–8.
[69] *The Silver Chair*, p. 145.
[70] Paul Ford, *Companion to Narnia*, p. 321.

lived his life, and, in particular, to the appreciation of the imaginative faculty that he was increasingly coming to have. In other words, his stated philosophical worldview and his *effective* worldview were at odds with one another. Puddleglum demonstrates through brute force – he stamps out the Witch's fire with his webbed foot – and sheer obstinacy of belief that he is simply not prepared to live his life as the Witch's postmodern theories dictate. Her position does not make sense of the memories, experience, language, and images – in other words, the worldview – that he has. Nor does it offer any degree of hope. Similarly for Lewis: he is not prepared to accept the implicit nominalism of Ogden and Richards or King and Ketley. Furthermore, in Lewis' view the Green Witch – and thus, by implication, the atheistic rationalists, nominalists (and deconstructionalists, if you accept Gene Edward Veith's point) – have got their epistemology the wrong way round: the lamp hanging from the cave's roof reminds us of the sun; the cat is perceived as being similar but smaller to Aslan, and so on. For logically, of course, the projection-theory parodied in the position of the Green Witch has no more to support it than the metaphysical and supernaturalist worldview of people like Lewis.[71] Moderate realism may seem, to those who have not really thought it through, at only one stage removed from nominalism, but it is a crucial stage – the assertion that there *is* reality, objective and knowable, beyond merely the physical world around us; the assertion that language does, even in its universal concepts, point to and correspond with something real. For Lewis, then, metaphor and metaphysics must be bound together by some kind of a psycho-physical parallelism since to believe otherwise would render our thinking nonsense and we simply cannot live like that.

Imagination and the End Time

In his article, 'Imagination for the Kingdom of God', Trevor Hart notes that the chapters of Deutero-Isaiah (Isaiah 40–55)

---

[71] For a good exposition of why this is the case see Hans Küng, *Eternal Life?*, p. 49.

depict not only the 'understandable lament' of a people forced to live in a foreign land but also 'the green and vigorous shoots of new hope bursting through the arid and seemingly inhospitable soil of exile'. He goes on to say:

> In his imagination the prophet sees beyond the given to an unexpected and surprising future, a future in which his fellow Jews are able to find hope even in the midst of despair, renewed purpose in the face of servitude and an identity as the people of God which exile had threatened to obliterate. Holding firm to such a vision, the present suffering loses its ultimacy and hence its capacity to crush the spirit.[72]

Hart sees a similar dynamic in the New Testament's Book of Revelation, where the author consoles a persecuted Church and 'discloses through its imaginative form a transcendent perspective on this world and the events of contemporary history, setting them in the wider and fuller context of God's ultimate purposes for the coming of his kingdom'.[73] Of course, biblical exegesis has long understood this assuring and consoling endeavour of apocalyptic literature to be its primary aim: the promise of a better future made to a people in the midst of suffering and persecution. Peter Stanford claims that 'The history of heaven ... reveals how we have coped with the lot we have been dealt with in life, and how we have dreamed of making it better or achieving some form of redress for injustices suffered.'[74] Whereas this might be true of many popular, and particularly secular, visions of the afterlife, it dramatically underestimates the purpose of what Richard Bauckham has classed as 'prophetic apocalypse' in the Scriptures. As Bauckham says of the Revelation of St John:

---

[72] Trevor Hart, 'Imagination for the Kingdom of God? Hope, Promise, and the Transformative Power of an Imagined Future', in Bauckham, *God will be All in All*, pp. 52–3.
[73] Ibid. p. 53.
[74] Peter Stanford, *Heaven*, p. 351.

> It is not that the here-and-now are left behind in an
> escape into heaven or the eschatological future, but that
> the here-and-now look quite different when they are
> opened up to transcendence.[75]

In other words, the data given in Christian apocalyptic literature is not so much the hope of better times to come, but rather
the promise that, despite all appearances to the contrary,
better times have already come: already the victory is won,
already God is acting definitively in human history. As Hart
says of the Book of Revelation:

> The challenge to the Christian Church in the midst of the
> all-too-real discomfort and danger of actuality is, as
> always, to live in the light of this alternative vision rather
> than submitting to the dominant ideology, even when the
> latter is backed up with military and political force.[76]

And the key category for making sense of this 'hopeful living
towards God's future', he says, is imagination because 'we have
the capacity through imagination to call to mind objects,
persons, or states of affairs which are other than those which
appear to confront us'. In other words, imagination allows us
to understand reality as it *is*, not as it necessarily presents itself
here and now. Another key role for the imagination, according
to Hart, is its 'capacity to interpret, to locate things within
wider patterns or networks of relationships which are not
given, but which we appeal to tacitly in making sense of things'.
This is surely what C. S. Lewis meant when he described imagination as the organ of meaning.

That imagination has a key role to play in eschatological
discourse is, I think, self-evident. It is not only the apocalyptic
prophets who have recourse to figurative language in speaking
of the coming of the kingdom. The evangelists, too (and
thereby, we can conclude, to some extent Jesus himself), used
simile and metaphor in their descriptions of the End Time. For

---

[75] Richard Bauckham, *The Theology of the Book of Revelation*, pp. 7–8.
[76] Trevor Hart, 'Imagination', p. 54.

example, Matthew 25:31–46 depicts the final judgement in terms of the separation of sheep and goats and uses royal court imagery with the 'Son of Man' presented as an absolute monarch. Luke 13:28 portrays perdition in terms of the 'weeping and grinding of teeth'. John 14:2 illustrates the beatific vision in terms of ready-prepared rooms in some kind of celestial mansion. And Revelation. 21:2 uses the imagery of a New Jerusalem for the new creation and picks up on the bridal imagery and the enthronement theology of late Judaism. Damnation is explained in terms of a second death through immersion in 'the burning lake of sulphur' (Revelation 21:8). Similarly, patristic and later theology employed the imaginative faculty, variously describing heaven as the perfect city, a garden paradise, family reunion, sexual ecstasy, a bridal chamber, and so on. Writers, poets, artists, and architects, too, have used vivid imagery to capture and educate the imaginations of their Christian confreres. One has only to think of Dante's *Divine Comedy* and the frescoes of Orvieto Cathedral based upon it by Signorelli, or of Fra Angelico's *Last Judgement,* or even of the architecture of Chartres Cathedral itself.[77] It is clear, then, that in depicting that which is beyond depiction, imagination is the key category. It is plain, too, that within a literary imagination metaphor and simile remain amongst the most essential of the tools at our disposal. Luis Alonso Schökel demonstrated the linguistic and epistemological effectiveness of imagination and reason working together when he compared a theology manual's treatise on the statement 'God loves his people' with the Scriptural pericope at Hosea 11:1–9. 'The words of Hosea,' argued Alonso Schökel, 'which include a series of statements whose predominant function is informative, actuate the other two elemental functions of language.'

> God expresses Himself and I am deeply impressed. After having read the propositions of the thesis, I can still remain cold or indifferent. If the passage from Hosea leaves me cold or indifferent, it is simply because I have

---

[77] Cf. Peter Stanford, *Heaven* and Alister McGrath, *A Brief History of Heaven.*

never really read it. Granted that the language of Hosea is symbolic and even anthropomorphic; still, it is an analogy which confers real understanding.[78]

Underlying this analysis is Karl Bühler's distinction of the three principal functions of language: statement (i.e. to communicate facts, things, events, etc.), expression (i.e. to communicate our interior state, emotions, feelings and so on), and address (i.e. communicating with another to provoke response). Alonso Schökel (as did Lewis) also distinguished between common language, technical language and literary – or poetic – language. Of the latter he argued that literary language is not some specialised or purified digression from common language, but proceeds 'by raising it to a new power'.

> Common language is unable to confer on such realities as adequate objectivity ... Literary language does not have to resign itself to this dilemma, but attempts to actualize experience and make it fully objective, exploiting all the functions of language by causing them to yield their maximum productivity.[79]

Where Lewis is important in this regard is in his reminding us that all language is radically metaphorical.[80] We make a

---

[78] Alonso Schökel, *The Inspired Word*, p. 140.

[79] Cf. Ibid. pp. 134–5, 159–60.

[80] I have already commented on how Lewis followed the theory of Owen Barfield in this. Lyle Smith points out, 'Although this idea did not originate with Barfield, it is not a very old one.' He goes on: 'It is romantic, going back to Rousseau's *Essay on the Origin of Languages,* in which he argued that "figurative language was the first to be born". Nietzsche, writing "On Truth and Falsity in Their Ultramoral Sense", agrees with Rousseau on the primacy of figurative language, going on to claim that our experience and our very thought processes themselves come to us metaphorically.' Smith argues that 'today it is widely accepted that language and metaphor are inseparable' and that 'the notion of the metaphorical nature of language, then, is widely shared among modern theorists and is the starting point for any discussion of what role metaphor plays in language.' See Smith, 'C. S. Lewis and the Making of Metaphor', p. 24.

mistake if we convince ourselves that referring to God as a perfect substance, say, is in any way more literal – or indeed, more theological – than calling him, 'Father'. Our use of language in theology is, of course, important, but what Lewis served to underline was the need for us to be aware of the images – whether deliberate or implied – that that language may convey. He warned us too: 'Not all our words are equally metaphorical, not all our metaphors are equally forgotten', and, 'The truth we won by metaphor could not be greater than the truth of the metaphor itself.' In the light of such limitations of metaphorical language, a note of caution was offered:

> We have in our hands the key of metaphor, and it would be pusillanimous to abandon its significant use, because we have come to realize that its meaningless use is necessarily prevalent. We must indeed learn to use it more cautiously.[81]

Earlier I noted that Lewis was hesitant in following Barfield's linguistic and epistemological theories to their full conclusion. As we have seen, he distinguished his own position with the dictum: 'Reason is the natural organ of truth; but imagination is the organ of meaning.'[82] Lyle Smith comments of this Lewisian position:

> Lewis' view of metaphor is, not surprisingly, consistent with his adherence to Platonism. Far from thinking of metaphor as a creator of 'new truth' or even new categories that create new insights, he held that metaphor does its work by showing resemblances – revealing categories that have been there all the time, but that human minds must uncover discursively.[83]

Whereas Barfield understood the recognition of resemblances and analogies as fundamental to human knowledge – he

---

[81] Cf. 'Bluspels', pp. 264–5.
[82] Ibid. p. 265.
[83] Lyle Smith, 'C. S. Lewis and the Making of Metaphor', p. 14.

referred to language as a 'kind of storehouse' in which we build up our ideas and are so enabled to 'become "conscious", as human beings, of the world around us'[84] – Lewis argued that only reason could provide the necessary discursive critique with which to guarantee the imagination's veracity. Therefore, although it is true that we cannot abandon metaphor altogether nevertheless our imagination needs to be employed in tandem with our reason or else we are in danger of spouting nonsense. Theologically speaking, we might say that our metaphors need to be underpinned by our metaphysics. To demonstrate this Lewis gave the example of contrasting Christian and pantheistic doctrine. Both, he argued, agree that God is present everywhere.[85] Similarly, both Christianity and pantheism agree that creation is contingent upon God and intimately related to him. But whereas Christianity's images define this relationship in terms of Creator and creation, pantheism understands our dependency in terms of emanation or evolution and so on. Whilst one may obviously hold to pantheistic theory and be quite coherent in one's imagery and metaphysics, it would be inconsistent for a Christian theologian to present an eschatology, for example, that was basically pantheistic in its imagery. This, for Lewis, was why reason was so important to epistemology. Equally, however, Lewis argued that we must beware of 'paying God ill-judged metaphysical compliments'. In other words, we need to be wary of the imagery induced by our metaphysical attributes. For example,

> If by using the word 'infinite' we encourage ourselves to think of Him as a formless 'everything' about whom nothing in particular and everything in general is true, then it would be better to drop that word altogether.[86]

Imagination and reason, then, have to work together. 'Reason knows that she cannot work without materials,' as Lewis said in *Miracles*. But the materials that imagination furnishes – the

---

[84] Owen Barfield, *Poetic Diction*, p. 57.
[85] Cf. *Miracles*, p. 88.
[86] Ibid. pp. 90–1.

resemblances and analogies – give meaning and not truth, and this must always be remembered.[87]

The Cataphatic versus the Apophatic

Lyle Smith has suggested that, in his sermon on *Transposition*, C. S. Lewis moved towards a more tensive view of the mechanism of metaphor than previously he seemed to have held. As he explains,

> [Lewis] points out that metaphoric resemblance ... presents not *only* resemblance but implicitly an understanding that resemblance is not identity; a thing can resemble another thing only if it is not that thing, and only if the difference between the two is apparent.[88]

In fact Smith argues that Lewis 'chartered a path of his own' in the territory of metaphysical theory, steering a middle road between what are sometimes called collusion and collision theories. In collusion theory, metaphor is believed to work primarily through resemblance and reference. Collision, sometimes called tensive theory, argues that metaphor works by holding two concepts together in tension. Using Lewis' own example of the metaphorical application of fatherhood to God, Smith notes that a 'tension between the biological metaphor "father" and the non-physical nature of God' is created. 'The resulting cognitive dissonance,' he argues, 'sustained throughout the history of theological discourse, makes for a far more sophisticated understanding of the complex and ultimately mysterious nature of God than does any attempt at metaphor revision (or demythologising) that seeks to narrow the gap between the word and the thing.'[89] Whilst Lewis was certainly aware of this collision of image, particularly in theological language – 'if absurd images meant absurd thought, then we

---

[87] Cf. ibid. p. 94..
[88] Lyle H. Smith, 'C. S. Lewis and the Making of Metaphor', p. 27.
[89] Cf. ibid. pp. 26–7.

should all be thinking nonsense all the time,' he noted[90] – he was not, Smith believes, presenting 'a theory of metaphoric interaction as such' but rather 'implicitly presenting one of the correlatives of the tensive theory: the necessity of keeping both the metaphorical and the literal meanings of the terms of a metaphor in view simultaneously'.[91] As Lewis himself explained:

> Christians themselves make it clear that the images are not to be identified with the thing believed. They may picture the Father as a human form, but they also maintain that He has no body. They may picture Him as older than the son, but they also maintain the one did not exist before the other, both having existed from all eternity.[92]

To be able to apprehend the truth in such collision of imagery, of course, requires reason once more working alongside imagination. But, in *Transposition*, Lewis seemed to take this collision theory one step further. Engaging in eschatological speculation, Lewis said:

> How far the life of risen man will be sensory, we do not know. But I surmise that it will differ from the sensory life we know here, not as emptiness differs from water or water from wine but as a flower differs from a bulb or a cathedral from an architect's drawing.[93]

What we have here is an appreciation that eschatological metaphor, although working through resemblance, must – like any metaphors for God himself – sit in tension with the understanding that resemblance is not identity. But I also think what we have here, in Lewis' understanding, is not merely a collision of the metaphorical and the literal, but also a specific awareness that in eschatological language we must always hold to the

---

90 *Miracles*, p. 76.
91 Lyle H. Smith, 'C. S. Lewis and the Making of Metaphor', p. 27.
92 *Miracles*, p. 76.
93 'Transposition', p. 84.

dictum: both continuity and newness. Lewis, in this passage from *Transposition*, was in my view trying to express what St Paul similarly struggled with when trying to give a description of the resurrection of the body, and coined the much debated term, 'spiritual body" (1 Corinthians 15:44).

This tensive approach to metaphor is useful when we are considering the various claims of apophatic and cataphatic theology, particularly in the area of eschatology. 'The mystery of blessed communion with God and all who are in Christ is beyond all understanding and description,' notes the Catechism. But then it goes on to admit: 'Scripture speaks of it in images: life, light, peace, wedding feast, wine of the kingdom, the Father's house, the heavenly Jerusalem, paradise.'[94] Peter Stanford has argued that the Christian Churches have increasingly moved away from an anthropocentric and cataphatic eschatology in favour of a theocentric and apophatic one, precisely at a time when secular society is clamouring for the former. The truth, as I see it, is somewhat more sophisticated. As the Catechism demonstrates, Christian tradition has long held in tension the truths of both apophatic and cataphatic, both anthropocentric and theocentric. True apophatic theology – sometime referred to as the *via negativa* – still employs imagery: it merely highlights dissimilarity rather than similarity. It says, 'This is unlike', rather than the cataphatic, 'This is like'. What Lewis underlined for language is true of theology also: there is no getting away from metaphors and imagery. Paucity of image – whether we adopt the positive or negative theological route – is no excuse for not speaking. The challenge is to ensure that our images are many and that they are appropriate. The apophatic and cataphatic ways are not, of course, contradictory approaches to theology. They are rather complimentary; they symbolise both the continuity and newness of all eschatological discourse. As Dermot Lane has noted, 'Negative theology is more a point of arrival than a point of departure. We need to arrive at a state of learned ignorance *(docta ignorantia)* in most matters theological and this is particularly the case in eschatology.'[95] 'Imagination,' as

---

[94] *Catechism*, p. 1027.
[95] Dermot Lane, *Keeping Hope Alive*, p. ix.

Lewis wrote in 'Bluspels and Flalansferes', 'the producing of new metaphors or reviving old, is not the cause of truth but its condition.'[96] Thus the role of metaphor, it would seem, has as firm a foundation in eschatology as that of metaphysics.

[96] 'Bluspels', p. 265.

Chaper 5

The Problem of Eschatological Imagery

It was Hans Küng who, quoting from the painter Max Beckmann, wrote in the preface to his own work on eschatology, 'If we want to grasp the invisible, we must penetrate as deeply as possible into the visible.' He went on to suggest that for himself, personally, the most fruitful meditation upon the Last Things had arisen not from theological textbooks on the subject but from the work of poets, philosophers, doctors and scientists.[1] 'Familiar images from the world around us,' notes Alister McGrath, the Professor of Historical Theology at Oxford University, 'become windows of perception into the nature and purposes of God.'[2] In the Old Testament and in the New, and in particular in the parables of Jesus, we find analogies drawn, images provoked, and understanding enhanced. Interestingly, however, this role of the imagination has something of a chequered history in the Christian tradition. Certainly there is much truth in Sally Ann McReynolds' point that, although Plato himself rather distrusted symbols and metaphor ('as mere shadows of the eternal ideas'), it was the more positive neo-Platonic approach to symbol, ritual and image that eventually found itself imbedded in Christian spirituality through the influence of Augustine and Pseudo-Dionysius.[3] However, I feel a more accurate assessment is made by Stephen Happel who argues that Christian attitudes

---

[1] Cf. Hans Küng, *Eternal Life?*, p. 11.
[2] Alister McGrath, *A Brief History of Heaven*, p. 4.
[3] Cf. Sally Ann McReynolds, 'Imagination', in *The New Dictionary of Catholic Spirituality*, p. 532.

toward the imagination were rather more mixed right from the beginning. For example, he claims that the iconoclastic controversies of the eastern Churches in the eighth and mid-ninth centuries were 'paradigmatic of the successive ascetical "purifications" of image in the Churches'. Listing the Cistercian criticisms of Benedictine ornament in architecture and liturgy in the twelfth century, the early Franciscan rejection of luxury and their attempted life of abject poverty, the Catharist heretics who 'angrily refused the delights of the senses', and the late medieval and *devotio moderna* emphases on artistic purity and simplicity of life, as well as the resurgent iconoclasm of Zwingli and, later, the English Puritans, Happel observes: 'All these reforming movements have their origins in the same ascetic impulse that motivated desert monks, like Anthony of the Desert, to flee the pleasures of the city and to seek out a quiet, unadorned life.' With its intellectual roots in the neo-Platonism of Augustine in particular, he believes, such unworldly zeal found itself with not only a dislike of artistic images but with an uncertain attitude towards the imagination itself. 'True beauty could lead one to God – as long as what was beautiful was intellectual and not sensible.' [4]

Augustine's own position, certainly, was very much a mixed bag. On the one hand he 'developed a theology of beauty derived from Plato and neo-Platonic thought that saw human making (art) as able to participate in divinity when it shared in the appropriate measure'. On the other, he 'mistrusted the sensible as seductive and illusory, able to tie us down to earthly things'.[5] Similarly, Pseudo-Dionysius held something of an ambivalent view. He was to admit, in his work *The Celestial Hierarchy*, that 'It is quite impossible that we humans should, in any immaterial way, rise up to imitate and to contemplate the heavenly hierarchies without the aid of those material means capable of guiding us as our nature requires. Hence any thinking person realizes that the appearances of beauty are signs of an invisible loveliness.' [6] Yet elsewhere he urged his readers to

---

[4] Cf. Stephen Happel, 'Imagination, Religious', in J. Komonchak, M. Collins, and D. Lane, *Dictionary of Theology*, pp. 505–6.

[5] Ibid. p. 506.

[6] Pseudo-Dionysius, *The Celestial Hierarchy*, I, 3 in idem, *The Complete Works*, p. 146.

'Leave behind ... everything perceived and understood, every-thing perceptible and understandable, all that is not and all that is,' in order to ascend 'with your understanding laid aside' to 'him who is beyond all being and knowledge.'[7] With this understanding of a God so utterly beyond, transcending all affirmations and negations – and with his Platonic interpreta-tion of the hierarchy of being – it is no surprise that, as Yves Congar observed, Pseudo-Dionysius, like Origen some time before him, '*suppose qu'une expression imageé constitue une certaine trahison du spirituel.*'[8] The legacy of the Pseudo-Areopogite was also to enthrone within mysticism – and to a certain extent within theology – the apophatic way: that images from, and analogies with, this corporeal world, whilst necessary up to a point, must eventually give way to the 'ray of the divine shadow which is above everything that is'.[9] Given the influence of both Augustine and Pseudo-Dionysius upon medieval thought, it is no surprise to find that some of their ideas should have filtered through into St Thomas. Both find themselves quoted by the Angelic Doctor in his examination of the use of metaphor and the role of imagination.[10] Thomas, like Pseudo-Dionysius,

---

[7] Pseudo-Dionysius, *The Mystical Theology*, I, 1 in idem, *The Complete Works*, p. 135.

[8] Yves Congar, *La foi et la théologie*, p. 31.

[9] Pseudo-Dionysius, *The Mystical Theology*, I, 1 in idem, *The Complete Works*, p. 135. Jeffrey Burton Russell has commented of the Pseudo-Areopogite's position: 'Dionysius combined the idea of our kinship with God with the understanding that God is wholly other. God is completely beyond anything that we might understand about him, partly because our own reason is tiny and restricted, but more because he is himself beyond all reason. In order to be taken up in union with the divine reality that underlies appear-ances, we must strip all predicates away from God; we must renounce knowledge in order to understand; we must give ourselves over to longing. Whatever we say about God is metaphorical, and Dionysius preferred metaphors of distance and otherness in order to lessen the danger of confusing substance with shadow. It is safer to call God a stone than fire or fire than Perfect Beauty, for the reason that the closer we get to the truth, the more we forget we are using metaphor.' Jeffrey Burton Russell, *A History of Heaven: The Singing Silence*, p. 92.

[10] For example, cf. St Thomas, *Summa Theologiae*, I, pp. 1, 9 and I, pp. 17, 2.

appreciated the need for metaphorical language in Scripture but was equally wary of its limitations. For example, towards the beginning of the *Summa Theologiae* Thomas observed: 'It seems that Holy Scripture should not use metaphors. For that which is proper to the lowest science seems not to befit this science, which holds the highest place of all.' But he went on to argue that Scripture was right to utilise metaphorical language, since all our knowledge is based upon sense perception. 'Hence in Holy Writ, spiritual truths are fittingly taught under the likeness of material things. This is what Dionysius says (Coel Hier. I): "We cannot be enlightened by the divine rays except they be hidden within the covering of many sacred veils."'[11] However, whereas in poetic language metaphor and images are employed for their own sake and beauty, in Scripture Thomas believed their use to be purely functional and of necessity. Furthermore, Thomas argued, the inadequacy of human metaphors for approaching any real likeness to God was an advantage, as was the fact that metaphorical language was language in its lowest form. 'It is more fitting that divine truths should be expounded under the figure of less noble than of nobler bodies,' he noted, 'for then it is clear that these things are not literal descriptions of divine truths ... [and] similitudes drawn from things farthest away from God form within us a truer estimate that God is above whatsoever we may say or think of Him.'[12] In other words, the image – being so obviously insufficient for the task – reminds us that it is only a metaphor and not a literal description. However, this positive reception of the use of imagery in Scripture is balanced a little later by what Thomas says of the imaginative faculty in general:

> Falsity is attributed to the imagination, as it represents the likeness of something even in its absence. Hence when anyone perceives the likeness of a thing as if it were the thing itself, falsity results from such an apprehension; and for this reason the Philosopher [Aristotle] says that

[11] Cf. St Thomas, *Summa Theologiae*, I, pp. 1, 9.
[12] Cf. ibid.

shadows, pictures, and dreams are said to be false inasmuch as they convey the likeness of things that are not present in substance.[13]

So it seems that classical theology came to take a rather tentative approach to imagination. At one level it had a necessary function in allowing us to expound eternal truths in an analogical way. But at another level it was somewhat suspect on two counts: the risk of idolatry and the danger of falsity. On the one hand, it was supposed, the image carries the risk of itself becoming the primary object of our contemplation, rather than the truth it conveys. And on the other, there is an equal danger that the image might be entirely false and convey no higher reality at all.

Contemporary theology has, to an extent, re-evaluated the role that imagination has to play in the apprehension of eternal truths. As Stephen Happel has noted:

Imagination and related aesthetical categories have clearly established themselves as a crucial factor in Catholic theology. Parallel to the ongoing investigations of philosophy, psychology, and the natural sciences, theology has studied the ways in which metaphor, symbol, and the language of imagination have been operative in Christian life.[14]

Likewise Sally Ann McReynolds has commented on the role that imagination has played in the development of the existential approaches of the likes of Lonergan, Rahner and Schillebeeckx. 'Imagination not only shapes the symbolic universe that is constitutive of human experience,' she contends, 'but it is essential to interpreting its meaning and sharing that interpretation with others.'[15] Rahner, in particular, stressed the need to remythologise rather than demythologise the language of Scripture. As Peter Phan has observed:

[13] Ibid. I, p. 17, 2, ad 2.
[14] Stephen Happel, 'Imagination, Religious', p. 507.
[15] Sally Ann McReynolds, 'Imagination', p. 534.

[Rahner] rejects Bultmann's demythologising program insofar as it implies a stripping away of biblical mythical images. Indeed, for Rahner, no thinking is possible without images, as is shown by Aquinas's doctrine of *conversio ad phantasma,* which Rahner brilliantly retrieves.[16]

Similarly, as Happel notes, Von Balthasar developed 'an extended theological aesthetics that overarches nature and history, unites secular and religious literature, and correlates interior movements of grace and the exterior products of imagination'.[17] And, perhaps most recently, there has been renewed interest in the interconnection of theology and literature in the work of, for example, the Oxford theologian, Paul Fiddes, and the use of narrative as a key theological category by the Jesuit, John Navone.[18] But, despite these modern appreciations, Happel points out that the use of religious images has become increasingly complicated.

The overpowering rapidity with which images change in our culture, the pervasive presence of images and non-verbal communication, the way in which such images are manipulated by governments, advertising agencies, and corporate boards make appeal to imagination as a process and symbols as their product somewhat difficult.[19]

It is clear, then, that the role of the imagination within Christian tradition in general – and within theology in particular – is an enormous subject worthy of its own dedicated study: certainly far too wide for me to do it any justice here.

In its 1979 letter, *Recentiores episcoporum synodi,* the Sacred Congregation for the Doctrine of the Faith (SCDF) warned:

16 Peter Phan, 'Current Theology: Contemporary Context and Issues in Eschatology', in *Theological Studies*, p. 517. Cf. Karl Rahner *Spirit in the World*, and St Thomas, *Summa Theologiae*, I, pp. 84, 7.
17 Stephen Happel, 'Imagination, Religious', p. 507.
18 Cf. Paul Fiddes, *The Promised End: Eschatology in Theology and Literature*, and John Navone, *Seeking God in Story*.
19 Stephen Happel, 'Imagination, Religious', p. 507.

> When dealing with man's situation after death, one must especially beware of arbitrary imaginative representations: excess of this kind is a major cause of the difficulties that Christian faith often encounters.[20]

It went on, of course, to acknowledge the respect due to biblical imagery of this kind and here it advised that we should discern the 'profound meaning' without 'overattenuating' the images themselves, 'since this often empties of substance the realities designated by the images'. We have seen already how Lewis deployed imaginative representations in his own eschatology, and how he understood the relationship between imagination and reason, and metaphor and metaphysics. In the light of the Congregation's concerns, then, it seems appropriate to examine in some further detail this specific problem of eschatological imagery.

The Images of Heaven in Christian Tradition

Within Christianity's tradition of heavenly imagery there are, broadly speaking, two approaches that can be identified: the theocentric and the anthropocentric. As its name suggests, the theocentric understanding focuses on the relationship between God and the individual soul, its imagery reinforcing the rather more abstract concept of beatific vision. The anthropocentric presentation, on the other hand, emphasises the communal character of salvation, drawing upon the doctrines of the communion of saints and the promise of a new heavens and a new earth. As Peter Stanford observes, 'The first has appealed most to theologians and mystics – somewhere we spend eternal solitude with God alone.'[21] The second, as Colleen McDannell and Bernhard Lang have suggested, appeals more to those who would ask the question, 'Why would a world be created at all if the divine intended everlasting life to leave no room for non-religious concerns?'[22] The two are not necessarily mutually

---

[20] SCDF, 'The Reality of Life After Death', p. 502.
[21] Peter Stanford, *Heaven*, p. 14.
[22] Colleen McDannell and Bernhard Lang, *Heaven: A History*, p. 355.

exclusive, however, and there are examples of Christian writers and artists who both depict a theocentric heaven at one stage in their work and an anthropocentric one at another, and those who blur the distinction between the two, portraying a largely theocentric view that has anthropocentric elements. As Stanford has described this latter approach:

> Somewhere to be with God alone, yet also a place where the imagination inevitably wanders into providing some shape and form, usually a garden, and to other relationships which may continue from earth.[23]

Equally, there is no real evidence to suggest that either of the models comes to dominate the entire theological or artistic scene to the detriment of the other, although, as McDannell and Lang note, 'one of them can generally be considered the dominant view for a given time and place'.[24] In his own study of the subject, Peter Stanford has tended to equate the theocentric view of heaven in particular with an apophatic school in theology and prayer. I have already commented, in the last chapter, on how any dialectic placement of the apophatic and the cataphatic in Christian tradition is somewhat simplistic. But perhaps we can let C. S. Lewis underline this point when, in *Letters to Malcolm*, we observe his remarks that the theocentric description of heaven as seeing God 'face to face' is in fact not only metaphorical (and in that sense cataphatic), but actually anthropocentric in its terminology. 'As if God and I could be face to face, like two fellow-creatures,' Lewis noted, 'when in reality He is above me and within me and below me and all about me.'[25] Jeffrey Burton Russell makes the same point when he acknowledges the ineffability of heaven but maintains, 'We have no way of discussing heaven except in the only speech we

---

23   Peter Stanford, *Heaven*, p. 5. In fact Stanford argues that this hybrid of the two approaches to heavenly imagery is itself an alternative view. I prefer to see it as merely the acceptable overlapping of two polar strands of thought on the subject, rather than as some new way all of its own.
24   Colleen McDannell and Bernhard Lang, *Heaven*, p. 357.
25   *Letters to Malcolm*, p. 19 (Letter 4).

know, human language.' Whether we choose to say what heaven is like or what heaven is unlike – or, perhaps, a mixture of the two – we have to use human language and therefore metaphor.

> Metaphors of heaven, expressing the reality of heaven, are written in the language of earthly delight: sound (melody, silence, conversation); sight (light, proportion); taste and smell (banquet, sweetness); touch (embracing the beloved).[26]

Thus, for both the anthropocentric and the theocentric approach to heaven, it is important to recognise the radically metaphorical nature of the images or language being deployed.

In their book, *Heaven: A History*, Colleen McDannell and Bernhard Lang have traced the theocentric and anthropocentric visions of heaven throughout Christian history. 'Despite the vacillation between the two directions,' the authors note, 'no simple repetition of images occur. Shifting models does not mean the mere restoration of the opposite. Whatever traditional elements are reused or revitalized, the result is a unique formulation.'[27] The theocentric model finds its clear foundation in Scripture. The image of the New Jerusalem in chapter twenty-one of Revelation is entirely God-centred. 'I could not see any temple in the city,' records St John, 'since the Lord God Almighty and the Lamb were themselves the temple, and the city did not need the sun or the moon for light, since it was lit by the radiant glory of God, and the Lamb was a lighted torch for it' (Revelation. 21:22–23). Similarly, the heavenly liturgy described in chapter nineteen, although descriptive of elements of a celestial choir, nevertheless has the worship of God seated on his throne as its focal point. Again, in both chapters nineteen and twenty-one, there is the bridal imagery in

---

[26] Jeffrey Burton Russell, *A History of Heaven*, p. 6.
[27] Colleen McDannell and Bernhard Lang, *Heaven*, p. 357. For a wide and varied anthology of heavenly images found in literature, see *The Book of Heaven: An Anthology of Writings from Ancient to Modern Times*, ed. Carol Zaleski and Philip Zaleski.

which the Lamb is married to the people for whom he was slain. All these images find their way into the theocentric tradition. As McDannell and Lang have observed, Augustine, in his earlier work, reaffirmed this model but also redefined it somewhat.

> In a different cultural climate, the original charismatic inspiration gave way to more intellectual, philosophical concerns that focus on 'God and the soul'. The 'flight in solitude to the Solitary' emphasized the privatised nature of heaven. Even the community of psalm-singing saints takes a second place to the individual's relationship with God.[28]

This process of privatisation of the salvific image continued in medieval scholasticism and was combined with the cosmological model of its time. Thus, as again McDannell and Lang point out, 'God and the soul meet in the empyrean: a transcendental, light-filled place outside of, but enveloping, the universe.'[29] Interestingly, C. S. Lewis devoted some considerable thought to this model in his work *The Discarded Image* and in a lecture delivered in Cambridge in 1956 and now published as *Imagination and Thought in the Middle Ages*. He described the structure as follows:

> A motionless Earth at the centre, transparent spheres revolving round it, of which the lowest, slowest, nearest and smallest carries the Moon, and thence upwards in the order Mercury, Venus, the Sun, Mars, Jupiter, Saturn; beyond these, all the stars in one sphere; beyond that, a

---

[28] Colleen McDannell and Bernhard Lang, *Heaven*, p. 354. This neo-Platonic idea of the flight in solitude to the Solitary can be found in Plotinus, *Enneads*, pp. 6, 9. McDannell and Lang note that early monasticism adopted such mystical asceticism, which in its turn inspired the early Augustine. 'Augustine's spiritual heaven,' they argue, 'was the continuation of an ascetic retired life. It was a world of immaterial, fleshless souls finding rest and pleasure in God.' See ibid. pp. 56–7, 59.

[29] Ibid. p. 354.

sphere which carries no light but merely imparts movement to those below it; beyond that, the Empyrean, the
boundary of the *mundus*, the beginning of the infinite true
'Heaven'.[30]

The artistic fruit of this mix of scholastic theocentricism and
medieval cosmology is to be seen in the extraordinary dimensions of height and space in Gothic architecture. As Stanford
wrote of his visit to Chartres Cathedral:

> The initial effect of the soaring Gothic style of the interior
> is to make the visitor feel very small. Humankind's physi-
> cal insignificance before God is an oft-repeated biblical
> theme ... Like its old spire, the whole momentum of
> Chartres Cathedral is to direct the eye upwards, in the
> medieval view of the universe, towards heaven ... Those
> cavernous, misty upper reaches of the cathedral seemed
> to take on their own mystery and life, far beyond
> anything I could touch, see or even comprehend. As a
> symbol of heaven, it was a neat fit.[31]

In literature we find the combination borne out in Dante's
geography of heaven and his use of the imagery of light in the
Paradiso. Medieval mystics, meanwhile, tended to be drawn
rather to the idea of Christ as bridegroom. Peter Stanford
notes that Hildegaard of Bingen's favourite image of heaven
was that of the bridal chamber. Likewise, Mechthild of
Magdeburg 'used language similar to that used by Hildegaard',
describing heaven as being on three levels, the third level – 'the
one on which she concentrated' – being both 'God's throne-
room and Christ's bridal suite'.[32] With such imagery, the

---

[30] C. S. Lewis, 'Imagination and Thought in the Middle Ages', in
Studies in Medieval and Renaissance Literature, p. 45.
[31] Peter Stanford, *Heaven*, p. 139.
[32] Cf. ibid. pp. 151–2. McDannell and Lang quote Mechthild's vision:
'She knelt down, thanking him for his favour. She took her crown
from her head and placed it on to the rose-coloured scars of his
feet and wished that she could come closer to him. He took her
into his divine arms, placed a paternal hand unto her breast and

process of privatisation continued and a theocentric heaven was presented in which the union of Christ with the individual soul is described rather than the more communitarian account given in Scripture of Christ with his elected people. Of the shift in emphasis from medieval scholasticism to medieval mysticism, McDannell and Lang have noted, 'Intimate union transcends the intellectual joys of the vision of God. Christ in heaven meets the soul as friend, companion, and lover.'[33]

The anthropocentric model of heaven, meanwhile, interpreted Revelation's 'new heavens and a new earth' as a transformation, or a transfiguration even, of the original heaven and earth. Therefore it looked to whatever points of continuity it could find between the two creations with which to express its hope in the age to come. One such point was the reference to 'trees of life' in Revelation 22:2, which immediately provided a link with Genesis 2:9 and allowed an interpretation of heaven as a return to paradise, further underscored by Jesus' promise of paradise to the repentant thief from the cross in Luke 23:43. Thus, as Jeffrey Russell comments, 'Heaven is a return to paradise, and the imagery of the earthly paradise and celestial paradise are drawn together by typology, allegory, and eventu-

---

beheld her face. And in a kiss, she was elevated above all the angelic choirs.' Colleen McDannell and Bernhard Lang, *Heaven*, p. 101. Cf. Mechthild, *The Flowering Light of the Godhead*, 3, 1. Stanford comments of this passage: 'The image of being kissed by God is a startling one, and overall the imagery makes for uncomfortable reading in the twenty-first century, especially the mixture of paternalism and eroticism – a father with his hand on his daughter's breast in a bridal chamber. However, applying a post-Freudian literalism is bound to distort the medieval mystical mind with its emphasis on a ceaseless outpouring of unconditional love.' Stanford, *Heaven*, p. 153. Stanford is right to question such post-Freudian analysis of medieval texts, but he has also highlighted quite effectively the difficulty of using any images in a rapidly changing culture and thus underlined Stephen Happel's caution made earlier.

[33] Colleen McDannell and Bernhard Lang, *Heaven*, p. 354.

ally artistic representation.'[34] Another point of contact found between the finite realm and its promised eschatological goal is the reference to a thousand year period in Revelation 20:1–6. Here we are told that, prior to the final judgement, Christ will establish his rule on earth for one thousand years, together with the martyrs and those who have withstood the allure of the beast. In the second century, St Irenaeus developed these points of contact with his doctrine of recapitulation and his proposal of a millennial reign. Like the book of Revelation itself, the context for Irenaeus' vision of heaven was one of persecution, suffering and martyrdom in the Church. Thus Stanford argues,

> Irenaeus' response was to calm ... fears and, in the process, fashion a theology of heaven which presented it explicitly as the reward for indignities suffered in God's name on this earth. A decent reward, if it was to have the desired effect, needed to be specific, so Irenaeus spoke not in vague, imaginary tones but in tangible terms of a cleaned-up version of this life.[35]

Perhaps Stanford has somewhat neglected the concern for theological tidiness that was also typical of the period. Wanting to 'close the circle', so to speak, inevitably led to Irenaeus making use of earthly, paradisal and anthropocentric imagery in his portrayal of heaven. Interestingly, given his earlier adoption of the neo-Platonic concept of the soul's escape 'in solitude to the Solitary', St Augustine too moved towards a more anthropocentric approach in later life. In *The City of God* he attempted to explain the vision of God in corporeal and anthropocentric terms. In the heavenly city, for sure, God will be the source of our satisfaction, the goal of all our longings, and we 'shall see him forever; we shall love him without satiety; we shall praise him without wearying'.[36] But perhaps this beatific vision, suggested Augustine, might take place in and through the communion of saints.

---

[34] Jeffrey Burton Russell, *A History of Heaven*, p. 43.
[35] Peter Stanford, *Heaven*, p. 87.
[36] St Augstine, *City of God*, XXII, p. 30.

> God will be known to us and visible to us in each one of
> us, perceived in one another, perceived by each in
> himself; he will be seen in the new heaven and new earth,
> in the whole creation as it then will be; he will be seen in
> every body by means of bodies, wherever the eyes of the
> spiritual body are directed with their penetrating gaze.[37]

Later, in the medieval period, the images of paradise and the
heavenly city find themselves combined. A popular theology
manual of that period, *Elucidation*, for example, depicts heaven
as a restored paradise in which there is a city and its royal
court. Anthropocentricism is maintained through the saints'
enjoyment together of paradise, whilst the theocentric dimension is ever present through the centrality of the divine court
and city. With the Renaissance, McDannell and Lang argue,
the 'Ciceronian hope of heavenly reunion assumed centre
stage. The separation of God's own heaven from an earthly
paradise enabled theologians, humanists, and artists to human-
ize the other world.'[38] These medieval and Renaissance models

---

[37] Ibid., XXII, p. 29. McDannell and Lang note of this anthropocentric conversion that whilst the neo-Platonic inspired notions of
heaven 'made sense to monks, hermits, and philosophers who all
preferred the life of the spirit to that of the flesh', it made less
sense to 'those urban Christians, like Irenaeus, who hoped for
compensation for their earthly trials'. A celibate priest, and
initially attracted to the monastic life, Augustine found himself
appointed bishop in 396 and thus 'responsible for a large number
of people who lived "in the word". These fourth and fifth-century
believers were the heirs to those second-century Christians who
had experienced the goodness of the world. Thus Augustine came
to be closely related to the world of business, politics, families, and
ambition. Toward the end of his life, Augustine revised his view of
heaven.' Cf. C. McDannell and B. Lang, *Heaven*, p. 59.

[38] Cf. C. McDannell and B. Lang, *Heaven*, p. 356. The 'Ciceronian
hope of heavenly reunion' refers to the Cicero's, dialogue, *Scipio's
Dream*. In this dream Scipio enters paradise and there is reunited
with, firstly, leading Roman citizens, and then his dead father. As
Alister McGrath comments: 'This classic scenario of a family
reunion in the world to come impacted on Christian writings of
the era. Cyprian of Carthage, a martyr-bishop of the third
century, tried to encourage his fellow Christians in the face of
suffering and death at times of persecution by holding before

are then rejected in the Protestant Reformation and Catholic counter-Reformation, and a more determinedly theocentric vision becomes predominant once again until the eighteenth century and the work of Swedenborg.

In this broad overview there is, of course, the danger of misreading the history of heaven as 'a simple alternation between theocentric and anthropocentric models'. This is inaccurate, as is the view that the theocentric and anthropocentric approaches stand in some way for biblical purity and human wishful thinking respectively.[39] What we do find, however, is the recurrence – on both sides – of a number of images, such as a garden paradise, the heavenly city, and the bride and bridegroom. In Alister McGrath's study of these images, he is keen to understand how such analogies come to be used in the first place. For example, he suggests:

> In turning to consider how a city came to be an image of heaven, we must appreciate that the ancient world saw the city as far more than an aggregate of streets and buildings. A city offered security; its gates and walls protected it population against their enemies, whether these took the form of marauding wild animals or invading armies.[40]

In addition to this symbolism of security, the image of the city had (for Greeks) the added dimension of corporate and communal identity and (for Jews) the sense of settlement. Their 'period of wandering was over,' notes McGrath; 'a period of permanent inhabitation of a definite geographical region had begun.'[41] Of course, historically, the idea of a New Jerusalem had grown out of the exilic period and as a result of

---

in which they would see the martyrs and apostles face to face.' A. McGrath, *A Brief History of Heaven,* p. 140. However, the dominant concept remained rather more theocentric until the renaissance period and then later, in the eighteenth century, with the writing of Emanuel Swedenborg.

[39] Cf. Colleen McDannell and Bernhard Lang, *Heaven,* pp. 357–8.
[40] Alister McGrath, *A Brief History of Heaven,* p. 7.
[41] Ibid. p. 8.

the destruction of the temple in 586 BC, with all the catastrophic implications that that event held for Hebrew theology.
With the destruction of the second temple in AD 70, and with
the Christian community finding itself under persecution, this
hope for (and vision of) a New Jerusalem was taken up into
Christian eschatology. Significantly, Revelation's description
has no new temple, for in Christ the old dispensation with its
laws and sacrifices has been definitively fulfilled. Furthermore,
as McGrath comments, this image of the heavenly city
'resonates strongly with one of the leading themes of Paul's
theology – that Christians are to be regarded as "citizens of
heaven" (Philippians 3:19–21).'[42] Similarly, the representation
of heaven as garden paradise – perhaps most famously
portrayed in Milton's epic poem, *Paradise Lost* – has a somewhat deeper background to it than merely the desire for
continuity and theological tidiness in tying together protology
and eschatology through the Genesis picture of Eden. McGrath
points out that the word 'paradise' is most probably derived
from the ancient Persian word, *paradeida*, meaning 'an
enclosed garden' or 'royal park'. And he points to Mircea
Eliade's observation of 'the abiding importance of "nostalgia
for paradise" in human thought and literature'. The garden
paradise, then, becomes a symbol of innocence and harmony,
an existence prior to, or away from, the destructive capabilities
of mankind. It is 'a place of peace, rest, and fertility'.[43] This
concept of fertility carries with it too the connotations of new
life. Likewise the description of beatific vision in terms of
conjugal love – the bride and bridegroom imagery so beloved
of the medieval mystics – also has roots sunk deep in the biblical and ancient near eastern traditions. Jeffrey Russell has
argued, 'The idea of a union with God comparable in intensity
to that of spouses in loving intercourse was reinforced by
Bernard's commentary on the Song of Songs.'[44] But, in fact,
the imagery goes further back than that and can be found in
the Judaic understanding of God's covenantal relationship with

---

[42] Ibid. p. 12.
[43] Cf. ibid. p. 40–3.
[44] Jeffrey Burton Russell, *A History of Heaven*, p. 144.

his chosen people, which in its turn is arguably a rather sophisticated development of the pagan notion of a fertility god. It would, then, be somewhat unfair to label such established imagery as 'arbitrary imaginative representations'. But, as is so often the case, the devil is to be found in the detail. The heavenly city, the garden paradise, and the bridal chamber – however biblically inspired – can each still run into problems through their particular manifestation. Russell, for example, has commented on how the mystics, theologians and artists of the medieval period, finding themselves in a rapidly changing world, undertook every effort to present the world beyond as rather more fixed and stable. And the fixtures appear to be more informative of their own prejudices than illuminative of the joys of heaven.

> Some arrangements placed Christians and Jews in different parts of heaven; some arranged souls by geographical origin. Other arrangements were by types of sin or virtue, by social classes, or, rarely, by family. Monks, of course, continued to put monks first ... Male clergy usually constructed rankings, placing themselves higher in heaven – that is nearer to God – than women and the laity. ... Mechthild of Magdeburg would see hell as populated by powerful temporal and spiritual figures, mostly male.[45]

With the publication of Emanuel Swedenborg's eschatological visions in the eighteenth century, McDannell and Lang argue, 'A major shift occurred in the perception of heavenly life.' They go on: 'While the majority of Christians during that time took little notice of the Swedish visionary, the cultural climate supported the general perspective of his views.'[46] Swedenborg reacted to the prevailing theocentricism of the post-

---

[45] Ibid. p. 123.

[46] Colleen McDannell and Bernhard Lang, *Heaven*, p. 183. For the text of Swedenborg's writings, see Emanuel Swedenborg, *Heaven and Hell*. McDannell and Lang acknowledge that although elements of Swedenborg's heaven can be detected 'in the paradise of Renaissance artists, their view contained little supporting theological framework'.

Reformation theology and presented a vision of heaven in which family relationships, social structure – including education and employment – and detailed geography took pride of place. As Carol and Philip Zaleski have observed, 'Swedenborg's revelations about the harmonious ordering of marriage, friendship, work, leisure, and education in heaven profoundly influenced eighteenth and nineteenth-century social critics.'[47] It also provided sufficient imaginative 'furniture' to encourage the development of what we might call the modern, secular, image of heaven. McDannell and Lang suggest that there are four characteristics to this 'modern' view of heaven. Firstly, scant attention is given to the associated eschatological concepts of judgement, purgatory, sleeping in death, resurrection, and so on. Secondly, heaven is viewed, effectively at least, as an enhanced continuation of our earthly and material existence. Thirdly, although referred to as a place of rest, heaven appears to be one of incessant activity on the part of its inhabitants. And fourthly, with its strong emphasis on familial ties and reunion, the primacy of divine love and beatific vision in any meaningful sense is lost.[48] In the light of this modern, secular image of heaven as the prevailing alternative to contemporary theology's rather more vague (at least in the imaginative detail) theocentric propositions, it is no surprise that the Congregation came to make the warning that it did. And Lewis, we know, was similarly wary of such utopia-inspired dreams. 'All that stuff about family reunions "on the further shore", pictured in entirely earthly terms,' he argued in *A Grief Observed*, 'is all unscriptural, all out of bad hymns and lithographs.'[49]

Turning to Lewis' eschatological imagery, then, the question arises: which of the models did he employ? In terms of focal point there are good examples of both anthropocentric and theocentric emphasis. *The Four Loves*, for example, attempting to answer the theological queries about whether we know one another in heaven, or whether our this-worldly bonds of love

---

[47] Carol and Philip Zaleski, *The Book of Heaven*, p. 266.
[48] Cf. Colleen McDannell and Bernhard Lang, *Heaven*, p. 183.
[49] A *Grief Observed*, p. 23.

survive the grave, asserts: 'It may depend what kind of love it had become, or was becoming, on earth.'

> For, surely, to meet in the eternal world someone for whom your love, in this, however strong, had been merely natural, would not be (on that ground) even interesting. ... In Heaven, I suspect, a love that had never embodied Love Himself would be equally irrelevant. For Nature has passed away. All that is not eternal is eternally out of date.[50]

This is theocentric language, essentially a variation of the bridal-chamber image with its accent on the exaltation of love. Arguably, it is even a re-working of Augustine's proposal that the beatific vision might in some way be mediated through the communion of saints and the new creation. Lewis has turned this idea on its head and argued that it is not other people who will reveal to us the vision of God, but that the vision of God may illuminate the presence of other people, insofar as their presence is no distraction or irrelevance. In *The Great Divorce*, on the other hand, Lewis' imagery is almost entirely anthropocentric, with only the merest hint of a beatific vision available in the mountains of deep heaven. Likewise, in *The Last Battle*, the triumphant procession through the Narnia within Narnia to Aslan's country, although led by the Lion himself, is nevertheless largely characterised by the reunion of old friends, loyal Narnians, and the recognition of familiar territory. Only at the end is there the suggestion that heaven is something much more than merely a continuation of our existing life on a slightly grander scale:

> And as [Aslan] spoke He no longer looked to them like a lion; but the things that began to happen after that were so great and beautiful that I cannot write them.[51]

---

[50] *The Four Loves*, p. 131.
[51] *The Last Battle*, p. 171.

In both these works Lewis adapted the garden paradise motif. In *The Problem of Pain* we return to a theocentric position, with Lewis again playing a variation of the bridal theme. Our souls have 'a curious shape because it is a hollow made to fit a particular swelling in the infinite contours of the Divine substance', he asserted. 'God will look to every soul like its first love because He is its first love,' he believed.[52] Perhaps a more implicit theocentricism is found in *Miracles*, where Lewis used both rural and royal imagery in his description of our spiritual bodies as being like 'winged, shining and world-shaking horses'. The whole purpose and point of having such horses is to be able to 'gallop with the King'.[53] And, again, in *Mere Christianity*, where Lewis described our eternal destiny in terms of being turned into 'a god or goddess, a dazzling, radiant, immortal creature ... a bright stainless mirror which reflects back to God perfectly (though, of course, on a smaller scale) His own boundless power and delight and goodness'.[54] J. A. T. Robinson once commented that it was 'noticeable that those who have been most successful in communicating [the Christian message] in our day – Dorothy Sayers, C. S. Lewis, J. B. Phillips – have hesitated least in being boldly anthropomorphic'.[55] However, my own assessment is that overall the thrust of Lewisian imagery is rather more towards the theocentric school. For, at one level, *The Great Divorce* is merely fleshing out in anthropocentric terms the theocentric point Lewis made in *The Four Loves*; the last chapter of *The Last Battle* is simply depicting in more vivid detail the theme of homecoming so prevalent elsewhere in his thought. And, in *A Grief Observed*, Lewis used most powerfully and movingly the idea of the flight in solitude to the Solitary.[56]

[52] Cf. *The Problem of Pain*, p. 122.
[53] *Miracles*, p. 173.
[54] *Mere Christianity*, p. 170.
[55] J. A. T. Robinson, *Honest to God*, p. 15.
[56] Cf. *A Grief Observed*, p. 14.

Resisting the Move Towards a Modern Minimalism

The objection to the Swedenborg-style vision of the celestial hierarchy and, to a lesser extent, to most anthropocentric representations of heaven is that they tell too much and in too earth-bound a way. An example of Lewis' own dissatisfaction with the extremes of this approach is found in an early letter to his friend, Cecil Harwood. The context for the letter was Harwood's recent conversion to anthroposophy and Lewis' problems with certain aspects of this creed. It is not that he doubted, Lewis maintained, the possibility of our intellectual faculties having atrophied or being found undeveloped, and thus not in possession of their full potential; nor did he doubt, necessarily, the likely existence of 'huge tracts of reality that slip through the meshes of the intellect'. What Lewis did find difficult, however, and where his scepticism did begin, was 'when people offer me explicit accounts of the super-intelligible and in so doing use all the categories of the intellect . . . as if it were a nice slice of the intelligible'.[57] He made a similar point in his attack on Spiritualism in *A Grief Observed*: 'How well the Spiritualists bait their hook! Things on this side are not so different after all.' There are cigars in Heaven. For that is what we should all like. The happy past restored.'[58] Such uninspired pictures, such precise yet so this-worldly a utopia, must be radically differentiated from Lewis' own imaginative aim. The Swedenborg school, and in particular the syrupy, secular heaven that sprang from it, is a perfect example of that over-attenuation of images that the Congregation warned us about. There is a thinness, an unbelievable literalism, in what these writers attempt to portray. Lewis, on the other hand, was in the business of creating contemporary Christian myth. Multiplicity of metaphor and not literal translation was his aim. He employed rich imagery and lots of it so that, even in the process of cataphatic illumination, he was implicitly reminding his readers of the deeper, apophatic mystery at its heart: God himself. As he noted:

---

[57] C. S. Lewis, *Collected Letters*, Volume 1, *Family Letters 1905–1931*, pp. 670–1 (Letter dated 28 October 1926).
[58] *A Grief Observed*, p. 23.

If you're approaching Him not as the goal but as a road, not as the end but as a means, you're not really approaching Him at all. That's what was really wrong with all those popular pictures of happy reunions 'on the further shore'; not the simple-minded and very earthly images, but the fact that they make an End of what we can get only as a by-product of the true End.[59]

This, of course, was what even Lewis' most anthropocentric of imagery pointed to: God as our end and goal and everything else thrown in. But, as he constantly reminded us, we cannot use God as the means to the 'everything else'.

McDannell and Lang have suggested that the 'modern heaven – exemplified by the visions of Swedenborg, the writings of Elizabeth Stuart Phelps, and Mormon theology – has become the minority perspective during the twentieth century'.[60] Generally they are correct, with theologians preferring more sophistication and most lay people, as Peter Stanford has observed, preferring to seek – should they seek at all – for a heaven in the image of their own reaction to the world.[61] Nevertheless, I think it would be wrong to underestimate the prevalence of this soft-focus hope for an eternity based on little more than a spruced up version of the life we now know. Karl Rahner once wrote:

There can be no doubt that belief in eternal life as a consequence of survival after death has grown weaker in the consciousness of modern people ... Today, even among Christians, what was once a basic Christian conviction is largely threatened. There are Christians who are sure of the existence of God and who lead lives according to the tenets of their religion, but who do not think it

[59] Ibid. p. 58.
[60] Colleen McDannell and Bernhard Lang, *Heaven*, p. 322. Elizabeth Stuart Phelps was an American author who died in 1911 and whose book, *The Gates Ajar*, was a bestseller in its day. For an extract of that book and an example of her style, see Carol and Philip Zaleski, *The Book of Heaven*, pp. 135–47.
[61] Cf. Peter Stanford, *Heaven*, p. 351.

necessary to show any great interest in the question of an eternal life that is simply not identical with life here and now.[62]

This loss of eschatological awareness amongst Christians is, perhaps, the legacy of what Lewis called Christianity-and-water: 'The view that which simply says there is a good God in Heaven and everything is all right – leaving out all the difficult and terrible doctrines about sin and hell and the devil, and redemption.'[63] It is the Swedenborg influence, which portrays heaven as so little different from our current social and economic experience that it is hardly worth thinking about; except, of course, in times of pain and grief, during which we all too readily comfort ourselves with the panacea of an unthreatening, anthropocentric hereafter. Perhaps this danger of a watered down eschatology is what lies behind the International Theological Commission's criticism of much modern preaching today: that homilists at funerals tend to treat 'salvation as a kind of quasi-automatic consequence' of death.[64]

Theologically speaking, the twentieth century did witness a reaction to the anthropocentric highpoint of the mid-eighteenth and nineteenth centuries. Following the excesses of Swedenborg many theologians attempted to reduce their images of the afterlife to a minimum with the aim of developing something seemingly more rational and hence more intellectually acceptable. This reductionist approach is exemplified in the work of Reinhold Niebuhr, Paul Tillich, and the infamous Father of demythologising, Rudolf Bultmann. Niebuhr argued that the biblical symbols for eternity 'cannot be taken literally because it is not possible for finite minds to comprehend that which transcends and fulfils history'.[65] Biblical metaphors are revealed and, as such, point us in the

---

[62] Karl Rahner, 'Eternity from Time', in idem, *Theological Investigations,* Volume XIX, p. 169.

[63] *Mere Christianity*, p. 33.

[64] ITC, 'Some Current Questions in Eschatology', p. 237.

[65] Reinhold Niebuhr, *The Nature and Destiny of Man: A Christian Interpretation*, p. 299.

direction of eternal reality and arousing hope, but they do not give us any knowledge as such.

> Thus wisdom about our destiny is dependent upon a humble recognition of the limits of our knowledge and our power. Our most reliable understanding is the fruit of 'grace' in which faith completes our ignorance without pretending to possess its certainties as knowledge; and in which contrition mitigates our pride without destroying our hope.[66]

Similarly, Tillich criticised the 'literalist distortion' of the symbols of eternal life, and argued that such references to what heaven might be like were entirely unnecessary. Indeed, perhaps aware of Feurbach's influence, Tillich warned, 'Religious symbols can easily be misunderstood as products of man's wishful thinking.' This is especially the case, he believed, of such eschatological symbols as the afterlife.[67] In other words, with Niebuhr and Tillich, there was a determined move towards the establishment of a modern minimalism when it came to eschatological discourse. Tillich, for example, was willing to discuss the theological concept of the symbol – although 'he would deny that one can ever fully get behind the symbol to its "nonmetaphorical" sense' – but only through use of what he termed 'negative metaphorical language': a language that employed paradox, contradiction, and metaphor to describe what eternal life is not.[68] Such negative linguistics has tended, however, to make Tillich's concepts quite obscure. But nevertheless, as Stanford sums up:

---

[66] Ibid. p. 332.
[67] Paul Tillich, *Systematic Theology*, Volume 3: *Life and the Spirit, History and the Kingdom of God*, p. 452
[68] Colleen McDannell and Bernhard Lang, *Heaven*, p. 328. For a fuller treatment of Tillich's position, see Paul Tillich, *Systematic Theology*, pp. 420–52 and idem, 'Existential Analyses and Religious Symbols', in *Contemporary Problems in Religion*, pp. 37–55.

For Tillich, afterlife was a state that combined group and individual fulfilment, this world and eternity in God's presence. Beyond that he did not go.[69]

Rudolf Bultmann, meanwhile, spoke of the need to demythologise biblical data, thus making the Word of God both relevant and operative within our given situation. On this basis he similarly argued for a minimalism when it came to images of eternal life. As McDannell and Lang explain:

> For the modern mind, he argued, the concept of a translation to a heavenly world of light, in which the self is destined to receive a celestial vesture, a spiritual body, is not merely incomprehensible by any rational process but totally meaningless.[70]

This is not to say that Bultmann rejected any belief in an afterlife. Heaven is a transcendent reality, he wrote in a letter in 1973, which we can only speak of only 'once we realize that our individual existence cannot find its authenticity in this world'.[71] Perhaps it is important to clarify that the point of the minimalists in this regard was not to deny the reality of life after death as such but to be suspicious of its symbols and detail. But, as Lewis demonstrated in his parable of the erudite limpets, minimalism can lead to just as many distortions as the over-attenuated imagery of Swedenborg. When we come 'limping after' the great prophets and saints whose intuition of God has led them to talk about him transcending 'those limitations which we call personality, passion, change, materiality, and the like', we do so with a naïve negativity 'unchecked by any positive intuition'. Thus our understanding is no more enlightened than if we had used more constructive imagery in the first place. Like the erudite limpets, who concluded that the supreme mode of existence is to be 'a famished jelly in a dimensionless void', we too believe that any image suggesting something a little more concrete must be

---

[69] Peter Stanford, *Heaven*, p. 305.
[70] Colleen McDannell and Bernhard Lang, *Heaven*, p. 331.
[71] Ibid.

nothing but 'a crude, materialistic superstition'.[72] A similar point is made in *Till We Have Faces* where, throughout the novel, the sophisticated philosophy of the Fox is contrasted with the cruel barbarism of the popular religion of Ungit. When Orual finds herself before the gods in judgement, it is her old tutor, the Fox, who pleads on her behalf:

> She never asked me (I was content she shouldn't ask) why the people got something from the shapeless stone which no one got from that painted doll of Arnom's. Of course, I didn't know; but I never told her I didn't know. I don't know now. Only that the way to the true gods is more like the House of Ungit ... oh, its unlike too, more unlike than we yet dream, but that's the easy knowledge, the first lesson; only a fool would stay there, posturing and repeating it.[73]

Clearly the images aren't the reality. 'My idea of God is not a divine idea,' Lewis noted in *A Grief Observed*. 'It has to be shattered time after time.'[74] But there is a difference between recognising that metaphors are as much unlike as they are like and arguing that eschatological symbolism is simply incomprehensible or to be avoided altogether.

In his article on the hermeneutics of eschatological language, Karl Rahner argued that this minimalism – and the whole demythologising controversy, as he called it – highlighted what is a very real problem for theology. He believed that some fundamental principles of eschatological interpretation needed to be worked out as a framework within which any theological statement or imagery could be judged.[75] Of images in particular, he stressed:

---

[72] Cf. *Miracles*, p. 93.
[73] *Till We Have Faces*, p. 224.
[74] *A Grief Observed*, p. 55.
[75] Cf. Karl Rahner, 'The Hermeneutics of Eschatological Assertions', pp. 323–5. Indeed, Rahner proposed seven theses as provision of such a hermeneutic which dealt with: (1) the futurity of eschatological statements – i.e. they do concern a future reality and are not merely existential statements; (2) the possibility of eschatological revelation; (3) the dialectic of the essential hiddenness of the

No assertion about the thing is possible without some sort of image, and in this sense a 'myth' can only be replaced by another, but not by language utterly devoid of images. And here of course one will not be so naïve as to think that the thing had once been thought of without images but that this lofty concept had then been clothed in 'imagery" for the sake of the weaker brethren. Thought is always image as well, because there is no concept without imagination.[76]

Here we have a familiar echo of Lewis' emphasis on the radically metaphorical nature of language, and of the role of imagination as the organ of meaning. Rahner went on to refer to St Thomas who, he said, maintains that 'There is no concept without a *conversio ad phantasma*, that is, a concept must be exteriorised and embodied in the imagination and the image, and hence too in "picturesque" language.'[77] Since it is impossible to 'rid oneself of the picturesque diction to reach a sphere where the thing itself appears as it is in itself', argued Rahner, the aim of eschatological assertion should not be to attempt to rid itself of these images but to multiply them and in their multiplication – and in the light of other hermeneutical principles – discern what pertains to content and what to form. Perhaps Lewis put it more clearly in *Letters to Malcolm*. Imagery, he accepted, must always be subjected to and 'balanced by all manner of metaphysical and theological abstractions'. But the limitation of such abstractions needs to be remembered too.

Never, here or anywhere else, let us think that while anthropomorphic images are a concession to our weakness, the abstractions are the literal truth. Both are

---

parousia and the historicity of man; (4) the existential implications of the hope raised by eschatology's future promise; (5) eschatological statements as Christological and concerned with the salvific event; (6) the consequences of this hermeneutic; and (7) the role of imagery in eschatological assertions. Cf. ibid., pp. 323–46.

[76] Ibid. p. 344.
[77] Ibid. Cf. St Thomas, *Summa Theologiae*, I, 84, 7.

equally concessions; each singly misleading, and the two together mutually corrective.[78]

Indeed, Lewis suggested two of his own hermeneutical principles for this problem of eschatological imagery: first, that one should 'never take the images literally'; and second, that 'When the *purport* of the images – what they say to our fear and hope and will and affections – seems to conflict with the theological abstractions, trust the purport of the images every time.'[79]

In this discussion I have quite deliberately concerned myself primarily with the imagery of heaven, to the neglect of some of the quite colourful presentations of judgement, purgatory, hell and so on. Partly this has been for reasons of time and space; partly because I believe that the general principles concerning eschatological imagery are the same for each. I have chosen to dwell on the celestial imagery, furthermore, to underline a theological point that will be drawn out more fully in the next chapter: we have only one eternal predestination, to beatific vision through the gift of grace offered to all in Jesus Christ. It seems to me appropriate, then, that if our discussion must be limited in any way, it should be limited to this eschatological goal. However, to highlight the transferable validity of what has been said, it might be worthwhile to look briefly at some comments Jürgen Moltmann has made concerning a recent document of the Church of England. In 1995 the Doctrine Commission of the General Synod published *The Mystery of Salvation: The Story of God's Gift* in which they replaced the fires of hell with the concept of non-being.

> Hell is not eternal torment, but it is the final and irrevocable choosing of that which is opposed to God so completely and so absolutely that the only end is total non-being ... Annihilation might be a truer picture of damnation than any of the traditional images of the hell of eternal torment.[80]

---

[78] *Letters to Malcolm*, p. 19 (Letter 4).
[79] Ibid. pp. 49–50 (Letter 10).
[80] Doctrine Commission of the Church of England, *The Mystery of Salvation: The Story of God's Gift*, p. 199.

Moltmann believes this shift in presentation to be significant. Not that he laments the move away from the 'atrocious and terrifying visions' of the Middle Ages, for example, but because the change itself mirrors an alteration in contemporary fears of what constitutes the worst possible catastrophe. As Moltmann observes,

> This belief [in hell fire] held its ground right down to the day when the bomb fell on Hiroshima in August 1945. But since Hiroshima, the imagination of modern men and women has been fascinated no longer by burning but by annihilation. So it is nothing out of the way that the Church of England's Doctrine Commission should replace the hell fire of old by the annihilation of modern times. 'Fire' and 'annihilation' are merely the metaphors for an inescapable remoteness from God, or for a Godforsakenness from which there is no way out.[81]

C. S. Lewis, we have seen, argued that there was a real danger of 'speaking as if we had two methods of thought open to us: the metaphorical, and the literal'. In fact, he believed, 'It is abundantly clear that the freedom from a given metaphor which we admittedly enjoy in some cases is often only a freedom to choose between that metaphor and others.'[82] This is exactly what has happened in the Doctrine Commission of the Church of England's publication. Thinking that they had moved away from the metaphorical presentation of hell as some kind of fiery torment, the Commission have unwittingly adopted a new metaphor, that of annihilation. And Moltmann has identified the change. In the Middle Ages, fire was a 'religious method for destroying heretics. The end of the world was imagined as the day when the world will go down to destruction in a great conflagration'.[83] But with the advent of modern warfare and the proliferation of weapons of mass destruction,

---

[81] Jürgen Moltmann, 'The Logic of Hell', in Richard Bauckham, *God will be All in All*, pp. 43–4.
[82] 'Bluspels', p. 261.
[83] Moltmann, 'The Logic of Hell', p. 43.

annihilation – nuclear or otherwise – has become a much graver threat in the contemporary imagination. Thus once again we find two key ideas of Lewis being put into practice: firstly, the radically metaphorical nature of language, and secondly – and following on from that nature – the importance of recognizing the metaphorical import that any language can have, even such seemingly innocuous and metaphor-free expressions as 'non-being' and 'annihilation'.

The Mythopoeic in Lewisian Eschatology

In the next chapter I will offer an examination of the contemporary eschatological debate and attempt to assess what contributions Lewis' thought may have to offer. But it seems to me that already we can surmise that one major contribution lies in the area of eschatological imagery. Not only did Lewis effectively foreshadow Rahner's call to remythologise but he actively attempted such a remythologisation. In his conclusions to his study, *The Image of Man in C. S. Lewis*, William Luther White has remarked:

> For more than forty years Lewis produced imaginative literature reflecting his keen understanding of myth and metaphor as the essential language of religion. C. S. Lewis was a Christian remythologizer par excellence.[84]

This is an important point. Lewis not only presented an eschatology which, as we have seen, stands up to theological scrutiny. He presented one with all the rich and memorable imagery of a modern day Christian mythmaker. Paul Fiddes, for example, has argued that Lewis' distinctive contribution to the call to remythologise lay not so much in his theory about myth but in the 'practical arena' of his own mythmaking.[85] Nevertheless, Rolland Hein has observed that Lewis' concept of

---

[84] William Luther White, *The Image of Man in C. S. Lewis*, p. 213.
[85] Paul Fiddes 'C. S. Lewis the Myth-Maker', in A. Walker and J. Patrick, *Rumours of Heaven*, p. 135.

myth was 'markedly different from that of many in the literary community at large ... With Lewis, myth was a vehicle by which supernatural reality communicates to man'.[86] As Lewis himself expressed it:

> What flows into you from the myth is not truth but reality (truth is always *about* something, but reality is that *about which* truth is), and, therefore, every myth becomes the father of innumerable truths on the abstract level.[87]

Behind this understanding lies the insight, recorded in *Surprised by Joy*, that Lewis got from reading Samuel Alexander's *Space, Time and Deity*: that there is a distinction to be made between enjoyment and contemplation. As Lewis explained it, 'In introspection [i.e. contemplation] we try to look "inside ourselves" and see what is going on. But nearly everything that was going on a moment before is stopped by the very act of our turning to look at it.'[88] Lewis gave the example of hoping and thinking about hoping. When we hope for something, he argued, our focus is on the goal of our hope – what we long for. When we think about hoping, our focus has moved from the goal to the process by which we hope. 'As thinkers,' Lewis believed, 'we are cut off from what we think about. ... The more lucidly we think, the more we are cut off: the more deeply we enter into reality, the less we can think.'[89] Abstract theological propositions, then, are thoughts *about* God: as such, they are a step back from the divine encounter in order to analyse it. They are the truths *about* Truth. But in myth, Lewis believed, such thought is in some way transcended. 'In the enjoyment of a great myth we come nearest to

[86] Rolland Hein, *Christian Mythmakers: C. S. Lewis, Madeleine L'Engle, J. R. R. Tolkien, George MacDonald, G. K. Chesterton & Others*, pp. 205–6.

[87] C. S. Lewis, 'Myth Became Fact', in *God in the Dock*, p. 35.

[88] *Surprised by Joy*, p. 170. Alexander's distinction uses these terms in a technical way. Enjoyment is the act of apprehending or experiencing the reality and contemplation the introspection that can then take place.

[89] 'Myth Became Fact', p. 34.

experiencing as a concrete what can otherwise only be understood as an abstraction.'[90] And whereas myth transcends
thought so the incarnation transcends myth, so that at 'the
heart of Christianity is a myth which is also a fact. The old
myth of the Dying God, *without ceasing to be myth,* comes down
from the heaven of legend and imagination to the earth of
history. It *happens* – at a particular date, in a particular place,
followed by definable historical consequences.'[91] If God has
chosen to be so mythopoeic, argued Lewis, can we refuse to be
so also? For, indeed, myth in its method (story) 'does what no
theorem can quite do. It may not be "like real life" in the
superficial sense: but it sets before us an image of what reality
may well be like at some more central region'. It provides us
with a net 'whereby to catch something else'.[92] We apprehend
eternal reality in a way that we cannot merely through theoretical abstraction. This appreciation of the mythopoeic is
similarly drawn out in *An Experiment in Criticism.* Listing the
defining characteristics of myth, Lewis noted that one such
distinguishing feature was that the experience of myth is 'not
only grave but awe-inspiring. We feel it to be numinous. It is as
if some great moment had been communicated to us'. Another
characteristic was that it is what Lewis called 'extra-literary'. In
other words, the myth's essential content transcends the
confinements of its particular storytelling. This is evinced by
the fact that a basic myth may have a number of versions in
which significant details might be changed but the essence
remains the same.[93] Mineko Honda put it this way: 'Lewis is
conscious of the limit of language in expressing reality, and
thinks that a pictorial and mythical presentation sometimes

---

[90] Ibid. p. 35.
[91] Ibid. p. 36. Paul Fiddes comments of Lewis' assertion that in the
incarnation myth becomes fact: 'The Christian story of the becoming flesh of the divine Logos is both historical *and* imaginative. He
[Lewis] would surely have agreed with the theologian Wolfhart
Pannenberg that the meaning ('God was in Christ') is inherent
within the event itself, so that history is revelatory, and yet still
there is a widening horizon of interpretation from age to age.'
Fiddes, 'C. S. Lewis the Myth-Maker', p. 135.
[92] 'On Stories', pp. 15, 18.
[93] Cf. *Experiment in Criticism*, pp. 43–4.

conveys the reality better.'[94] However, Lewis was also aware that 'the same story may be a myth to one man and not to another'.[95] Honda has argued that in this sense Lewis could be considered 'a forerunner of receptionist theory'.[96] Certainly Lewis distinguished between the use of a work of art and its reception. 'When we "receive it,"' he observed, 'we exert our senses and imagination and various other powers according to the pattern invented by the artist. When we "use" it we treat it as assistance for our own activities.'

> 'Using' is inferior to 'reception' because art, if used rather than received, merely facilitates, brightens, relieves, or palliates our life, and does not add to it.[97]

But I think that here, though, we are back to Samuel Alexander's distinction between enjoyment and contemplation. Thus, if we try to analyse the mythopoeic we loose the reality it conveys; we descend into abstraction once again. As Lewis wrote to Arthur Greeves: 'The doctrines we get *out of* the true myth are of course *less* true: they are translations into our *concepts* and *ideas* of that wh[ich] God has already expressed in a language more adequate, namely the actual incarnation, crucifixion, and resurrection.'[98] The purpose, then, of any remythologisation is to enable an encounter with God, rather than transmit a lot of information *about* him. In a footnote in *Miracles* Lewis argued that myth is not misunderstood history, diabolical illusion, or priestly lying but potentially a 'gleam of divine truth falling on human imagination'.

Peter Schakel has observed that in the mid 1940s Lewis began to expand his conception of myth and turned more to imaginative representation than logical argument in his writings. Schakel suggests a number of factors for this, but

---

[94] Mineko Honda, *The Imaginative World of C. S. Lewis: A Way to Participate in Reality*, p. 38.
[95] *Experiment in Criticism*, p. 44.
[96] Honda, *The Imaginative World of C. S. Lewis*, p. 39.
[97] *Experiment in Criticism*, p. 88.
[98] *They Stand Together*, p. 428 (Letter dated 18 October 1931).

significantly he comments: '[Lewis'] turning to myth is not a rejection of his earlier mode, but an effort to go beyond it and to offer a reader not "knowledge" of God but a "taste" of Divine Reality'.[99] Certainly his aim in the Narnia Chronicles was not to catechise children through allegory but to submit his young readers to the Christian myth in another version, one in which, once stripped 'of their stained-glass and Sunday school associations', might allow the full potency of the Reality behind the myth to be encountered.[100] In his essay, *On Three Ways of Writing for Children*, however, I think Lewis himself provided a reason for the shift in writing style that he undertook in later life. 'I see pictures,' he said. 'I have no idea whether this is the usual way of writing stories, still less whether it is the best. It is the only one I know: images always come first.'[101] The methodology of myth is the conveyance of pictures: those mental images evoked of characters, events, and scenery. Of his own mythmaking, he said: 'Let the pictures tell you their own moral. For the moral inherent in them will rise from whatever spiritual roots you have succeeded in striking down during the whole course of your life.'[102] And this is the point. We could just as easily transpose the word 'eschatology' for 'moral' in Lewis' comments. I believe that the shift to the mythopoeic in the later Lewis represents not only his realisation that myth is the best vehicle for conveying the Christian message, but also the deepening of his own Christianity from the rather theoretical, intellectual and propositional understanding he had at his conversion. In attempting to create modern Christian myth, Lewis did not, I believe, deliberately set out to convey eschatological truths. Rather through his writing he revealed his own deeply held Christian *Weltanschauung*. In other words, in his later writings, Lewis' medium became his message: that 'the very essence of our life as conscious beings all day and every day consists of

---

99 Peter Schakel, *Reason and Imagination in C. S. Lewis: A Study of Till We Have Faces*, p. 150.

100 Cf. 'Sometimes Fairy Stories May Say Best What's to Be Said', in *Of Other Worlds*, p. 37.

101 *On Three Ways of Writing for Children*, pp. 32, 33.

102 Ibid. p. 33.

something which cannot be communicated except by hints, similes, metaphors, and the use of those emotions (themselves not very important) which are pointers to it'.[103]

[103] 'Language of Religion', p. 265.

Chapter 6

The Contemporary Debate

Back in 1957 Hans Urs Von Balthasar spoke of eschatology as being the storm zone of contemporary theology. Twenty years later Joseph Ratzinger was to observe: 'Today it appears to dominate the entire theological landscape.'[1] Certainly, in comparison with the place classical theology had given to the subject, eschatology underwent a near revolution in the last century.[2] Far from being merely a theological appendage of 'Last Things', theology was to see a renewal in the eschatological appreciation of Jesus' message and subsequently in the meaning of Christian hope. And yet, no so long ago – 1996 to be precise – the theologian Dermot Lane was to suggest: 'It is something of an understatement to suggest that a theological vacuum exists in relation to eschatology today.'[3] Since that time, and with the passing of a new millennium, there has been a noticeable upsurge in eschatological publications. But even today, in 2007, Lane is surely right when he notes, 'Given the amazing number of books published in theology on Jesus, the Church and the Trinity over the last thirty years, it is quite extraordinary that so little has been written on escha-

---

[1] J. Ratzinger, *Eschatology*, 1. Cf. Hans Urs Von Balthasar, 'Eschatologie' in *Fragen der Theologie heute,* ed. J. Feiner, J. Trütsch, and F. Böckle, (Einsiedeln: Benziger Verlag, 1957), p. 404.

[2] For an excellent and concise overview of this revolution see Christoph Schwöbel, 'Last Things First? The Century of Eschatology in Retrospect', in David Fergusson and Marcel Sarot, *The Future as God's Gift*, pp. 217–41.

[3] Dermot Lane, *Keeping Hope Alive*, p. 112.

tology.'[4] Lane goes on to argue that the formulations of past theologies seem to command very little credence in our modern world. Nevertheless, the questions that caused such theologies to arise still demand answers: 'Issues about the meaning of life and death, about the range of hope, and about the destiny of the world simply will not go away.'[5] In this chapter I want to examine those issues a little more closely and see what contribution – if any – Lewis' own eschatology might have to make to the contemporary theological debate.

The Meaning of Life and Death

In 1979, the Sacred Congregation for the Doctrine of the Faith reiterated the 'importance of [the] final article of the baptismal creed', expressing as it does the 'goal and purpose of God's plan'. As the Congregation went on:

> If there is no resurrection, the whole structure of faith collapses, as Saint Paul states forcefully. If the content of the words 'life everlasting' is uncertain for Christians, the promises contained in the Gospel and the meaning of creation and redemption disappear, and even earthly life itself must be said to be deprived of all hope.[6]

Our understanding of the Last Things, it would seem, clearly gives meaning to our experience of the present reality and opens up for us the horizon of hope. But, as Zachary Hayes has noted of life after death, 'Whatever experience awaits us, it is not a return to space and time experience, nor is it an endless continuation of our temporal existence in another world.'[7] The precise meaning of the credal affirmations of the resurrection and life everlasting, then, are valid subjects for theological

---

[4] Ibid. p. ix. Although Lane goes on to say: 'It might be argued that it is not surprising that so little has been published on this subject because there is very little that can be known about eschatology.'
[5] Ibid. p. 112.
[6] SCDF, 'The Reality of Life After Death', pp. 500–1.
[7] Zachary Hayes, *Visions of a Future*, p. 103.

discussion. Indeed, the Congregation itself made precisely this point when it acknowledged that there is no question of 'restricting or preventing theological research that the faith of the Church needs and from which it should profit'.[8] However, it did outline seven clarifications concerning existing eschatological teaching; in other words, seven non-negotiable points of parameter within which contemporary Catholic theology must conduct its debate. Firstly, the Congregation reminded theologians that the Church believes in the resurrection of the dead. Secondly, this resurrection is to be understood 'as referring to the whole person'. Thirdly, the Church 'affirms that a spiritual element survives and subsists after death, an element endowed with consciousness and will, so that the "human self" subsists'. This element is traditionally called the soul. Fourthly, the *lex orandi* of the Church must inform the *lex credendi*; in other words, that theology is not free to go off on some eschatological tangent that takes it away from the traditional prayer of the Church. Fifthly, the expectation of the parousia is a vital component of Christian eschatology and that this 'glorious manifestation of our Lord, Jesus Christ' is believed to be 'distinct and deferred with respect to the situation of people immediately after death'. Sixthly, eschatological theology must be careful not to 'deprive the Assumption of the Virgin Mary of its unique meaning', in particular the idea that Mary's fate is an 'anticipation of the glorification that is the destiny of all the other elect'. And finally, the Church understands hell as the eternal punishment of sinners – 'who will be deprived of the sight of God, and that this punishment will have a repercussion on the whole being of the sinner' – and purgatory as the possibility of a purification for the elect 'before they see God', a purification which is to be understood as 'altogether different from the punishment of the damned'.[9]

---

[8] SCDF, 'The Reality of Life After Death', p. 501.

[9] Cf. ibid. pp. 501–2. Of the clarification concerning the *lex orandi* and the *lex credendi*, Joseph Ratzinger has noted: 'Because the "fundamental truths of faith" belong to all believers, and are, as a matter of fact, the concrete content of the Church's activity, the fundamental language of faith can not be regarded as something for experts to work out. And for the same reason, that language

The context for the Congregation's clarifications was an eschatological debate of the 1970s concerning what was called the interim, or intermediate, state and the meaning of the resurrection of the body. Certain theologians, unhappy with what they saw to be the dualism of classical theology, had proposed an eschatology which did away with the intermediate state and the need to speak of the soul's subsistence after death. Initially G. Greshake and G. Lohfink were the major protagonists of this new theology.[10] As Zachary Hayes has commented: '[Greshake's] thesis is expressed most pointedly in the claim that resurrection takes place in death and not at some future time at the end of history.'[11] These ideas began to be of considerable interest especially among German theologians who, Hayes notes, found that such an approach made 'the meaning of the traditional symbol of resurrection of the flesh more understandable in the context of contemporary understandings of human nature'.[12] Even Karl Rahner was to admit, 'It is by no means certain that the doctrine of the intermediate state is anything more than an intellectual framework.'[13]

---

which is the bearer of unity cannot be manipulated at will. Theology as an academic discipline needs technical language; as interpretation, it tries to translate its shared materials in ever new ways. But in both of these respects theology is beholden to the basic language of faith, a language which can only be developed in peaceful continuity with the common life of the praying Church, and which cannot endure sudden ruptures.' See J. Ratzinger, *Eschatology*, p. 244.

[10] For example, cf. G. Greshake, *Auferstehung der Toten*, (Essen, 1969) and G. Greshake and G. Lohfink, *Naherwartung – Auferstehung – Unsterblichkeit*, (Frieburg, 1976). By 1988 and the English edition of Ratzinger's book, *Eschatology,* the debate had widened to include a wider range of theologians, notably amongst them, H. Küng, H. Vorgrimler, F. Nocke, J. Auer, and M. Kehl. Cf. J. Ratzinger, *Eschatology*, p. 262.

[11] Zachary Hayes, *Visions of a Future*, p. 164.

[12] Ibid.

[13] Karl Rahner, 'The Intermediate State', in idem, *Theological Investigations,* Volume XVII p. 115. Rahner went on to explain: 'So whatever it [i.e. the intermediate state] has to tell us (apart from statements about the commencement through death of the final form of man's history of freedom, and about the inclusion of the

However, one German theologian in particular was to mount a vigorous defence of the classical position against this new eschatological approach. Joseph Ratzinger, in the 1977 publication of *Eschatologie – Tod und ewiges Leben*, attacked what he saw as inconsistencies in the positions of Greshake and Lohfink. After the Congregation's 1979 statement he returned to the theme again, with notable relish, in two later appendices to his work. At the heart of the issue, admits Ratzinger, is a problem with the traditional Christian concept of the soul. But this is a problem, he identifies, that betrays a deeper issue of 'a quite general crisis of Catholicism itself', brought about by the reception of the historical-critical method under Pius XII and, in particular, since Vatican II. Indeed, at one stage Ratzinger suggests that theology's 'intercourse of the historical-critical method with its object may be compared with a kind of necrophilia'.[14]

> Once the Jesus of the 'Sayings-Source' has been located, everything of later provenance can be explained away as a human garnish, its ingredients analysed and combined. The true key-master of so archeologically conceived a Gospel can only be the historian. People forget that there might be in history a continuous Subject, in whom development is faithful to an Origin whose plenary authority the Subject carries within her own life.[15]

---

body in this final form) does not necessarily have to be part of Christian eschatology itself. We might put the matter differently and say: no one is in danger of defending a heresy if he maintains the view that the single and total perfecting of man in "body" and "soul" takes place immediately after death; that the resurrection of the flesh and the general judgement take place "parallel" to the temporal history of the world; and that both coincide with the sum of particular judgements of individual men and women.' Later Rahner concluded, 'In my view, the idea of the intermediate state contains a little harmless mythology, which is not dangerous as long as we do not take the idea too seriously and do not view it as binding on faith.' See ibid. pp. 115, 123.

14 Cf. J. Ratzinger, *Eschatology*, pp. 248–9.
15 Ibid. pp. 249–50.

Nevertheless, under the historical-critical approach – and since the traditional understanding of soul is not a strictly biblical term – the classical formulations of the immortality of the soul and the resurrection of the body appear to be 'a betrayal of the biblical and modern recognition of the unity of man'. Ratzinger notes that they can be seen to be a 'kind of fall from out of the biblical thought-world into a Greek dualism which split the world into spirit and matter'.[16] And whereas in the sixteenth century Martin Luther, who himself had raised precisely this debate, attempted to resolve it by recourse to the biblical notion of man as 'asleep' between death and resurrection, twentieth-century Catholic theologians have preferred to take the atem-poral route.[17] Peter Phan has been quite condemning of

---

[16] Ibid. p. 50.

[17] Of Luther's position, Ratzinger comments: 'But what hope, then, remains for the human being after death, if the distinction of body and soul is thus denied? Luther had at least got to grips with the issue by representing man between death and resurrection as "asleep", But the question arises, Who is it that is asleep? The concept of sleep can hardly be employed to describe the gradually disintegrating body. But if there is something distinct from the body which goes on living, why should it not be called the soul? If, on the other hand, the term "sleep" is meant to express the tempo-rary suspension of the existence of a human being, then that human being in his self-identity simply exists no longer. The reawakening of resurrection would be for him a new creation. The man who rises at the resurrection may be like the man who died but he cannot be the same as he – since it necessarily follows that with death the man who was has reached his definitive end.' See ibid. p. 251. As an example of contemporary Protestant thinking in this area, Hans Schwarz combines an atemporal approach *and* the use of the biblical concept of sleeping in death: 'As people cross the borderline of time at different points and leave our chronological time, it is legitimate to use the New Testament imagery and say that the dead "sleep" until Judgement Day. But we also know that in God all the different points of time coincide. For God there is no sooner or later, not even a too late. In God's eternal presence there is no distinction between past, present, and future. This distinction exists only for us as time-bound creatures, not for the creator. In death we cross the borderline of time and encounter God's eternal presence. We are then coeternal not only with God but also with all human creatures. Regardless of when

Ratzinger's contribution to this debate, describing his arguments in *Eschatology* 'as excessively sweeping' and as 'labouring under non-sequiturs'.[18] Nevertheless, I believe Ratzinger's objections are significant. Firstly, he suggests that the concept of resurrection in death is, in reality, little more than 'a camouflaged return to the doctrine of immortality on philosophically somewhat more adventurous presuppositions'.[19] We claim a resurrection of the body, argues Ratzinger, for someone whose body we see lying in death before us; indeed, for someone whose body has evidently begun the slow process of decay and disintegration. What, then, precisely is being raised up? And if what is raised incorruptible is *not* the material body – which we witness in corruption – then surely we have introduced once again 'something which, amid the spatio-temporal disintegration of the body, is distinguishable from the body'. As Ratzinger says, 'If there is such a something, then why not call it the soul?'[20] Secondly, Ratzinger expresses concern with the very concept of time being used in the atemporal approach. Death, the atemporalists argue, marks the leaving of time for eternity: a stepping into the eternal today of God. Thus 'The person who dies steps into the presence of the Last Day and of judgement, the Lord's resurrection and parousia.' But, asks Ratzinger, 'Are we really confronted with a choice between the stark, exclusive

---

we cross this line, we will appear on the "other side" at the "same moment" as everyone else. Thus the confrontation with God in death will result in the eternal judgement. This is not to be understood as an individualized act, because together with everyone else we will encounter God's eternal presence. As anything between death and resurrection is beyond space and time, we can only talk about the "transitory state" in approximations. When we call it a state of "bodiless sleep", this shows very drastically the limits of our conceptual tools. A "bodiless sleep" is an obvious contradiction, since we cannot conceive of sleep without thinking about a body. Yet in order to express that death and resurrection are not the same, and in order to attempt to relate our present experiences to the future we hope for, we have to resort to such inadequate, though necessary, concepts.' See Hans Schwarz, *Eschatology*, p. 301.

[18] Peter Phan, 'Current Theology', p. 527 n. 68.
[19] J. Ratzinger, *Eschatology*, p. 108.
[20] Ibid. p. 252.

alternatives of physical time on the one hand, and, on the other, a timelessness to be identified with eternity itself?' He goes on: 'Is it even logically possible to conceive of man, whose existence is achieved decisively in the temporal, being transposed into sheer eternity?'[21] The potential problem here lies in man's entry into eternity. Surely for the risen man eternity has a beginning: there was a time when he was not eternal. And yet the very meaning of eternity admits of no beginning or end.

> If, coerced by the logic of the position, one chose to deny this, then surely one would have to suppose that man has always existed in the risen state, in an eternity without beginning. But this view would abolish all serious anthropology. It would fall, in fact, into a caricature of that Platonism which is supposed to be its principal enemy.[22]

Of course, this raises issues beyond merely our own personal history. Again, as Ratzinger notes: 'How can history be, at one point (other than God!) already at its end, when in reality it is still unfolding? ... What future can history and the cosmos expect? Will they ever come to their fulfilled wholeness, or will an everlasting duality separate time from an eternity that time can never reach?'[23] In fact, Lohfink had attempted to deal with precisely this point – as Ratzinger acknowledges – with his adaptation of the concept of *aevum,* a medieval notion of time beyond time developed in the context of angelic existence.[24] More recently, Dermot Lane has attempted a modified concept

---

[21] Ibid. pp. 108, 109.

[22] Ibid. pp. 109–10.

[23] Ibid. p. 253.

[24] Ibid. p. 110. Karl Rahner was critical of the concept of *aevum* or similar ideas, saying they smacked of mythology. And he argued: 'Do they not blur what is really a radical difference – the radical difference between, on the one hand, a temporal state which is not merely our experience of time in the sense of physics, but which has freedom as its very essence; and on the other hand, the final consummation of the history of freedom which can then no longer be thought of in terms of time at all?' For Rahner the intermediate state – or even those immediate resurrection positions such as Lohfink's which tried to adopt a temporal concept after death –

of resurrection in death, proposing an individual resurrection in death, but one which is as yet incomplete until the second coming of Christ and the general resurrection.

> The Christian who undergoes individual resurrection in death continues to retain a relationship with the pilgrim people of God on earth and indeed with the creation itself. It is this underlying relationship which is completed and transformed in the general resurrection of the dead at the end of time in the *Parousia*.[25]

Lane claims that this proposal has a number of advantages. With its emphasis on the incomplete nature of the individual's resurrection in death it accommodates something akin to the intermediate state of classical eschatology. Similarly, it takes into account the International Theological Commission's concern that the future character of parousia be given sufficient attention in any theological speculation. However, unlike the classical formulation, it avoids any necessity of speaking about a subsisting soul and thus falling foul of any charge of anthropological dualism.[26] 'Furthermore,' Lane notes, 'it places the risen Christ at the centre of individual and collective eschatology and in doing so recovers the essential mediating role of Christ in the beatific vision.'[27] Whilst Lane's position is

---

raised serious questions concerning the important distinction between our freedom in time and our death as entry into a definitive state and the moment of our final consummation. See K. Rahner, 'The Intermediate State', p. 119.

25 Dermot Lane, *Keeping Hope Alive*, p. 159.

26 Cf. ibid. pp. 154–9. Peter Phan notes of the International Theological Commission's document, *Some Current Questions in Eschatology*, that it 'strongly rejects the recent theory of resurrection at the moment of death. While sympathetic to its aversion to Platonic dualism, it argues that the theory does not do justice to the *future* character of Christ's parousia with which the resurrection is professed to occur simultaneously. Violence is done to the New Testament texts, the document maintains, if Christ's parousia is interpreted as a permanent event consisting in the individual's encounter with the Lord in his or her death.' Peter Phan, 'Current Theology', pp. 509–10.

27 Dermot Lane, *Keeping Hope Alive*, p. 154.

an interesting attempt to reconcile what he identifies as two distinct resurrection traditions in the Pauline corpus[28] and, indeed, to find a compromise between the classical formulation and modern anthropology, nevertheless he fails to answer sufficiently Ratzinger's critique of the corporeal dimension to Christian hope. When we witness a body decomposing in death and yet affirm that it is raised, what exactly are we saying? And furthermore, how can any such resurrection in death be reconciled with the Church's prayer for the dead?[29] For, as Ratzinger points out, 'To be sure, one can bring the believer to

---

[28] 'How then are we to reconcile two apparently different traditions in Paul?' Lane asks. 'Must we collapse the biblical tradition about individual resurrection at the time of death into the tradition about the general resurrection at the end of time as classical eschatology seems to do, or must we conflate the tradition about the general resurrection of the dead at the end of time into "resurrection at death" as some modern German theologians have done? Is it perhaps possible to retain what is of value in these two traditions by introducing some additional important distinctions?' Ibid. p. 158. For his exegesis of Pauline texts see ibid. pp. 154–8.

[29] Karl Rahner attempted to deal with this problem of the *lex orandi*: 'Of course numerous objections can be raised … with the help of Scripture and tradition. There seem to be texts enough in which matter is described in such a way that there would seem to be an intermediate state of this kind – texts which in no way reckon with the possibility that the human body, too, could already be glorified at death. But, as we have already said, do these texts really intend to expound an intermediate state as a truth binding on faith? Or do they merely presuppose it because at the time when they were formulated, in the aftermath of Platonism and under the influence of a naively empirical view of the corpse and the grave, nothing else could be said with regard to what they had to expound clearly as being a genuine part of actual Christian faith?' See Rahner, 'The Intermediate State', p. 123. On the specific issue of prayer for the dead, Hans Küng argued: 'Prayer for the dead should not be a life-long prayer lacking deep faith (or going to the expense of Masses for the "holy souls") for individual souls in purgatory; nor should it be a scarcely understandable prayer "with" and "to" the dead. It is certainly appropriate to pray for the *dying*, while reverently and lovingly keeping alive the memory of *those who have died*, commending them to God's mercy, in the living hope that the dead are finally with God. *Requiescant in pace!* May they rest in peace!' See Küng, *Eternal Life?*, pp. 172–3.

the conclusion that there is no immortality of the soul. But no preaching idiom will ever make him understand that his dead friend is, *by that very fact,* risen from the dead.' Such ideas are, he says, 'A typical exercise of *lingua docta,* the language of academics with a historical theory on the brain. It is not a possible expression of the common, and commonly understood, faith.'[30] In other words, the *lex credendi* no longer seems connected with the *lex orandi.*

It is significant, I believe, that Lewis pre-empted many of these reservations. As I have already shown, C. S. Lewis dealt head on with the issues of immortality, the meaning of death, concepts of time, prayer for the dead, the relationship between body and soul, and the nature of our resurrection. And I have pointed out that Lewis was no atemporalist. 'The question is not whether the dead are part of timeless reality,' he noted, 'the question is whether they share the divine perspective of timelessness.'[31] Whether Lewis held to a theory of resurrection in death is perhaps another matter. However, in a letter dated 5 August 1960 he wrote, 'I believe in the resurrection ... but the state of the dead *till* the resurrection is unimaginable.'[32] And in *Letters to Malcolm* he expanded his position: 'I don't say the resurrection of this body will happen at once. It may well be that this part of us sleeps in death and the intellectual soul is sent to Lenten lands where she fasts in naked spirituality – a ghostlike and imperfectly human condition.'[33] This idea of the intermediate state as some kind of naked, spiritual fast is quite at odds with the affirmation of *Benedictus Deus* that the saved and purified soul enjoys beatific vision prior to the general resurrection. However, the suggestion of it being a ghostly and imperfectly human condition is perhaps an important one if we are not to succumb to a thor-

---

[30] J. Ratzinger, *Eschatology,* p. 254. The International Theological Commission made a similar point when it argued: 'Pastoral experience shows us that the Christian people are greatly perplexed when they hear sermons affirming that the dead person has already risen while his corpse is still buried.' ITC, 'Some Current Questions in Eschatology', p. 217.

[31] *Letters to Malcolm,* p. 106 (Letter 20).

[32] *Collected Letters,* p. 491 (Letter dated 5 August 1960).

[33] *Letters to Malcolm,* p. 117 (Letter 22).

oughly dualist anthropology, in which immortality of the soul takes preference over resurrection of the body. Elsewhere, in *The Great Divorce*, Lewis' imagery is powerfully corporeal – with its comparison between the ghost-like figures from hell's grey town and the bright and beautiful bodies of the saints – and it might be tempting to misinterpret this as Lewis postulating some kind of immediate resurrection. But here it needs to be remembered that Lewis was not attempting a detailed description of life after death. He was making an eschatological point about freedom and moral choice. And he was taking the opportunity to reiterate once again – this time in dramatic depiction – his familiar dogma that 'The ultimate spiritual reality is not vaguer, more inert, more transparent than the images, but more positive, more dynamic, more opaque. ... If we must have a mental picture to symbolise Spirit, we should represent it as something *heavier* than matter.'[34] Earlier I noted that, with his understanding of sin and death, Lewis opened himself up to a possible charge of dualism. It is interesting that Joseph Ratzinger has pinpointed the crux of the whole intermediate state discussion as to be derived from 'the fear, reaching almost panic proportions, of any accusation of dualism'.[35] Of course, any legitimate accusation of dualism against Lewis can only come from an overly scrupulous examination of one or two of his images. Overall his position seems entirely in tune with the Council of Vienna.[36] What Lewis had attempted to present was man as a 'composite being' who, because of the Fall and sin, experiences in himself a dualism,

---

[34] Ibid. pp. 95–6.

[35] J. Ratzinger, *Eschatology*, p. 250.

[36] Neuner and Dupuis have commented of this Council: 'There is, however, a deeper meaning in the doctrine of the Council: the spiritualistic movements [e.g. the "Spiritual" Franciscans who followed Peter John Olivi] tended to separate the spirit from the realities of nature and history and so split the human nature into two heterogeneous spheres. The Council doctrine affirming that the spiritual soul is by itself also the principle of organic life is a strong assertion of the unity of the person.' See J. Neuner and J. Dupuis, *The Christian Faith*, p. 164 (n. 404).

or a 'state of war', between his body and soul.[37] But this dualism was never our natural or intended state. Lewis perceived that the disruptive effects of sin had consequences beyond our relationship with God, and even our relationships with one another and with the rest of creation. Sin affects our very own make up. And this disruption extends into death itself. A difficulty with the atemporal eschatology – or with modern-day applications of the notion of resurrection in death such as that of Dermot Lane's – is that by stressing too strict a monism in human anthropology they unwittingly strip death of some of its force. For Lewis, the fragmentation and dualism caused by the Fall, and felt in the tensions between spirit and nature in human experience, ultimately leads to a fragmentation of the whole human being in death. Death, then, is truly a consequence of sin. As the International Theological Commission put it in 1992: 'Death intrinsically tears people asunder. Indeed, since the person is not the soul alone, but the body and soul united, death affects the person.'[38]

---

[37] Cf. *Miracles*, 132–3. Vatican II made the same point: 'Man, though made of body and soul, is a unity ... Nevertheless man has been wounded by sin. He finds by experience that his body is in revolt.' Vatican II, *Gaudium et Spes*, 14. The International Theological Commission preferred to speak of a duality of body and soul in Christian anthropology rather than a dualism, to avoid any confusion with neo-Platonic notions that would undermine the Christian doctrines of the immortality of the soul and the resurrection of the body. Similarly the Commission took up St Augustine and St Thomas' understanding that, precisely because the human being is *not* to be wholly identified as pure soul, the soul separated in death has an 'appetite for the body or for the resurrection'. Cf. ITC, 'Some Current Questions in Eschatology', pp. 224–5; St Augustine, *The Literal Meaning of Genesis*, pp. 12, 35; and St Thomas, *Super primam epistolam ad Corinthios*, c. 15, lectio 2, n. 924.

[38] ITC, 'Some Current Questions in Eschatology', p. 226. Peter Phan argues that this statement by the International Theological Commission still 'fails to elaborate how the soul is truly affected by death, short of ceasing to exist'. He goes on to say: 'It would seem that the Commission is still operating with the understanding of death as separation of the soul from the body and appears to be unaware that such a description of death, though legitimate in its emphasis on the immortality of the soul, is seriously inadequate in

A criticism of Ratzinger's own critique of the theory of resurrection in death might be that he takes too physicalist an approach. As Lewis noted in *Letters to Malcolm*, 'The old picture of the soul reassuming the corpse – perhaps blown to bits or long since usefully dissipated through nature – is absurd.'[39] This 'old picture', of course, has long been debated, finding considerable discussion even amongst the patristic Fathers as to what St Paul had meant by his distinction between the 'psychic' body and the 'pneumatic' body (Cf. 1 Corinthians 15:42–9). For example, it was Origen who, in an attempt to respond to both a 'crude literalism' on the one hand and 'the perverse spiritualism of the Gnostics and Manichees'[40] on the other, proposed an understanding of resurrection in which the *eidos* of the body rose from death rather than the physical particles of which it had once been composed. The Alexandrian's position was quite subtle and therefore subsequently misunderstood by Methodius, who condemned it as being a denial of the Christian doctrine of resurrection in favour of a some kind of Platonic concept of the immortality of the soul. Methodius, it seems, had taken Origen's concept of *eidos* literally and supposed he meant only the form or shape of the body being reunited with the soul.[41]

---

describing death as a *human* event.' Phan, 'Current Theology', 519. It seems to me that Phan here has fallen foul of his own charge of dualism, with his insistence that death must affect *both* the body and the soul. Death affects the *human person* through the tearing asunder of body and soul.

[39] *Letters to Malcolm*, p. 115 (Letter 22).

[40] J. N. D. Kelly, *Early Christian Doctrines*, p. 471.

[41] For example, *De resurrectione*, 3, 12 in *Translations of the Writings of the Fathers: Down to AD 325*, Volume XIV: *The Writings of Methodius, Etc.*, ed. Alexander Roberts and James Donaldson, p. 168: 'Origen therefore thinks that the same flesh will not be restored to the soul, but that the form of each, according to the appearance by which the flesh is not distinguished, shall arise stamped upon another spiritual body; so that everyone will again appear the same in form; and that this is the resurrection which is promised. For, he says, the material body being fluid, and in no wise remaining in itself, but wearing out and being replaced around the appearance by which its shape is distinguished, and by which the

In fact, Origen argued that the *eidos* represented our bodily identity, retained despite the changes made in our 'material substratum' which he understood as being 'in a state of constant flux'.[42] As Kelly explains:

> The development of a man from childhood to age is an illustration, for his body is identically the same throughout despite its complete physical transformation; and the historical Jesus provides another, since His body could at one time be described as without form or comeliness (Isaiah 53:2), whilst at another it was clothed with the splendour of the Transfiguration.[43]

---

figure is contained, it is necessary that the resurrection should be only that of the form.' Mark Edwards is at pains to show that, for all Methodius' later detractions, Origen *did* believe in a resurrection of the body. 'The hope of some continuance or revival of the body after death is expressed in works by Origen which need not be read through a Latin mediator. In the *Contra Celsum*, if anywhere, he might have been expected to disguise this Pauline stumbling-block; yet in fact he rather insists that it is faith in a corporeal resurrection that sets apart the Christian from the Greek (v. 18-19). Even in the treatise which Methodius quoted as proof of his injustice to the body [Cf. Origen, *De principiis*, 2, 10, 2 and Methodius, De resurrectione, 25, 2], he declares that it does not entirely perish, but transfers its form or *eidos* to the soul. Methodius takes his adversary to mean that the soul retains a mere appearance of the body without its underlying matter. Even if this thesis is coherent, it cannot be that of Origen, who defends the transformation of the body as the effect of God's authority over matter.' See Mark Edwards, 'Origen's Two Resurrections', in *The Journal of Theological Studies*, pp. 503–4.

[42] Cf. Origen, *De Principiis*, 2, 2, 1 and 3, 6, 1-6. For example, *De principiis*, 3, 6, 5 in *Origen on First Principles*, p. 251: 'Our flesh indeed is considered by the uneducated and by unbelievers to perish so completely after death that nothing whatever of its substance is left. We, however, who believe in its resurrection, know that death only causes a change in it and that its substance certainly persists and is restored to life again at a definite time by the will of its Creator.'

[43] J. N. D. Kelly, *Early Christian Doctrines*, p. 471.

Methodius, however, opted for a radically more literalist interpretation, based on his belief that Christ's glorified body was in
every sense – flesh and bones included – identifiable with his
earthly one.[44] Although our 'resurrected bodies will indeed
have heightened qualities', he believed, nevertheless they will
be 'materially identical with our present earthly bodies'.[45]
Methodius countered any objections concerning the loss over
time of the body's putrefied remains with an appeal to the
omnipotence of God. It seems to me that there are problems
with both positions. In modern terms we might say that whilst
Origen was proposing something akin to a resurrection of our
DNA, Methodius postulated a resuscitated corpse with special
powers, overlooking the fact that the molecules and atoms of
which our bodies are composed now have, at some stage, been
the basic building materials of many likely forebears and will be
for many more future progenies. In this last respect Anton Van
der Walle rather forcefully states the case:

> In earlier centuries, when people still had no awareness
> of the enormous extension of the human race in space
> and time and could think on a relatively small scale, such
> conceptions were evidently still acceptable. Today,
> however, things are quite different. When we realize that
> so far approximately seventy-seven thousand million
> human beings have lived and that countless millions more
> are still to be expected ... then any conception of a resur-
> rection of the body at the end of time, coupled with some
> thought of material identity, is sheer nonsense.[46]

Whereas it is true to say that the positions taken by Origen and
Methodius in some way marked the boundaries for subsequent
patristic debate, it ought to be observed that more elements of
Methodius' literalism found their way into later theology than

---

[44] Methodius, *De resurrectione*, pp. 3, 12–14.
[45] Kelly, *Early Christian Doctrines*, p. 476. Cf. Methodius, *De resurrectione*, 3, 16. For a good exposition of Methodius' thought and
rejection of Origen see Brian Daley, *The Hope of the Early Church: A
Handbook of Patristic Eschatology*, pp. 62–4.
[46] Anton Van der Walle, *From Darkness to the Dawn*, p. 26.

Origen's use of *eidos*.[47] Interestingly, however, contemporary eschatology has moved further away from Methodius' literalist line and, whilst not adopting Origen as such, has endeavoured to come to what it views as a more realistic and acceptable understanding of the spiritual body.[48] For example, Van der Walle – unsurprisingly given his view as expressed above – insists, 'Resurrection has nothing to do with corpses. Corpses do not come to life again at the resurrection. Resurrection is not resuscitation.'[49] It is probably safe to say that most modern theologians would agree with such a statement. As Karl Rahner noted in 1981:

> Probably no metaphysically thinking theologian would continue to maintain today (for either philosophical or theological reasons) that the identity of the glorified body and the earthly body is only ensured if some material fragment of the earthly body is found again in the glorified body.[50]

[47] For example, J. N. D. Kelly notes, 'For Augustine the resurrection of all men at the last day is an undoubted dogma of the Christian faith; and he is convinced that "this identical flesh will be raised which is buried, which dies, which is seen and touched, which must eat and drink if it is to go on existing, which is sick and subject to pain." ... His interpretation of the Apostle's promise that the risen body will be spiritual is, not that its substance will have undergone change, but that it will be in complete subjection to the spirit, and will thus rise superior to all sluggishness, weakness and pain.' See Kelly, *Early Christian Doctrines*, pp. 478–9.

[48] The International Theological Commission has noted: 'It is a novelty in the history of this dogma [i.e. the resurrection of the body] (novel at least since the overcoming of the tendency which appeared in the second century under Gnostic influence) that this realistic presentation should be subjected to criticism by some theologians in our day. To them the traditional representation of the resurrection seems too crude. In particular (they believe) that the too physicalist descriptions of the resurrection event raise a difficulty. Because of this they seek refuge in a certain kind of spiritualised explanation. And for this they demand a new kind of interpretation of the traditional affirmations about the resurrection.' See ITC, 'Some Current Questions in Eschatology', p. 215.

[49] Anton Van der Walle, *From Darkness to the Dawn*, p. 172.

[50] Karl Rahner, 'The Intermediate State', p. 120.

Indeed, the International Theological Commission itself has noted that the 'Church has never taught that the very same matter is required for the body to be said to be the same'.[51] But Van der Walle appears to want to go further.

> By bodily resurrection I mean resurrection or glorification of the person, of the human being *qua* human being ... So we are no longer talking of a disembodied soul which after death of the body is admitted to the blessed vision of God, but of a human being who at death is glorified by God in every respect of his or her humanity.[52]

For Van der Walle, then, it seems that Ratzinger's complaint against a theory of resurrection in death – that the decaying corpse is still to be seen – is something of a red herring. The material body is *not* the human being just as the idea of a bodiless soul awaiting its restoration of matter is equally as unlikely. Similarly, Hans Küng has argued: 'What is at stake here is not the continuity of my body as a physical entity, and subsequently scientific questions like those about the whereabouts of the molecules simply do not arise. What matters is the identity of the person.'[53] Likewise even Karl Rahner was sceptical of what he perceived to be an overly physicalist approach. 'For us, identity consists, now and in the future, of the free, spiritual, subject, which we call "soul",' he suggested. 'That is why even empirical experience of the corpse in the grave can no longer provide an argument for there having been no "resurrection".'[54] However, as the International Theological Commission has pointed out, in the Eleventh Council of Toledo (in 675) the Church has clearly rejected any view of resurrection that 'takes place "in flesh without the substance or any other kind of flesh".' Faith, it notes, refers to a 'resurrection in "the very same flesh in which we live, in which we subsist, and in which we move".' The Commission went on,

---

[51] ITC, 'Some Current Questions in Eschatology', p. 216.
[52] Anton Van der Walle, *From Darkness to the Dawn*, p. 173.
[53] Hans Küng, *Eternal Life?*, p. 139.
[54] Karl Rahner, 'The Intermediate State', p. 120.

Realism must be maintained in such a way that it does not exclude the transformation of the bodies of those living on earth into glorified bodies. But an ethereal body, which would be a new kind of creation, would not correspond to the reality of the resurrection of Christ and consequently would pertain to the realm of fables.[55]

Van der Walle and Küng have both argued that this realism can be accommodated provided we move away from an anthropology that identifies the human being in terms of body and soul. 'The dead live,' Van der Walle asserts, 'as the same people that they were before their death.' And this, he acknowledges, implies a bodily resurrection. But, like Küng, he goes on:

It is not a question of reincarnation, nor of the resuscitation of a body, but of the recreation of a human being who has realized his or her humanity in and through an essential corporeality, with all that this implies in terms of mutual relationships with everything and everyone in the universe. The body rises in humanized form, not in its material character, its extent, but precisely to the degree in which it is human, a self-possession, a self-realization.[56]

---

[55] ITC, 'Some Current Questions in Eschatology', p. 214.

[56] Anton Van der Walle, *From Darkness to the Dawn*, p. 190. Cf. Hans Küng, *Eternal Life?*, p. 139: 'Is it then a *bodily resurrection*, a raising up of man with his body? Yes and No. No, if we understand "body" in physiological terms as this actual body, the "corpse", the "remains", Yes, if "body" is understood in the New Testament sense as "soma", not so much physiologically as personally: as the identical personal reality, the same self with its entire history ... When we talk of the resurrection of the body, we mean then, as the Catholic theologian Franz Josef Nocke expresses it, "that not only man's naked self is saved through death, when all earthly history is left behind, all relationships with other human beings become meaningless; bodily resurrection means that a person's life-history and all the relationships established in the course of this history enter together into the consummation and finally belong to the risen person." Cf. also Franz Nocke, *Eschatologie*, (Düsseldorf, 1982), p. 123.

Nevertheless, it seems to me that the Council Fathers at Vatican II *were* keen to affirm a material component as essential to our corporeal relationship with all around us and for our risen life. As they put it:

> Through his very bodily condition [man] sums up in himself the unity of the material world. Through him they are thus brought to their highest perfection and can raise their voice in praise freely given to the creator. For this reason man may not despise his bodily life. Rather he is obliged to regard his body as good and to hold it in honor since God has created it and will raise it up on the last day.[57]

It seems strange to me for theology to assert this corporeal identity with the material world around us and then, when speaking of resurrection, to argue that the material nature is no longer quite so significant. But, as Peter Phan asks the question, 'What makes the body real? Blood and bones? Matter-energy? The individual's history of self-determination in freedom in and through the body?' Furthermore, to what extent are Scripture and theological tradition's emphasis on the resurrection of the *flesh* pertinent and binding, given our modern scientific insights into anthropology and matter. As Phan puts it,

> Even if it is determined that biblical, patristic, and conciliar authors do intend by 'body' the physiological entity as such, it still remains to be settled whether this intended sense necessarily belongs to the revealed message, since it may be part of a more naïve and prescientific worldview in which the message was formulated, and not the message itself.[58]

---

[57] *Gaudium et Spes*, p. 14. What makes this statement even less prone to an interpretation that could accommodate Van der Walle or Küng's position, or, indeed, any other theologian who seeks to downplay the material component in the corporeal dimension of resurrection is that the Council Fathers were explicitly affirming here an anthropology which spoke of man as being the unity of body and soul.

[58] Peter Phan, 'Current Theology', p. 522.

For myself, I still hold certain reservations over the position as put by Van der Walle. It seems to me that an interpretation of resurrection has been adopted for reasons of contemporary anthropology at the expense of a key piece of biblical data and against the prayer of the Church. If the material body – the corpse – plays no part in resurrection whatsoever, why then do the Gospels stress the empty tomb?[59] As Peter Phan has accepted, commenting on the position of the International Theological Commission's 1992 document, our 'interpretation of the resurrection of the dead must be based on our knowledge of the resurrection of Christ'.[60] And our knowledge of Christ's resurrection emphasises an empty tomb and the fact that Jesus' earthly body was not allowed to decay in a grave

[59] Hans Küng, in fact, plays down the significance of the empty tomb in the New Testament, arguing: 'It was not by the empty tomb, but by the "appearances" or "revelations" ... that Jesus's disciples came to believe in his resurrection to eternal life. The controversy about the empty tomb is therefore an unreal controversy. Even critical exegetes allow for the possibility that the tomb might have been empty. But what does that prove? An empty tomb is not as such a proof of resurrection. There are many explanations of it and even the evangelists mention a number of "possibilities" when opposing tendentious Jewish rumours, such as deception by the disciples, theft of the corpse, confusion in regard to the body, sham death. Which means that the empty tomb has no more to say than "he is not here". To this must be added expressly – what is by no means obvious – "he is risen".' See Küng, *Eternal Life?*, p. 131. Whilst I wholeheartedly agree with Küng's point that the empty tomb *without* the "appearances" is at worst meaningless and at best ambiguous, nevertheless I fundamentally disagree with his assertion that the empty tomb controversy 'is therefore an unreal controversy'. It was a very real controversy for the Early Church – and, indeed, for the disciples – or why else would the evangelists have made such a point of it and bother to delineate the 'tendentious Jewish rumours'? And it has a theological importance in that it dramatically demonstrates that the transformation – or glorification – of the whole person in resurrection affects precisely the *whole* person: God does not leave Jesus' corpse to rot in a tomb.

[60] This is because, 'Since eschatological assertions do not refer merely to the future but also to realities that have already occurred in Christ, made evident in his resurrection, the first principle of hermeneutics of eschatological assertions requires that we

after his resurrection. Again, if our material bodies in death play no part in resurrection, why, then, do we have a cult of relics? It is one thing to affirm – as did Lewis – that resurrection is not resuscitation but it is quite another to insist upon a complete discontinuity with the material body. Ratzinger's claim that such modern interpretations of resurrection in death are little more than a camouflaged return to a doctrine of the immortality, at first appearing perhaps a little simplistic and even possibly polemical, may well now stand.

At one stage Lewis seemed to approach a position very similar to Van der Walle and Küng. In *The Four Loves* he described the resurrection of the body in terms of 'what may be called our "greater body"; the general fabric of our earthly life with its affections and relationships.'[61] Later, in *Letters to Malcolm*, he postulated:

> We are not, in this doctrine, concerned with matter as such at all: with waves and atoms and all that. What the soul cries out for is the resurrection of the senses. Even in this life matter would be nothing to us if it were not the source of sensations.[62]

Thus he suggested that the glorified body might be conceived of as somehow 'inside the soul' – that 'in entering our soul as alone it can enter – that is, by being perceived and known – matter has turned into soul'.[63] It is important here to take Lewis' comments alongside what he said elsewhere, thus providing an essential balance to his thought. Certainly in *Reflections on the Psalms* he was keen to stress the corporeality of human existence, even in Hellenistic thought. As he noted of Homer's *Iliad*, 'It is the body, even the dead body which is the man himself; the ghost is only a sort of reflection or echo.'[64] In

fully accept truths which God, who has knowledge of the future, has revealed to us.' Cf. Peter Phan, 'Current Theology', pp. 509, 513 and ITC, 'Some Current Questions in Eschatology', p. 215.
61 *The Four Loves*, p. 130.
62 *Letters to Malcolm* p. 115 (Letter 22).
63 Ibid. pp. 116, 117 (Letter 22).
64 *Reflections on the Psalms*, p. 32.

Miracles he again stressed a corporeal dimension to resurrection when he affirmed, 'Those who attain the glorious resurrection will see the dry bones clothed again with flesh, the fact and the myth remarried, the literal and the metaphorical rushing together.'[65] And in 'Transposition' he re-stated what is essentially the classical Pauline approach: 'How far this the life of the risen man will be sensory, we do not know. But I surmise that it will differ ... not as emptiness differs from water or water from wine, but as a flower differs from a bulb.'[66] Furthermore, in a handwritten addition to the original manuscript for *Letters to Malcolm,* Lewis wrote:

> The old whimsical picture of the ghost returning to the long-forgotten grave and 'putting on' the body – stepping into your feet as if they were shoes and resuming you hands like gloves – is in one way not so wide of the mark. The soul will come back from the long Lent of her disembodiment and resume ... the riches of which penal and corrective death deprived her.[67]

Although he later crossed out this paragraph and did not intend its inclusion in the final publication, nevertheless it gives a clue to Lewis' overall thinking in this area. Elsewhere Lewis acknowledged the essential mystery that pertains to the doctrine. As he concluded in *A Grief Observed,* 'There is also, whatever it means, the resurrection of the body. We cannot understand. The best is perhaps what we understand least.'[68] And in a letter dated 8 September 1959, he stated, 'No one, I presume, can imagine life in the glorified body. ... Lor,' bless us, I can picture very few of the things I believe in.'[69] In my assessment, *The Four Loves* and *Letters to Malcolm* (published in 1960 and 1964 respectively), were simply attempts – perhaps

---

[65]   *Miracles*, p. 170.
[66]   Cf. 'Transposition', p. 84 and 1 Co 15:42–4.
[67]   Cf. Original manuscript and corrections of C. S. Lewis, *Letters to Malcolm: Chiefly on Prayer* held at the Bodleian Library, Oxford (Dep. d. 808).
[68]   *A Grief Observed*, p. 64.
[69]   *Collected Letters*, p. 482 (Letter dated 8 September 1959).

rather weak ones – to move away from a crude literalism and make the doctrine credible. For, as Lewis noted in a letter to an American lady written in 1962 and explaining his position over a likely animal eschatology, 'These particular guesses arise in me, I trust, from taking seriously the resurrection of the body: a doctrine which now-a-days is very soft pedalled by nearly all the faithful – to our great impoverishment.'[70] An attempt, then, to struggle with the mystery and indeed, 'Guesses, of course, only guesses,' as he again admitted at the end of *Letters to Malcolm.* My own preference in this matter is not to guess. But then, as Lewis himself concluded, 'If they are not true, something better will be. For we know that we shall be made like Him, for we shall see Him as He is.'[71]

The Range of Hope

Perhaps a more significant trend than this debate concerning the intermediate state and the resurrection of the body – at least in recent eschatology – has been the re-emergence of a theology of hope. Zachary Hayes makes the point: 'For many of our contemporaries, the word "hope" is associated with a sort of romantic inability to see and to deal with the pain and tragedy of human experience.'[72] The fundamental distinction of Christian hope is that it is made precisely in the light of such pain and tragedy. It is, as Dermot Lane powerfully argues in his book, *Keeping Hope Alive,* above all in the reality of the crucified and risen Christ that the shape of the future is prefigured. As he says:

---

[70] *Letters to an American Lady,* p. 110 (Letter dated 26 November 1962).

[71] *Letters to Malcolm,* p. 118 (Letter 22).

[72] Zachary Hayes, *Visions of a Future,* p. 22. John Polkinghorne defines hope as 'the negation both of Promethean presumption, which supposes that fulfilment is always potentially there, ready for human grasping, and also of despair, which supposes that there will never be fulfilment, but only a succession of broken dreams. Hope is quite distinct also from a utopian myth of progress, which privileges the future over the past, seeing the ills and frustrations of earlier generations as being no more than necessary stepping stones to better things in prospect.' John Polkinghorne, *The God of Hope and the End of the World,* p. 94.

Some contemporary eschatologies, especially those of the 1960s and 1970s, did not take sufficient account of the Cross; in retrospect some of these eschatologies now appear too sunny and optimistic – they did not face realistically the elements of tragedy and failure, suffering and death that are an intrinsic part of the human condition.[73]

Over forty years ago now, notes Zachary Hayes, Yves Congar pointed to what he saw as the beginnings of a shift in eschatology from an approach 'largely concerned with depicting the last events of history and the geography of the world beyond this one' to one understood 'principally in terms of the fulfilment of God's creative intent in humanity and in the world of God's creation'.[74] That shift has now for the most part been completed and with it has arisen a major area of tension within eschatological debate: the tension between a this-worldly theology and an other-worldly one. Michael Scanlon has helpfully sketched out the broad history of this debate in his article on hope in *The New Dictionary of Theology*. With the collapse of the Roman Empire in the fifth century and the realisation that the existing theological connections between eschatological hope and historical events were perhaps overly simplistic, Christianity found itself faced with the task of needing to be 'extricated from the fortunes and misfortunes of political arrangements'. This, argues Scanlon, was to be 'the task and the accomplishment of Augustine of Hippo'.

To protect Christian hope from the vicissitudes of historical progress and decline, Augustine both individualized and de-historicized its meaning. Hope is the personal hope for heaven after death. This Augustinian eschatology has been identical with doctrinal orthodoxy until its recent modification by a new understanding of the relation between time and eternity.[75]

---

[73] Dermot Lane, *Keeping Hope Alive*, p. 19.
[74] Zachary Hayes, *Visions of a Future*, p. 69.
[75] Michael Scanlon, 'Hope', p. 495.

With Augustine, then, hope during history is 'hope *for* eternity, a higher place of perfection above and beyond history. Such hope begets patience on earth as it focuses on heaven as its ultimate satisfaction'.[76] However, in recent times – and in particular due to the influence of the critique of the Marxist philosopher Ernst Bloch and a revival, or at least revision, of something of the approach of Joachim of Fiore[77] – theology has undergone 'something momentous'.

The centripetal ecclesiology of Augustine wherein the Church is a vessel of salvation for its members has given way to the centrifugal ecclesiology congenial to Joachim wherein the Church is 'the universal sacrament of salva-

[76] Ibid. p. 496.

[77] Joachim of Fiore was a visionary in the late twelfth century who described history in trinitarian stages. The 'age of the Son' had superseded the 'age of the Father' but this in turn was to be superseded by an 'age of the Spirit'. The implications of this idea undermine the definitive action of Christ in history and his role as mediator. As Scanlon notes, 'In his trinitarian teaching on the *Filioque* Augustine had intensified the Pauline connection between Christ and the Spirit. As the Spirit *of Christ,* the Holy Spirit is the divine power whereby God's redeeming work in Christ is appropriated by the Christian – the Spirit is not the principle of unmediated freedom granting direct access to God in a new age transcending Christ.' Of the influence of Joachim in Ernst Bloch's work, Scanlon comments: 'Although driven underground, the historicized hope of the Joachimite vision became a potent, if indirect, force in the subsequent history of revolutionary thought in the west ... For the "modern history of freedom" (the tradition of thought on the philosophy of history from Kant to Marx) it mediated the understanding (ultimately biblical) of reality *as history.* Because historicized, the Joachimite vision of hope was readily secularised in ideologies of immanent progress in history. For the twentieth century revisionist Marxist philosopher, Ernst Bloch, Joachimitism symbolised the authentic interpretation of the Judeo-Christian tradition as a powerfully evocative vision of utopia. Joachimite Christianity states the religious dream for a better tomorrow – Joachimitism demystified is authentic Marxism. Bloch indeed has become a catalyst for the retrieval of interest in Joachim.' See Michael Scanlon, 'Hope', p. 496. Cf. Ernst Bloch, *The Principle of Hope,* pp. 509–15.

tion' (LG48) ... Traditional hope for heaven has become
hope for earth. Other-worldly dualism has yielded to an
historicization of the Christian tradition.[78]

The International Theological Commission has highlighted
one of the consequences of this shift with regards to eschatology, suggesting that the 'rebirth of the tendency to establish an
innerworldly eschatology' has led to a silence or 'theological
obscurity' concerning the Last Things. It goes on:

> This tendency is well known in the history of theology,
> and beginning with the Middle Ages it constituted what
> came to be called 'the spiritual heritage of Joachim de
> Fiore'. This tendency is found in some theologians of
> liberation, who so insist on the importance of establishing
> the kingdom of God as something within our own history
> on earth that the salvation which transcends history seems
> to become of rather secondary interest.[79]

Thus Scanlon observes that to the question, 'What can we hope
for?' traditional Christians would answer, 'Eternal life after
death for the purified soul', while progressive Christians would
make the proviso: 'Yes, ultimately eternal life, but penulti-
mately a more just, more peaceful world order.'[80] Underlying
these answers are an implicit position on our understanding of
God in his relation to history and our appreciation of both
future and realised eschatology. As Dermot Lane has observed:
'If we operate with an image of God as absolutely transcendent,
then our eschatology will tend to be other-worldly. Likewise if
we understand the mystery of God solely as immanent, then our
eschatology will be principally this-worldly in orientation.'[81]

---

78 Michael Scanlon, 'Hope', p. 497.
79 Cf. ITC, 'Some Current Questions in Eschatology', p. 211.
80 Michael Scanlon, 'Hope', p. 497.
81 Dermot Lane, *Keeping Hope Alive*, p. 20. Lane later comments:
    'Christians are divided on how they answer this important ques-
    tion about hope, and most of the division derives from different
    perceptions of eschatology which affect a host of issues within
    practical theology such as the relationship between prayer and

In his own theology, Lane has been keen to take seriously the Marxist critique of religion as being 'the opium of the people'.[82] Ernst Bloch, for example, argued that, while hope is grounded in the difference between what we experience now and the dream of what we can be in the future, only human action in history can overcome this difference. 'Without the strength of an I and we behind it, even hoping becomes insipid,' said Bloch.[83] Thus, as Zachary Hayes explains, if hope is to be authentic for Bloch it must become 'the seed-bed of social revolutions'. Although Christianity's 'initial inspiration' had lain in an 'explosive messianism', nevertheless the Churches of Western Europe, at least, had betrayed such inspiration through 'lip-service and ecclesiastical compromise'.[84] Thus, according to Bloch's analysis, classical Christian eschatology is fraught with a false and fraudulent hope in that it has held up to its believers the promise of another world after death rather than a better one here and now.[85] In the light of such critiques, Lane believes that any coherent eschatological interpretation of experience must affirm the value of 'human actions and social praxis both for this life and the next', and

---

politics, liberation and salvation, the religious and social mission of the Church, and faith and justice. Ultimately these different views of eschatology evolve around the stubborn tension that exists between ... what is often called the elements of the "already" and 'the not yet' of the Christ-event.' See ibid. pp. 123–4.

[82] Cf. ibid. p. 3. Hans Küng asserts that it is Feuerbach's 'projection-theory' that 'provides the foundation, not only for Marx's opium-theory, but also for Freud's illusion-theory'. See Hans Küng, *Eternal Life?*, p. 47. For a good and concise overview of such 'projection-theory' cf. ibid. pp. 38–49.

[83] Bloch continued: 'There is never anything soft about conscious-known hope, but a will within it insists: it should be so, it must become so. The wishful and volitional streak vigorously bursts out within it, the intensive element in venturing beyond, in acts of overhauling.' Ernst Bloch, *The Principle of Hope*, p. 147.

[84] Zachary Hayes, *Visions of a Future*, p. 77.

[85] As Bloch put it: 'Even deception, if it is to be effective, must work with flatteringly and corruptly aroused hope. Which is also why hope is preached from every pulpit, but is confined to mere inwardness or to empty promises of the other world.' Ernst Bloch, *The Principle of Hope*, p. 5.

must have an 'emancipatory thrust' to it.[86] In his response to such a Marxist analysis Lane is by no means alone. As Zachary Hayes has observed: '[The] intellectual encounter between Christians and Marxists provided the occasion for many Christian theologians to develop their eschatological insights more explicitly.' He goes on:

> As early as 1960, K. Rahner had published his widely-influential essay on the interpretation of eschatological statements. J. Moltmann had taken up the provocative thesis of Bloch in his *Theology of Hope* first published in 1965. J. B. Metz and W. Pannenberg, each in his own way, had studied the question of the public and social dimensions of the Christian faith.[87]

Particularly relevant to the shaping of this contemporary debate are the contributions of Wolfhart Pannenberg and Jürgen Moltmann. For Pannenberg, the futurity of the proclamation of God's kingdom is essential to understanding the eschatological implications of Jesus' preaching and teaching. This is not to say that God's rule is 'simply in the future, leaving men to do nothing but wait quietly for its arrival', but rather that in 'Jesus' proclamation of the Kingdom of God that future and present are inextricably interwoven'.[88] In other words, as Zachary Hayes puts it, 'As perceived through the eye of the apocalyptic, human existence reveals a "proleptic structure". By this Pannenberg means that in the human search for meaning, the dynamic of human experience tends to anticipate the future.'[89] Underlying this 'proleptic structure' is Pannenberg's assertion

---

[86] Dermot Lane, *Keeping Hope Alive*, p. 17.

[87] Zachary Hayes, *Visions of a Future*, p. 131.

[88] Wolfhart Pannenberg, *Theology and the Kingdom of God*, p. 53.

[89] Zachary Hayes, *Visions of a Future*, p. 138. As an example of this, Pannenberg argues, 'A characteristic expression of this awareness [of the future] is man's ability to ask questions. Because man is able to distinguish the future from the present, he is ahead of himself and of the existent world. So he is able to dominate that world. It follows from this openness for the future as future that man can participate in the creative dynamic of the divine love.' Wolfhart Pannenberg, *Theology and the Kingdom of God*, p. 68.

that the God of the *coming* kingdom is the God who *is* future.

> If the Kingdom of God and the mode of his existence (power and being) belong together, then the message of the coming Kingdom of God implies that God in his very being is the future of the world. All experience of the future is, at least indirectly, related to God himself. In this case every event in which the future becomes finitely present must be understood as a contingent act of God.[90]

Thus Pannenberg's theology is based upon 'a reversal of the time sequence usually presupposed in notions of causality'.[91] As Hayes puts it, 'Reality is stamped by the future to which it is directed.'[92] Although it is probably fair to say that C. S. Lewis would have had little to do with such theological speculation, it is interesting to note that in *The Great Divorce* there can be found at least one point of contact with Pannenberg's ideas. In his preface, Lewis observed of those who attain heaven, 'It will be true for those who have completed the journey (and for no others) to say that good is everything and Heaven everywhere. But we, at this end of the road, must not try to anticipate that retrospective vision.'[93] This is not dissimilar to Pannenberg's point, where he notes, 'It is true that, from the viewpoint of our finite present, the future is not yet decided ... But ... what turns out to be true in the future will then be evident as having been true all along.'[94] Pannenberg's theology is a positive one, speaking as it does of 'a single future for all events', and thus can be included amongst those attempts of theologians from the 1960s and 70s to overcome the prevalent 'death of God' theology that preceded them.[95] It is, I suspect, one of those

---

[90] Wolfhart Pannenberg, *Theology and the Kingdom of God*, p. 61.
[91] Ibid. p. 70.
[92] Zachary Hayes, *Visions of a Future*, p. 138.
[93] *Great Divorce*, p. 8.
[94] Wolfhart Pannenberg, *Theology and the Kingdom of God*, pp. 62–3.
[95] Ibid. p. 59. Richard Neuhaus, in his preface to *Theology and the Kingdom of God*, observes: 'One promising spring morning in 1968, page one of *The New York Times* brought the news. The "death of God" thing was out. The theology of hope was in. The change was generally welcomed.' Ibid. p. 9.

overly 'sunny and optimistic' theologies of the period that Dermot Lane was marginally critical of in his own work, *Keeping Hope Alive*. 'To speak of the definitive unity of the world,' argues Pannenberg, 'means that events are moving ahead to meet, finally, a common future. In our experience, the existing connection of events and the fact of corporate unities direct us toward the unifying power of the future.'[96] Significantly, however, in terms of the this-worldly/other-worldly tension in contemporary eschatology, Pannenberg's was a move towards a more socially aware eschatology for the here and now. For, as Richard Neuhaus observes,

> In speaking of the future, Pannenberg is not merely accenting a neglected aspect of the Christian tradition, nor is he merely suggesting that the concept of the future should have priority in theological thought, although he would agree with both these contentions ... For Pannenberg, Christian theology cannot be narrowly theological. Theology either illuminates the public understanding of human existence or it has no worthy claim on our attention.[97]

Moltmann, too, emphasises the relationship between the future and the present but, whereas Pannenberg presented a theology in which 'God is understood as the power of the future who in his creative love lets a world be and become by drawing it into communion with himself',[98] Moltmann has taken a more dialectic line. He understands the eschatological category of future not as *futurum* but rather as *adventus*: the coming of Christ that marks the transformation of all things and thus provides the basis for Christian hope.[99] The future, then, promised in the coming of Christ stands over and above history and time. Thus, in fact, Moltmann is rather more apocalyptic in his eschatology than Pannenberg. Nevertheless, the hope

---

[96] Ibid. p. 59.
[97] Ibid. p. 12.
[98] Christoph Schwöbel, 'Last Things First?' p. 229.
[99] Cf. Jürgen Moltmann, *The Coming of God*, pp. 25–6.

that this *adventus* inspires has its own transformative nature. As Moltmann says in *Theology of Hope*: 'The theologian is not concerned merely to supply a different *interpretation* of the world, of history and of human nature, but to *transform* them in expectation of a divine transformation.'[100] As Zachary Hayes describes the position:

> Eschatological preaching, as Moltmann sees it, is a summons to enter into the pain of the suffering Messiah in an attempt to bring humanity to a new level of consciousness and eventually to bring about a new reality for the world.[101]

Hayes further notes that 'Cardinal Ratzinger has taken sharp exception to this approach', believing the entire project to run 'the risk of transforming the Gospel into yet another ideology of the future'. Actually, Ratzinger's position is far more nuanced than Hayes would have us believe. Whilst indeed, in *Eschatology*, he observed that the 'new manifesto'[102] of Moltmann's theology was eventually to lead to, or at least to inspire, the development of various political, liberation, and black theologies, nevertheless he was at pains to point out:

> Moltmann's theological model is so rich and complex that it would be inappropriate to try and weigh it up in terms of those consequences – and even more so to dismiss it hook, line, and sinker by the same token. Besides, in the theologies of liberation and revolution themselves there are here and there gleams of real gold.[103]

Ratzinger's critique of some of the later eschatological approaches that followed Moltmann's work concerned not so much the connection the Lutheran had made between eschato-

---

[100] Jürgen Moltmann, *Theology of Hope*, p. 84.
[101] Zachary Hayes, *Visions of a Future*, pp. 135–6.
[102] Ratzinger wrote: 'The new manifesto ran: put Christianity into practice by transforming the world, using the criterion of hope.' See J. Ratzinger, *Eschatology*, p. 58.
[103] Ibid.

logical hope and Christian praxis, but rather the interpretation of what that praxis might entail. As Ratzinger commented:

> If Christianity is to be interpreted as a strategy of hope, the question naturally arises: But *which* hope? The Kingdom of God, not being itself a political concept, cannot serve as a political criterion by which to construct in direct fashion a program of political action.[104]

Furthermore, he argued that the 'transformation of eschatology into political utopianism involves the emasculation of Christian hope', since, of course, the transformation of human nature necessary to transform the world 'is possible only as a miracle of grace'.[105] Significantly, Moltmann himself – particularly in more recent writings – has been keen to stress the ultimately transcendent nature of the transformative power of God's kingdom. 'With the American Declaration of Independence and the French Revolution of 1789 the age of utopias begins,' says Moltmann, 'utopias of justice and of social equality. Yet the clash between the right to liberty and the claim to equality remained.'[106] Similarly, he observes, 'The dream of the "new world" and the "new age" in world politics, of human rights and human dignity for every man and women, succumbed to the two European world wars of the twentieth century. Auschwitz, Hiroshima and Chernobyl are the names for the end of this messianic dream of the modern world.'[107] Only when such dreams of utopia inevitably come to nothing, argues Moltmann, do we learn the lesson: 'It is impossible to complete history within history.'[108]

---

[104] Ibid.
[105] Ibid. p. 59.
[106] Jürgen Moltmann, 'Is the World Coming to an End?' p. 134.
[107] Ibid. p. 135.
[108] Cf. ibid. On this point C. H. Dodd argued: 'In the supposed law of progress in history [some religious thinkers in the West, and in particular in the UK and America] have seen evidence of the immanent Spirit of God, leading humanity onwards to its goal, which they have identified with the Kingdom of God on earth. This however does not appear to be the view to which the teaching

It would be ridiculous to suggest that Lewis presented his readers with a coherent theology of hope with all the sophistication of, say, a Pannenberg or a Moltmann. Nevertheless, it is true to say that he did consider the tension between this-worldly and other-worldly claims and argued: 'A continual looking forward to the eternal world is not (as some modern people think) a form of escapism, but one of the things a Christian is meant to do.'[109] And he went on:

> It does not mean that we are to leave the present world as it is. If you read history you will find that the Christians who did most for the present world were just those who thought most of next. [110]

Thus Lewis steered a middle course and roundly rejected the Marxist critique of religion. The most inspiring reformers and 'revolutionaries' of Christianity – 'the Apostles themselves, who set foot on the conversion of the Roman Empire, the great men who built up the Middle Ages, the English Evangelicals who abolished the Slave Trade' – were all people, according to Lewis, who 'left their mark on Earth, precisely because their minds were occupied with Heaven'.[111] Neither a purely other-worldly aspiration nor a purely this-worldly praxis is appropriate, believed Lewis, because both positions in their extreme forms undermine the true Christian perspective. As he put it in *Mere Christianity*:

> It is since Christians have largely ceased to think of the other world that they have become so ineffectual in this.

---

of the Gospel points. There is no hint that the Kingdom of God is Utopia. The restored kingdom of David, which was the Utopia of popular Jewish hopes in the time of Jesus, is all but expressly rejected, and no alternative Utopia is suggested.' See C. H. Dodd, *The Parables of the Kingdom*, p. 206.

[109] *Mere Christianity*, p. 111.

[110] Ibid. In a way this prefigures the sentiments of the Council Fathers at Vatican II who argued: 'The expectation of a new earth must not weaken but rather stimulate our concern for cultivating this one.' See *Gaudium et Spes*, p. 39.

[111] *Mere Christianity*, p. 111.

Aim at Heaven and you will get earth 'thrown in': aim at earth and you will get neither.[112]

Anton Van der Walle makes a similar point when he argues, 'Heaven is only another word for God himself, and this God is active as a liberator in our human history.' It is, he suggests, up to believers themselves 'to do away with the misconception that faith in a beyond is a betrayal of life in this world'. [113] Indeed Van der Walle claims that it is precisely the Christian praxis in this world that lends any credibility to the hope for a world beyond.

> If believers do all that is humanly possible to make a bit of heaven for people here on earth, and in so doing come up against their own limitations and those of others, then they need not really be confused or ashamed to point to a future heaven which can mean everything for those who are not really helped by social justice.[114]

The whole thrust of Christian eschatology, then, cannot be reduced to either some other-worldly, personalised hope for beatific vision, or a purely this-worldly imperative to social action. Rather it is the making, by God himself, of a new heavens and a new earth. As John Polkinghorne puts it, 'A credible eschatology must find its basis in a "thick" and developed theology.' This means a richer theological base than simply some other-worldly concept of God as 'the Mind behind cosmic order'; and, again, a richer Christology than some this-worldly vagary 'which sees Jesus as no more than an inspired teacher, pointing humanity to new possibilities for self-realisation.'

> To sustain true hope it must be possible to speak of a God who is powerful and active, not simply holding creation in being but also interacting with its history, the one who

[112] Ibid.
[113] Anton Van der Walle, *From Darkness to the Dawn*, pp. 13, 15.
[114] Ibid. p. 15.

'gives life to the dead and calls into existence the things that do not exist" (Romans 4:17).[115]

As Anton Van der Walle notes of the situation in Latin America, 'For most people, liberation by heaven, by God, still means being stood on one's head, so complete a change and renewal that everything familiar is shaken up, so that a new earth and a new heaven come into view.'[116] The same should be able to be said, I believe, of authentic Christian experience in general.

In his own critique of aspects of liberation and other – for want of a better word – revolutionary theologies, Joseph Ratzinger has pointed to the 'emasculation of Christian hope' in the politicisation of Christian eschatology. 'Though to all intents and purposes that hope is simply being re-expressed in humanly realistic terms,' he goes on, 'in fact its own essential content is draining away, leaving behind nothing but a deceptive surrogate.'[117] Lewis, similarly, was to argue, 'A Christian cannot, therefore, believe any of those who promise that if only some reform in our economic, political, or hygienic system were made, a heaven on earth would follow.'[118] If political action becomes the content of eschatology and hope rather than that of ethics and charity, there will always be the danger of hope's true goal – beatific vision – being usurped by a purely this-worldly utopia. And, as Lewis observed, 'I think earth, if chosen instead of Heaven, will turn out to have been, all along,

---

[115] John Polkinghorne, *The God of Hope*, p. 95.

[116] Anton Van der Walle, *From Darkness to the Dawn*, p. 13.

[117] J. Ratzinger, *Eschatology*, p. 59. The International Theological Commission similarly warned against what it called 'temporal messianism', by which certain theologies emphasize so much the ideas of economic liberation and social emancipation that 'theological hope loses its full strength' because it is 'replaced by a political dynamism'. ITC, 'Some Current Questions in Eschatology', p. 211.

[118] *The Problem of Pain*, pp. 92–3. Indeed, as his novel *That Hideous Strength* was to demonstrate, Lewis believed firmly in the truth revealed through the story of Babel (Gn 11:1–9): that all purely human achievements are of their essence necessarily limited and that not to realise this fact is a potentially catastrophic act of hubris on our part.

only a region in Hell: and earth, if put second to Heaven, to have been from the very beginning a part of Heaven itself.'[119] Put another way, although political action must not be allowed to become the sum total of eschatological content, nevertheless the Christian political ethic must always be radically eschatological. Again, as Anton Van der Walle comments, we must not, as Christians, become scared of talking about politics, as if 'social injustice would ever come to an end without real specific political power'.[120]

In recent times there has been much evidence of a concerted drive to deepen the exchange of ideas between faith and science. John Polkinghorne and Michael Welker have referred to this 'currently expanding and intensifying dialogue' as having moved through its 'methodological phase' and its 'physics phase', now finding itself in a state in which 'theological topics and questions have become more and more important'.[121] In this respect, then, eschatology is ripe for discussion. Indeed, Polkinghorne and Welker's book, *The End of the World and the Ends of God*, is a testament to the ongoing mutual collaboration between science and religion in this regard, it being the fruit of a three year consultation held by scientists and theologians between the university of Heidelberg and Princeton Theological Seminary. For the range of human hope, modern science presents an enormous challenge. 'The proclamation by the sciences of the definite finitude of the world has come as a cultural shock,' note Polkinghorne and Welker. 'In the face of the environmental crisis, the continuing surge of global poverty, and threat by an age of increasing conflict, scarcity, and despair, many people around the world look to a future without hope or joy.' What then, they ask, of contemporary eschatology? 'Should theologians simply concede the scientific point, join the current mood, and thereby abandon all claims about God's involvement with and care for creation?'[122] Actually such questions are hardly

---

[119] *The Great Divorce*, p. 8.
[120] Anton Van der Walle, *From Darkness to the Dawn*, p. 13.
[121] John Polkinghorne and Michael Welker, eds, *The End of the World and the Ends of God: Science and Theology on Eschatology*, p. 1.
[122] Ibid. p. 7.

contemporary. As long ago as 1948 C. S. Lewis pointed to the scientific data that suggested nature was in inevitable entropy.

> The astronomers hold out no hope that this planet is going to be permanently inhabitable. The physicists hold out no hope that organic life is going to be a permanent possibility in any part of the material universe. Not only this earth, but the whole show, all the suns of space, are to run down. Nature is a sinking ship.[123]

Add to that the possibility of nuclear annihilation and the question is posed: how are we to live? Lewis argued that the question concerned not so much the novelty of our situation but rather whether we have any basis and ability to believe in reality beyond our current experience. Polkinghorne notes that it is not science's place 'to usurp theology's role in speaking of what God might do by way of a new creation'. However the current dialogue of faith and science in eschatology assumes that if the 'new creation is to be related to the present in a way that involves both continuity and discontinuity (as the Christian resurrection hope suggests), then science may have something to say about the conditions of consonance and credibility that the continuity aspect of the relationship might be expected to fulfil'.[124]

A further matter in question concerns the relationship of science and religion at a popular level. As the Jesuit and member of the Vatican Observatory Research Group, William Stoeger, has noted, in America at least, although there are 'influential religious constituencies', they rarely manage to 'present an adequate or compelling testimony of ultimate meaning and hope to our scientifically and technologically sophisticated culture – particularly when they ... call for the outright repudiation of scientific results and conclusions'.[125]

---

[123] 'On Living in an Atomic Age', p. 116.
[124] John Polkinghorne, 'Eschatology and the Sciences', in John Polkinghorne and Michael Welker, *The End of the World*, p. 17.
[125] William Stoeger, 'Cultural Cosmology and the Impact of the Natural Sciences on Philosophy and Culture', in John Polkinghorne and Michael Welker, *The End of the World*, p. 65.

Clearly one of the issues here is the problem of fundamentalism, both scriptural and dogmatic. But it is also true to say that
there exists, at least in the West, a deep scepticism of religion's
credentials vis-à-vis scientific endeavour – perhaps, lamentably,
the long-lasting legacy of the Galileo affair. Furthermore,
Donald Juel has suggested, 'Many people live their lives within
a world of 'common sense' that has little to do with what is
common and sensible among knowledgeable insiders in
various disciplines.'[126] In some respects it is true to say little has
changed since Lewis observed that whilst 'many theologians
and some scientists are now ready to proclaim that the nineteenth-century "conflict between science and religion" is over
and done with', nevertheless, 'if this is true, it is a truth known
only to real theologians and real scientists'. It would appear,
therefore, that one pressing concern for eschatology today is
how it can both participate constructively in contemporary
scientific research *and* present its subsequent theological reflections in a captivating and constructive way. As Juel puts it, 'It is
important that the testimony of the Church be truthful. It is
equally important that it be plausible and engaging.'[127] A
superficial reading of the Lewisian corpus might lead one to
assume that he would have had no truck with such inter-disci-
plinary dialogue. But in fact a closer reading demonstrates that
Lewis' aim was not to downplay science at all but to eradicate
scientism – the over-simplification and reduction of scientific
theories and their misrepresentation as somehow necessarily
and always in contradiction to Christian faith. Like the current
debate – although in a somewhat more apologetically polemical
style than would be acceptable now – C. S. Lewis endeavoured
precisely to prevent the divorce of religion from science and to
withstand any suggestion that faith might not be wholly reasonable.[128]

---

[126] Donald Juel, 'Christian Hope and the Denial of Death', in John
Polkinghorne and Michael Welker, *The End of the World*, p. 171.
[127] Juel, 'Christian Hope and the Denial of Death', p. 172.
[128] Cf. C. S. Lewis, 'Religion and Science', in *God in the Dock*, pp.
38–42; *Miracles*, pp. 47–64.

The Destiny of the World

The eternal destiny of the world – whether it be to salvation or perdition – has long aroused popular interest and artistic depiction, as well as (thankfully) a more balanced theological debate. 'Heaven and hell,' Dermot Lane notes, 'have a habit of appearing in surveys and in discussions about religion as if they were equal sides of the one coin and therefore of the same theological importance.'[129] Of course, they are not and it was Karl Rahner who made the point that, in Christian theology at least, the 'eschatology of salvation and of loss are not on the same plane'.[130] In a strict sense, then, there can be talk of only one predestination: to beatific vision through the gift of grace offered to all in Jesus Christ.[131] As G. Martelet put it,

> In speaking of love refused, we do not mean that God refuses his love to anyone, as if beings could be lost forever because God had not loved them sufficiently ... The absolute refusal of love (which is hell) exists, therefore, only in the case of him who eternally acknowledges and affirms no one but himself; and it is inconceivable that God could have anything to do with this grotesque possibility. [132]

Thus the eternal destiny of hell is to be understood, as Rahner put it, as the 'consequence of the inward obduracy of man' in which God is active 'only insofar as he does not release man from the reality of the definitive state which man himself has achieved on his own behalf'.[133] As we have seen in chapter two

---

[129] Dermot Lane, *Keeping Hope Alive*, p. 137.
[130] Karl Rahner, 'The Hermeneutics of Eschatological Assertions', p. 338.
[131] Ibid. p. 340.
[132] Quoted in Von Balthasar, *Theo-Drama*, p. 278. Cf. G. Martelet, *L'Au-dela retrouvé*, (Descleé, 1974), pp. 181, 188.
[133] Cf. Karl Rahner, 'Hell', p. 604. John Sachs underlines the point when he notes, 'Virtually all [contemporary Catholic] theologians emphasize the universal aspect of God's saving will and move beyond a view of divine justice which seems to separate it from and pit it against God's love and mercy. Many stress that while we

C. S. Lewis took a similar view, presenting an image of heaven – understood as communion with God – as being reality itself, whilst hell was little more than an eschatological footnote: a parasitical concept, not so much a place as a state, the inevitable consequence of our definitive and freely willed rejection of God and therefore self-imposed. However, to suggest that hell is merely an eschatological footnote is not to dismiss it altogether from the bounds of eschatological discussion. John Sachs has noted that the challenge for contemporary eschatology 'has been to identify the true meaning and the proper place of hell in the proclamation of the gospel about the world's salvation in Christ'.[134] Thus it has, in fact, become one of the more contentious issues of recent times, in particular with reference to the concept of apocatastasis.

It is well known that Origen developed a notion of the restoration (*apokatastasis*) of all things under Christ in his theology, and that this restoration included an eventual end to the punishment of the damned and even the possibility of salvation for the devil. This position – at least as put forward by later followers of Origen – was condemned in 543 at the Synod of Constantinople, which decreed:

If anyone says or holds that the punishment of the demons and of impious human beings is temporary, and

---

believe that heaven in indeed (already) a reality, hell is, at most, a real *possibility*.' John R. Sachs, 'Apocatastasis in Patristic Theology', in *Theological Studies*, p. 617.

[134] John R. Sachs, 'Current Eschatology: Universal Salvation and the Problem of Hell', in *Theological Studies*, p. 233. He explains the parameters of this challenge thus: 'In presenting and explaining the Church's doctrine, however, current theology tries to address two significant pastoral realities. First, for many centuries, the doctrine of hell has had an exaggerated place in the theology and preaching of the Church. For many Christians, the "good news" of the kingdom became the "bad news" about judgement and punishment. Then, in reaction to the excessively juridical and often monstrous images of God which had been prevalent for so long, it has become common to ignore the topic of hell altogether or to deny its existence outright as incompatible with God's love and mercy.' Ibid. p. 231.

that it will have an end at some time, or that there will be a complete restoration of demons and impious human beings, *anathema sit*.[135]

Interestingly, Origen's actual position was somewhat more cautious and theoretical, made 'rather by way of discussion than coming to definite conclusions'. For example, he wrote:

> We suppose that the goodness of God will restore the whole creation to unity in the end, through his Christ, when his enemies have been subdued and overcome ... Whether any of those orders [*viz. the opposing powers*] who act under the devil's leadership ... will be able in some future ages to be converted to goodness ... I leave to the reader's judgement.[136]

And of the devil, he speculated:

> When it is said that 'the last enemy shall be destroyed', it is not to be understood as meaning that his substance, which is God's creation, perishes, but that his purpose and hostile will perishes; for this does not come from God but from himself. Therefore his destruction means not his

---

[135] See J. Neuner and J. Dupuis, *The Christian Faith*, n. 2301. John Sachs has observed: 'It would be unfair to call the theses condemned [by the Synod of Constantinople in 543] fair representations of Origen's thought.' He notes that from the time of Origen in the first half of the third century until the mid-sixth century and the synod's condemnation, a movement of 'Origenism' had grown up 'which had less and less to do with the thought and spirit of the man whose name it bore'. The main reasons for this shift away from Origen's actual theology are to be found in the 'literalist interpretations of his writings, pre-occupations with certain extreme areas of speculation in his theology, and attempts to find within or force upon Origen's thought a rigid system (which could only ignore or deny the subtleties and ambiguities in his thought).' See J. Sachs, 'Apocatastasis in Patristic Theology', pp. 638–9.

[136] Cf. Origen, *De Principiis*, 1, 6, 1–4 in *The Early Christian Fathers*, ed. and trans. Henry Bettenson, p. 256.

ceasing to exist but ceasing to be an enemy and ceasing to be death. Nothing is impossible to omnipotence; ... there is nothing that cannot be healed by its Maker; ... and if things were made that they might exist they cannot become non-existent.[137]

Joseph Ratzinger has commented that this 'ambitious attempt to systematize Christianity', in which Origen proposed that 'given the logic of God's relationship with history, there must be a universal reconciliation at the End', was based on a tendency to downplay evil as 'nothingness', for only God is real. Although Origen later 'sensed much more acutely the terrible reality of evil', notes Ratzinger, he could never 'wholly let go of his hope that, in and through this divine suffering, the reality of evil is taken prisoner and overcome so that it loses its quality of definitiveness'.[138] This optimistic line of universal salvation was later followed in modified forms by people such as Gregory of Nyssa, Didymus of Alexandria, Diodore of Tarsus, Theodore of Mopsuestia, Evagrius Ponticus and – 'at least on one occasion', according to Ratzinger – by St Jerome.[139] It should be observed, as Dermot Lane has pointed out, that these later proponents of a modified apocatastasis did not find themselves questioned or condemned by the Church. In recent times perhaps the most famous advocate of universal salvation has been Hans Urs Von Balthasar. In his book, *Dare We Hope 'that All Men be Saved'?* published in 1988, Von Balthasar argued that not only *might* we hope for universal salvation, but that it is our *duty* to do so. Since Christ has expressed his ultimate solidarity with sinners through his entry into hell in the drama of Holy Saturday, Christian hope must mirror this solidarity in the hope that all may be saved. Hope of heaven for all is not an 'inducement to laziness in our ethical commitment but rather the heaviest demand upon all of us

---

[137] Origen, *De Principiis*, 3, 6, 5 in *The Early Christian Fathers*, p. 257.
[138] J. Ratzinger, *Eschatology*, pp. 215–16.
[139] For a good general overview of how the idea of apocatastasis can be traced in the thought of Clement of Alexandria, Origen, Gregory Nazianzus and Gregory of Nyssa, see J. Sachs, 'Apocatastasis in Patristic Theology', pp. 617–40.

that one can imagine: the decision for a patience that absolutely never gives up but is prepared to await infinitely long for the other'.[140] It is worthy of note, too, that Karl Rahner, although appearing to be somewhat disparaging of the subject, rather lamented towards the end of his life that he had not devoted more time and study to the idea.[141] Nevertheless, as Dermot Lane points out, 'Many students of Rahner's theology, such as John R. Sachs and Carmel McEnroy, have developed [his principles] into a modified form of *apokatastasis*.'[142] Sachs, in particular, has concluded that 'a properly understood Christian universalism is not only consonant with several strands of Christian belief, but is also profoundly relevant' to our current day, a sign of contradiction in a world that is increasingly fragmented through fundamentalism in religious belief, isolationism and prejudice in general. A hope that all will be saved, he argues, implies a realisation that 'already here and now all men and women are being saved'. And this in its turn 'demands a certain posture not only with respect to future fulfilment, but to present life'. Thus,

---

[140] Cf. Hans Urs Von Balthasar, *Dare We Hope 'that All Men be Saved?' With a Short Discourse on Hell*, p. 212. Von Balthasar was quoting here from Hans-Jürgen Verweyen, *Christologische Brennpunkte*, (Essen: Ludgerus, 1977), p. 119.

[141] Rahner argued, for example, 'True eschatological discourse must exclude the presumptuous knowledge of a universal apocatastasis and of the certainty of the salvation of the individual *before* his death, as well as certain knowledge of a damnation which has actually ensued.' Karl Rahner, 'Hermeneutics', p. 339. Similarly, in his article on hell, Rahner noted: 'In its official teaching, the Church has defined the existence of hell and its eternity against the doctrine of apocatastasis as put forward by Origen and other ancient writers.' Thus, he argued: 'The preacher must try to bring home to his hearers the seriousness of the threat to eternal salvation, with which the Christian must reckon without any sly look at a possible apocatastasis.' See Karl Rahner, 'Hell', pp. 602, 604. However Leo O'Donovan notes that in an interview given some years before his death, Rahner had remarked that he 'would still like to have written something about such a teaching on apocatastasis that would be orthodox and acceptable'. See Leo O'Donovan, 'Living into Mystery: Karl Rahner's Reflections at 75', in *America*, (1979), p. 179.

[142] Dermot Lane, *Keeping Hope Alive*, p. 163.

since 'we must truly live what we hope for', the eschatological hope for universal salvation demands a more inclusive and patient approach to those around us.[143]

J. N. D. Kelly has argued that the 'two guiding principles' behind Origen's theological system were 'the free will of man and the goodness of God'.[144] It seems to me that these two principles provide indeed the very framework within which any modern version of apocatastasis must be debated. Clearly, any appeal to universal salvation emphasizes the utter goodness and mercy of God and his will that nothing should be lost to him. But equally it must take seriously the nature of human free will and the possibility that the sinner may reject God's divine mercy. John Sachs has observed, 'Most Catholic theologians refuse to embrace a doctrine of universal salvation outright … because they believe it would be tantamount to denying the reality of human freedom.'[145] As Ratzinger puts it, positing the classical position, 'Heaven reposes upon freedom, and so leaves to the damned the right to will their own damnation.'[146] Lewis put it another way: the doors of hell are bolted shut, but from the inside.[147] Like Ratzinger, Lewis also could

---

[143] Cf. John Sachs, 'Current Eschatology', pp. 227, 254.

[144] Cf. J. N. D. Kelly, *Early Christian Doctrines*, p. 474.

[145] Sachs goes on to add: 'Most admit and insist upon a fundamental tension or dialectic between the sovereignty of God's universally saving act and human freedom which must embrace it freely. Within the limits of Catholic "orthodoxy" what is encouraged by most is a strong and active *hope* that all will be saved.' J. Sachs, 'Apocatastasis in Patristic Theology', p. 617.

[146] J. Ratzinger, *Eschatology*, p. 216.

[147] Cf. *Preface to Paradise Lost*, p. 105; *The Problem of Pain*, pp. 104–5. Jürgen Moltmann takes to task this particular understanding and emphasis of human freedom. 'The logic of hell,' he notes, 'seems to me not merely inhumane but also extremely atheistic: here the human being in his freedom of choice is his own lord and god. His own will is his heaven – or his hell. God is merely the accessory who puts that will into effect. If I decide for heaven, God must put me there; if I decide for hell, he has to leave me there. If God has to abide by our free decision, then we can do with him what we like. Is that the "love of God"? Free human beings forge their own happiness and are their own executioners … After a God has perhaps created us free as we are, he leaves us to our fate. Carried

not see how an affirmation of universal salvation could ultimately be reconciled with the gift of human free will. For, as he
argued in *The Problem of Pain*,

> I would pay any price to be able to say truthfully, 'All will
> be saved.' But my reason retorts, 'Without their will or
> with it?' If I say, 'Without their will', I at once perceive a
> contradiction; how can the supreme voluntary act of self-
> surrender be involuntary? If I say 'With their will', my
> reason replies, 'How if they *will not* give in?'[148]

Furthermore, Lewis was at pains to demonstrate that the existence of hell in no way undermines the utter mercy of God.
Christianity, he argued, presents a God 'so full of mercy that
He becomes man and dies by torture to avert that final ruin
from His creatures'. The point, the terrible paradox that the
reality of human sin (and not God) represents, is thus: 'so
much mercy, yet still there is Hell'.[149] And, indeed, as Joseph

---

to this ultimate conclusion, the logic of hell is secular humanism,
as Feuerbach, Marx and Nietzsche already perceived a long time
ago.' See Moltmann, 'The Logic of Hell', p. 45. This argument is
uncharacteristically simplistic of Moltmann and, as I have shown
already in this study – and will endeavour to demonstrate again in
this chapter – does not reflect at all the classical position of hell as a
condition of the possibility of free will. Human freedom is the
freedom to reject or accept divine grace, which *then* leads to
heaven. It is not a freedom to 'forge our own happiness' as such.
Thus Moltmann is quite wrong when he suggests that such a
concept of hell is Pelagian rather than Augustinian. Cf. J.
Moltmann, 'The Logic of Hell', p. 44.

[148] *The Problem of Pain*, p. 97.

[149] Ibid. pp. 97, 98. Ratzinger has argued: 'The specificity of
Christianity is shown in this conviction of the greatness of man.
Human life is fully serious. It is not to be denatured by what Hegel
called the 'cunning of the Idea' into an aspect of divine planning.
The irrevocable takes place, and that includes, then, irrevocable
destruction. The Christian man or woman must live with such seriousness and be aware of it. It is a seriousness which takes on
tangible form in the Cross of Christ.' See J. Ratzinger, *Eschatology*,
pp. 216–17. In *Perelandra* Lewis made a similar point in his discussion of the serious implications of sin despite the *Felix peccatum
Adae*. 'Whatever you do, He will make good of it. But not the good

Ratzinger rather forcefully points out, the idea of an eternity of hell holds a considerable place not only in theological tradition but in the scriptural accounts of Christ's teaching too:

> No quibbling helps here: the idea of eternal damnation, which had taken ever clearer shape in the Judaism of the century or two before Christ, has a firm place in the teaching of Jesus, as well as in the apostolic writings. Dogma takes its stand on solid ground when it speaks of the existence of Hell and of the eternity of its punishments.[150]

Acknowledging, then, that any theory of apocatastasis 'seems to require a reappraisal of the innumerable biblical passages that speak of the twofold result of the Last Judgement and of the eternity of the pains of hell', Hans Urs Von Balthasar went on to maintain:

> However, before we draw this apparently inevitable conclusion, we must frankly admit that a great number of passages really do speak in favour of universal salvation; we must give this fact its appropriate place and, as Schleiermacher demands, grant it 'at least equal right' to exist.[151]

He had prepared for you if you had obeyed Him. That is lost for ever. The first King and first Mother of our world did the forbidden thing; and He brought good of it in the end. But what they did was not good; and what they lost we have not seen. And there were some to whom no good came nor ever will come.' See *Perelandra*, p. 121. Cf. also the texts that deal with the Lewisian refrain that reality never repeats itself: e.g. *Prince Caspian*, p. 125; *A Grief Observed*, p. 23; *Perelandra*, p. 214.

150 J. Ratzinger, *Eschatology*, p. 215. I have already commented on how Lewis stressed this teaching as being in the nature of moral exhortation rather than detailed and definitive description. See *The Problem of Pain*, p. 97: 'When they have roused us into action by convincing us of a terrible possibility, they have done, probably, all they were intended to do.'

151 Hans Urs Von Balthasar, *Theo-Drama*, pp. 269–70.

Interestingly, a close reading of the patristic texts – including those that have a universalist slant – demonstrates pointedly the early Church Fathers' concerns to uphold both the existence of hell (and its dreadful punishments) and the concept of free will. For example, John Sachs has noted that Clement of Alexandria believed not only that the damned could be led to conversion *through* the punishments of hell and thus achieve apocatastasis, but also that God could accomplish this without abrogating their free will. Similarly, Origen argued that, due to the infinite goodness of God and his will that nothing should be lost, punishment of the damned was to be seen as remedial rather than punitive, and therefore not eternal. It had a pedagogical nature, or persuasive power. And thus, again, free will is respected.[152] Even in the patristic period, it seems, the idea of universal salvation required a more careful nuance than simply the affirmation that 'all men will be saved' (1 Timothy 2:4). In the final volume of his work, *Theo-Drama: Theological Dramatic Theory*, Hans Urs Von Balthasar attempted to develop precisely this sort of nuance. The Cross of Christ, he noted, is 'the decisive Judgement because here the Son undercuts and undergirds the world's sin'. He went on: 'If all sins are undercut and undergirded by God's infinite love, it suggests that sin, evil, must be finite and must come to an end in the love that envelops it.'[153] Thus he echoed some of the patristic ideas that we have already discussed. But 'is this not too simple?' he asked.

> After all, it is not simply a question of taking something that has been isolated from the sinner and making it disappear: it is a question of the sinner's own free refusal, which God, if he respects the freedom he has given to man, cannot overrule simply because his absolute freedom is more powerful that created, finite freedom.[154]

The task for theology, then, as Von Balthasar identified it, is

---

[152] Cf. John R. Sachs, 'Apocatastasis in Patristic Theology', pp. 619, 628.
[153] Hans Urs Von Balthasar, *Theo-Drama*, pp. 282, 283.
[154] Ibid. p. 285.

how to reconcile the all-encompassing, universal scope of Christ's redemptive act as described in the New Testament with the acknowledgement that, as individuals, we might choose to reject such an act. For surely such a rejection, he speculated, would be that unforgivable sin against the Spirit that Christ warned us about (Matthew 12:32). What theology must not do, he believed, is present an apocatastasis in which Christ's work is turned into 'some sort of blurred collective redemption. Such a way of dealing with sinners would be unworthy of the human being. If we refuse to allow Christ to accept us, we remain in our sin, and the separation (of us from our sins), which can be performed only in him, becomes impossible'.[155] But neither must theology present our eternal destiny as a double predestination, in the simplistic and dualist terms that God ordains some of us for heaven and some for hell. Since any rejection of God is the personal exercise of human free choice – in which the Saviour does 'not positively thrust [the sinner] from him ... but will negatively leave the sinner to his blinded will' – hell must be understood as self-judgement and therefore 'only seriously entertained as a personal and existential question'.[156] Thus one may speak in *hope* for the restoration of all things and of universal salvation (at least of humans, if not the devil), whilst admitting of the possibility of eternal hell for ourselves alone as the existential consequence of our own rejection of God's grace.[157] This presentation of

---

[155] Ibid. p. 288.

[156] Cf. ibid. p. 299.

[157] As the question is raised in Von Balthasar, *Dare We Hope*, p. 211: 'If the threats of judgement and the cruel, horrifying images of the gravity of the punishments imposed upon sinners that we find in Scripture and Tradition have any point, then it is surely, in the first instance, to make *me* see the seriousness of the responsibility that I bear along with my freedom. But do Scripture and Tradition also force me to assume from these threats of judgement, beyond what concerns me, that even only *one other* besides me has met ruin in hell or is destined to do so?' A similar position is put forward by the International Theological Commission, where it argues: 'The Church takes seriously both human liberty, and the divine Mercy which gives people the liberty which is a condition for obtaining salvation. Since the Church prays for the

universal salvation, thus nuanced, speaks (as did Origen, in fact) of apocatastasis in terms of persuasion rather than compulsion. Hell remains a possibility, for the sinner is always ultimately free to reject God's goodness, but God's mercy is so rich and his love so abounding that even the most recalcitrant sinner could not fail to be moved to repentance and the acceptance of divine grace. In the theology of Von Balthasar this merciful, rich and abounding love is expressed most dramatically through Christ's descent into hell on Holy Saturday. 'Into this finality (of death) the dead Son descends, no longer acting in any way, but stripped by the cross of every power and initiative of his own,' meditated Von Balthasar. Christ is truly dead and therefore one with the dead. In this expression of utter solidarity, even unto death, God demonstrates his will that nothing should be lost to him. And thus 'exactly in that way he disturbs the absolute loneliness striven for by the sinner.' As Von Balthasar reflected:

> The sinner, who wants to be 'damned' apart from God, finds God again in his loneliness, but God in the absolute weakness of love who unfathomably in the period of nontime enters into solidarity with those damning themselves.[158]

This position, too, seems to have its theological problems. Von Balthasar appears to be admitting of second chances after death, an admission that raises important issues for our under-

---

salvation of all people living, by that fact it is praying for the conversion of all. God wants 'all men to be saved and to come to the knowledge of the truth' (1 Tm 2:4). The Church has always believed that such a universal salvific will on God's part has an ample efficacy. The Church has never once declared the damnation of a single person as a concrete fact. But, since hell is a genuine possibility for every person, it is not right – although today this is something which is forgotten in the preaching at exequies – to treat salvation as a kind of quasi-automatic consequence.' ITC, 'Some Current Questions in Eschatology', pp. 236–7.

[158] Hans Urs Von Balthasar, *The Von Balthasar Reader*, p. 153.

standing of human freedom and of death as our final and definitive state. Of second chances, Lewis commented, 'I believe that if a million chances were likely to do good, they would be given.' But then, 'Finality must come some time.'[159] The question here is really: how free are we after death? Or rather, how free are we when finally we encounter God face to face? Surely the whole point of death, as understood theologically, is that here at last we will not only see God as he really is, but ourselves too. And, once we are in this state, how can there be any talk of freedom in the sense of room for manoeuvre? Lewis argued in *The Great Divorce*: 'If ye put the question from within Time and are asking about possibilities, the answer is certain. The choice of ways is before you.' But, on the other hand, 'If ye are trying to leap on into eternity, if ye are trying to see the final state of all things as it *will* be (for so ye must speak) when there is no more possibilities left but only the Real, then ye ask what cannot be answered to mortal ears.'[160] In other words, can we really speak of freedom in terms of a choice between alternatives, once we 'know as fully as we are known' (cf. 1 Corinthians 13: 12)? Our definitive state is our definitive state. As Lewis argued elsewhere:

> It will be too late then to choose your side. There is no use saying you choose to lie down when it has become impossible to stand up. That will not be the time for choosing: it will be the time when we discover which side we really have chosen, whether we realised it before or not.[161]

Surely, then, there can be no room for the restoration of impious souls *after death* unless there is some sort of abrogation of their free will. And, as Lewis saw it, any abrogation of free will was not simply a matter of divine self-contradiction (in the sense that God has, in creation, already chosen to grant us free will) but strikes at the very nature of heavenly reality. To the complaint that 'the final loss of one soul gives the lie to all the

---

159 *The Problem of Pain*, pp. 101–2.
160 *The Great Divorce*, pp. 114–15.
161 *Mere Christianity*, p. 54.

joy of those who are saved',[162] Lewis argued that we must follow through the implications of such a sentiment, that we must see what lurks behind it: 'The demand of the loveless and the self-imprisoned that they should be allowed to blackmail the universe: that till they consent to be happy (on their own terms) no one else shall taste joy: that theirs' should be the final power; that Hell should be able to *veto* Heaven.'[163] If a man refuses to allow God to transform him into a saint, how else can he then become a saint, unless sainthood and heaven loses all value and meaning? Heaven resides on freedom, Ratzinger observed, and Lewis would have agreed with him. Indeed, freedom is the essential component to that kenotic pattern found in the inner life of the Trinity, that pattern which gives all reality its very structure. It is surrender's pre-requisite. Self-surrender can be demonstrated, can be called for, but ultimately it cannot be anything other than freely and self-given. And thus we see what Lewis meant when he said, towards the end of *The Great Divorce*, 'Freedom: the gift whereby ye most resemble your Maker and are yourselves parts of eternal reality.'[164]

Von Balthasar's meditation on Holy Saturday overcomes any notion of compulsion precisely through its emphasis on the weakness of Christ in his entry into hell. Here is no triumphant God but the broken, crucified Saviour, stripped of all heavenly and human glory and left in death. This expression of utter solidarity with sinners – by which God demonstrates, through total self-surrender, his commitment even to those creatures who have resolutely rejected him – is, hopes Von Balthasar, enough to make them finally repent. As he observed:

> The freedom of the creature is respected, but it is retrieved by God at the end of the passion and seized again in its very foundations. Only in absolute weakness

---

[162] Interestingly, St Thomas argued just the opposite and suggested that the saints will rejoice in heaven upon witnessing the fate of the damned, realising the misery they have escaped. Cf. St Thomas, *Summa Theologiae*, III, *supplementum*, pp. 94, 3.

[163] *The Great Divorce*, pp. 110–11.

[164] *The Great Divorce*, p. 115.

does God will to mediate to the freedom created by him the gift of love that breaks from every prison and every constraint: in his solidarity from within with those who reject all solidarity.[165]

John Sachs has further developed this idea by questioning our understanding of human freedom. Although he admits that freedom, understood as the capability to reject God finally and irrevocably, is 'clearly presupposed by doctrinal pronouncements concerning universal salvation and the existence of hell', nevertheless it has, he believes, never 'been the object of dogmatic definition'.[166] Thus, in the light of the eschatological hermeneutic that heaven and hell are not parallel but that there is only one eternal predestination, Sachs argues that our freedom as exercised in hell is not definitive in the same way as it is when exercised in heaven. Hell, understood now as a state of *persistent* rejection, entails 'an active effort against the power of God's inviting, forgiving love, and something quite different from the final rest of human freedom which freely and finally surrenders to the power of that love'.[167] Theoretically the sinner is free to persist in this rejection forever, in which case the reality of hell does become eternal (and the Synod of Constantinople's *anathema* against those who deny the eternity of hell's punishments can stand). But Sachs believes that Christians may legitimately hope that such persistence, when set against the all-encompassing love of God, is ultimately unlikely. What interests me here – beyond a personal attraction both to Sachs and Von Balthasar's theologies of universal salvation – is how C. S. Lewis' own thought can be reconciled. Let me make myself plain: I don't believe that Lewis held to a universalist position. And I don't believe he considered human freedom in the terms with which Sachs presents it. Nevertheless, Lewis' examination of moral choice and its eschatological implications in *The Great Divorce* provides uncanny dramatic depiction to Sachs' idea. In Lewis' *supposal*, the ghosts

165 Hans Urs Von Balthasar, *Reader*, p. 153.
166 John R. Sachs, 'Current Eschatology', p. 247.
167 Ibid. p. 248.

from the grey town have the opportunity to travel to heaven. Once there, it is only *their* rejection of the invitations, cajoling and persuasion to stay that will lead to their return to the grey town. 'You need never come back unless you want to,' says their bus driver. 'Stay as long as you please.'[168] Should they persist in their rejection, the grey town becomes hell; indeed, all of their experiences will have been hell. But, should they choose to stay, all of it will have been merely part of a purgatorial process in which they will have learnt, finally, to surrender themselves to the divine Mercy. For Sachs, and for Von Balthasar before him, the firm hope is that all will surrender eventually. But for Lewis – at least in *The Great Divorce* – it is significant that only one character responds. The man who has been weighed down all his life by lust suddenly finds himself transformed, with his erotic urges restored to their rightful place as the very charger on which he will ride into the mountains of deepest heaven. All the others – the murderer's self-righteous boss, the nagging and ambitious wife, the intellectual cleric, the possessive mother, the painter, the manipulative husband – opt to persevere in their wrapped up little lives. But Lewis was writing, here, as a moralist and aiming to stem the tide of our small, petty, daily sins which, he believed, might one day become, as Screwtape would put it, 'A hard, tight, settled core of resolution to go on being what it is ... rejection of what the Enemy [God] calls Grace.'[169] For Hans Urs Von Balthasar, on the other hand, for John Sachs and, indeed, for myself, (none of us, I think, moralists) the hope will always be that the depths of God's love – displayed upon the Cross of Christ and in his entry into hell – will in the end persuade us against settling upon such a selfish resolution.

[168] *The Great Divorce*, p. 28.
[169] *Screwtape Proposes a Toast*, p. 6.

Epilogue

In the introduction to his book, *Keeping Hope Alive*, the theologian Dermot Lane has argued that there are four good reasons for presenting a contemporary eschatology. First, to lead people to a 'learned ignorance' on the subject and so to avoid its simplistic dismissal; second, to correct classical eschatology's tendency to 'claim too much' and seem 'far too certain'; third, to proffer a vision of hope to a world desperately in need; and finally, to correct the prevalent assumption that eschatology is only about life after death.[1] In the course of this book I have, I hope, demonstrated not only the existence of a Lewisian eschatological position, but also its coherence, its firm philosophical and theological underpinnings, and its ability to speak to the current debate. At the outset I argued that it might be seen as somewhat spurious to suggest that C. S. Lewis was an eschatologist and yet boldly I made that claim. I now contend that eschatology provides such a framework within which to understand the Lewisian corpus that it is almost impossible to understand fully his thought and work without taking it into account. Perhaps the single most striking thing about encountering eschatological motifs in Lewis' writings is their pervasiveness. After his conversion to Christianity, eschatology – and in particular the hope of heaven – coloured all else he wrote about. Lewis, as I have said before, presented a worldview. Indeed, this worldview is in evidence even when he was writing about other, seemingly unrelated, subjects. For Clive Staples Lewis, eschatology was not simply one more theological

---

[1] Cf. Dermot Lane, *Keeping Hope Alive*, p. ix.

viewpoint among many; it was the Christian perspective *par excellence*. Perhaps the one remaining question to be answered here, then, is how – if at all – his presentation of this Christian perspective might stand up to Lane's four criteria.

Throughout the book I have consciously attempted to draw on eschatological references from amongst the whole range of the Lewisian corpus. In part this has been to exhibit the full role and scope of Lewis' eschatology. But I had a further motive. In *Letters to Malcolm* C. S. Lewis warned us never to mistake the abstract theological concept as in some way being more literal, or in some sense truer, than the anthropocentric image. 'Both are equally concessions,' he noted; 'each singly misleading and the two together mutually corrective.'[2] As we have seen, in his own writings Lewis chose to employ *both* abstract concept and anthropomorphic image. Thus, in one sense, the medium became his message. What was limited and inaccurate in one way was to be compensated and corrected in another. What was an abstract and theoretical proposition in one place was to be fleshed out in myth and metaphor else-where. Furthermore, in my chapter on eschatological imagery, I picked up on Peter Schakel's observation that, in later life, Lewis' writing had moved towards a more consistently mythopoeic style. And I suggested that here, too, the medium was the message: that the use of story and rich imagery, the attempt to produce a modern day myth in which 'a real though unfocused gleam of divine truth' might fall on our human imagination, was itself reflective of Lewis' belief that our whole lives consist of such glimmers and hints of our glorious destiny beyond. So then, in this medium-message, did Lewis open himself up to the charge of claiming to know too much? Is his eschatological presentation so naïve as to provoke only simplis-tic dismissal? I think not. Indeed, rather the reverse. Lewis steered clear of presenting eschatological imagery with all the over-certainty of, for example, Swedenborg (who claimed he really had seen heaven and spoken with angels). Equally, however (and unsurprisingly, given that the two are often related), Lewis also avoided producing images so utterly thin

---

[2] *Letters to Malcolm*, p. 19 (Letter 4).

and unbelievable that the reader would immediately dismiss them as nonsense or sheer fantasy. Zachary Hayes has argued: 'The primal levels of the language of hope are characteristically the language of image, picture, and metaphor rather than the language of precise definition.' But, for all that, the language of hope (and thereby of eschatology) is not one of 'an empty, idle dream'.[3] The credibility of Lewisian eschatological imagery, we have seen, lay in that 'morganatic' marriage of reason and imagination which I have earlier discussed. But there is more than mere credibility here. There is a deep humility too. For, as Lewis admitted in *Surprised by Joy*, the 'lower life of the imagination is not a beginning of, nor a step towards, the higher life of the spirit, merely an image'. But nevertheless, as he added rather significantly in a footnote, the image *can* be the step towards the spirit: 'God can cause it to be such a beginning.'[4] In his work, the rich imagery with which C. S. Lewis presented his eschatological worldview was anything but an attempt to say what the End Time might actually be like. Rather he furnished us with a cataphatic springboard from which to enter into the apophatic mystery at the heart of God himself. Lewis offered a magnificent application of analogous imagination, in which we are reminded that the best we can picture and hope for here and now, in our limited finite way, is ultimately as nothing compared with the glory we are promised. A true *via negativa*, then, must have as its foundation the firm belief that every negation will only be the reverse side of a fulfilling.

One of Lewis' great bugbears was what he called, 'Christianity-and-water', in which 'all the difficult and terrible doctrines' are left out in favour of the 'view which simply says there is a good God in Heaven and everything is all right'.[5] Certainly, at parochial level, there is a real danger of our eschatology becoming diluted, often simply because of the perceived difficulties of presenting its doctrines to ordinary people in the pew. Judgement, purgatory and hell, in particu-

---

[3] Cf. Zachary Hayes, *Visions of a Future*, pp. 93–4.
[4] *Surprised by Joy*, p. 130.
[5] Cf. *Mere Christianity*, p. 33.

lar these days, run the risk of becoming Cinderella subjects in the light of our preached hope for heaven. It is a concern that the International Theological Commission raised back in 1992, with its criticism of those funeral homilies that treat eternal salvation as some kind of a quasi-automatic consequence of death.[6] John Sachs has commented that such homilies are simply a reaction to the exaggerated emphasis on hell of earlier times.[7] Undoubtedly we turn God into a sort of juridical monster if our accent is only on hell-fire and damnation, but ignoring the process of judgement, purification and the possibility of perdition is just as inaccurate. By thus demoting the reality of human freewill, and underestimating the seriousness of sin, we diminish the enormity of God's saving love for us and the immensity of Christ's sacrifice on Calvary. For if human freedom isn't taken seriously, if hell isn't a very real condition of the possibility of that freedom, then the salvific act essentially becomes a game. We know that Lewis was, from the very outset of his conversion, rather critical of the perceived carrot and stick approach to Christianity. One might argue, of course, that carrot *and* stick have rarely been seen together in the preaching of heaven and hell. It has tended to be either all stick, or more recently, all carrot. What Lewis managed to achieve, however, was an authentic, popular presentation of theology in this regard. Heaven is our unalloyed promise and goal. But hell is its necessary footnote, should we want to persist in our wrapped up earthly lives. Similarly, it seems, the notion of purgatory gets scant mention these days, except perhaps come November and the rush to have Masses said and souls sprung from their temporary torment. This mechanistic approach to mercy needs constant challenging but, yet again, ignoring the topic throughout much of the liturgical year is not the answer. Lewis, following the rich tradition of Catherine of Genoa and John Henry Newman, offers us the mental furniture with which to challenge it appropriately. As Dermot Lane has pointed out, a contemporary eschatology should aim to proffer hope to a fallen world. Genuine Christian hope is not the same as secular society's search for some ultimate panacea.

[6] ITC, 'Some Current Questions in Eschatology', p. 237.
[7] Cf. John R. Sachs, 'Current Eschatology', p. 231.

Sooner or later, those 'difficult and terrible doctrines' have to come back in.

Lane's final criterion was that a current theology should correct the assumption that eschatology is only about life after death. In the course of this study much has been made of what I have termed Lewis' moral eschatology. In fact the synthesis of moral and dogmatic themes in the light of the End Time is, perhaps, Lewis' greatest contribution to theology. There is a real danger that the division of theological disciplines becomes a divorce. Moral theology, in particular, runs the risk of separating itself from its ultimate objective. Morality is more than just a jumping through hoops in the hope of some eternal Grand Prize. Our life, here and now, has definitive, ontological consequences. Our moral actions have bearings on our future being. The legacy of Lewisian eschatology in this regard is to be a constant reminder to modern day moral theology to keep that End Time in view. 'We are half-hearted creatures,' preached C. S. Lewis, to a packed University Church in Oxford on 8 June 1941, 'fooling about with drink and sex and ambition when infinite joy is offered us, like an ignorant child who wants to go on making mud pies in a slum because he cannot imagine what is meant by the offer of a holiday at the sea. We are far too easily pleased.'[8] With this most famous of Lewis' addresses, it seems to me that we have, summed up, the whole thrust of the Lewisian endeavour: to awaken in us an awareness of our eschatological destiny, to help us understand and appreciate more deeply our life's desires in the light of this end, and to give us the metaphorical tools by which we can glimpse – if only ever so faintly – the glory to which we are called.

[8] *Weight of Glory*, p. 26.

Acknowledgments

In writing a book such as this I am inevitably indebted to a great number of people who have supported and advised me throughout this project. I am honoured that Walter Hooper should have written the foreword to this work. I am deeply grateful to him, not only for his personal assistance during my time of research, but also for his own lifetime's work in Lewis studies which has made possible a commentary such as this. I am grateful, too, to Professor Luke Dempsey OP of the Angelicum University in Rome. Luke was a gentle but persuasive director of my doctoral studies and pushed me (I must say, somewhat unwillingly!) into exploring areas that I would have otherwise left alone. I believe the finished product is all the richer for his intervention. A huge debt of thanks is owed to Professor Robert Christian OP, again of the Angelicum University, for leading me to Luke and for his unstinting friendship and faith in me over the years. During the 'Oxford stage' of my studies, I owe thanks to the staff of the Bodleian Library, to the Dominicans of Blackfriars (and in particular to David Sanders OP), and to the parish of Our Lady & St Thomas More in Kidlington and their then parish priest, Fr Mervyn Tower. Throughout, two good friends who kept me sane were John Udris and Regan O'Callaghan: my gratitude to you both. Finally, I must thank Archbishop Peter Smith who, as the Bishop of East Anglia at the time, had enough faith in my academic ability to grant me study leave and keep me financially solvent.

All Scripture quotations, unless otherwise noted, were taken from the New Jerusalem Bible, published in the UK by Darton, Longman, and Todd Ltd, © 1985, and published in the USA

Selected Bibliography

WORKS C. S. LEWIS

Published Sources

The Abolition of Man: Or Reflections on Education with Special Reference to the Teaching of English in the Upper Forms of Schools (London, Oxford University Press, 1943, Fount, 1999).

The Allegory of Love: A Study in Medieval Tradition (Oxford, Clarendon Press, 1936. New York, Galaxy Books, 1958).

All My Road Before Me: The Diary of C. S. Lewis 1922–1927, Walter Hooper (ed.) (London, HarperCollins, 1991, Fount, 1993).

Boxen: The Imaginary World of the Young C. S. Lewis, Walter Hooper, (ed.) (London, Fount, 1985).

The Case for Christianity. First published as Broadcast Talks: Reprinted with Some Alterations from Two Series of Broadcast Talks ('Right and Wrong: A Clue to the Meaning of the Universe' and 'What Christians Believe') given in 1941 and 1942. (London, Geoffrey Bles, 1942. New York, Touchstone, 1996).

Collected Letters, Volume 1: Family Letters 1905–1931, Walter Hooper (ed.) (London, HarperCollins, 2000).

The Collected Poems of C. S. Lewis, Walter Hooper, (ed.) (London, Fount, 1994).

Compelling Reason: Essays on Ethics and Theology (London, Fount, 1996, 1998).

The Dark Tower and Other Stories, Walter Hooper (ed.) (London, Collins, 1977, Fount, 1998).

The Discarded Image: An Introduction to Medieval and Renaissance Literature (Cambridge, Cambridge University Press, 1964, 1994).

English Literature in the Sixteenth Century, Excluding Drama. Volume 3 of The Oxford History of English Literature, F. Wilson and B. Dobrée. (eds) (Oxford, Clarendon Press, 1954).

Essay Collection and Other Short Pieces, Lesley Walmsey. (ed) (London, HarperCollins, 2000).

Essays Presented to Charles Williams (London, Oxford University Press, 1947. Grand Rapids, Eerdmans, 1966).

An Experiment in Criticism (Cambridge, Cambridge University Press, 1961, 1992).

The Four Loves (London, Geoffrey Bles, 1960, Fount, 1998).

George MacDonald, An Anthology: 365 Readings (London, Geoffrey Bles, 1946. San Francisco; HarperSanFrancisco, 2001).

God in the Dock: Essays on Theology, Walter Hooper (ed.) (London, Geoffrey Bles, 1971, Fount, 1998).

The Great Divorce: A Dream (London, Geoffrey Bles, 1946, Fontana, 1972).

A Grief Observed (London, Faber & Faber, 1961, 1966).

The Horse and His Boy (London, Geoffrey Bles, 1954, HarperCollins, 1980).

The Last Battle: A Story for Children (London, Bodley Head, 1956, HarperCollins, 1980).

The Latin Letters of C. S. Lewis: C. S. Lewis and Don Giovanni Calabria, Martin Moynihan (ed. and tr.). First published as *Letters, C. S. Lewis, Don Calabria: A Study in Friendship*, (Ann Arbor, Michigan, Servant Books, 1988. Indiana, St Augustine's Press, 1998).

Letters of C. S. Lewis. Edited, with a Memoir, by W. H. Lewis, (London, Geoffrey Bles, 1966). Revised and enlarged edition edited by Walter Hooper (London, Collins, 1988. San Diego; Harcourt Brace, 1994).

Letters to an American Lady, Clyde Kilby (ed.) (Grand Rapids,Eerdmans, 1967, 1971).

Letters to Children, Lyle Dorsett and Marjorie Lamp Mead (eds) (New York, Macmillan, 1985, Touchstone, 1995).

The Lion, the Witch and the Wardrobe: A Story for Children, (London, Geoffrey Bles, 1950, HarperCollins, 1980).

The Magician's Nephew (London, Bodley Head, 1955, HarperCollins, 1980).

Mere Christianity. A Revised and Amplified Edition, with a New Introduction, of the Three Books, 'Broadcast Talks', 'Christian Behaviour' and 'Beyond Personality' (London, Geoffrey Bles, 1952, Fount, 1997).

Miracles: A Preliminary Study (London, Geoffrey Bles, 1947, Fount, 1998).

Narrative Poems, Walter Hooper (ed.) (London, Geoffrey Bles, 1969, Fount, 1994).

Of Other Worlds: Essays and Stories, Walter Hooper (ed.) (London, Geoffrey Bles, 1966. New York; Harvest, 1975).

Of This and Other Worlds, Walter Hooper (ed.) (London, Collins, 1982, Fount, 2000).

Out of the Silent Planet (London, Bodley Head, 1938. New York, Scribner, 1996).

Perelandra: A Novel London, Bodley Head, 1943. (New York, Scribner, 1996).

[with E. M. W. Tillyard] *The Personal Heresy: A Controversy* (London, Oxford University Press, 1939, 1965).

The Pilgrim's Regress: An Allegorical Apology for Christianity, Reason and Romanticism (London, J. M. Dent, 1933, Fount, 1998).

Prayer: Letters to Malcolm. First published as *Letters to Malcolm: Chiefly on Prayer* (London, Geoffrey Bles, 1964, Fount, 1998).

A Preface to Paradise Lost (London, Oxford University Press, 1942, 1961).

Prince Caspian: The Return to Narnia (London, Geoffrey Bles, 1951, HarperCollins, 1980).

The Problem of Pain (London, Geoffrey Bles, 1940, Fount, 1998).

Reflections on the Psalms (London, Geoffrey Bles, 1958, Fount, 1998).

The Screwtape Letters (London, Geoffrey Bles, 1942, Fount, 1998).

Screwtape Proposes a Toast and Other Pieces (London, Fontana, 1965, Fount, 1998).

Selected Literary Essays, Walter Hooper (ed.) (Cambridge, Cambridge University Press, 1969).

The Silver Chair (London, Geoffrey Bles, 1953, HarperCollins, 1980).

Studies in Medieval and Renaissance Literature, Walter Hooper (ed.) (Cambridge, Cambridge University Press, 1966, 1979).

Studies in Words (Cambridge, Cambridge University Press, 1960, 1967).

Surprised by Joy: The Shape of My Early Life (London, Geoffrey Bles, 1955, Fount, 1998).

[with Charles Williams] *Taliessin through Logres, The Region of the Summer Stars, and Arthurian Torso. First published as Arthurian Torso: Containing the Posthumous Fragment of 'The Figure of Arthur' by Charles Williams and 'A Commentary on the Arthurian Poems of Charles Williams' by C. S. Lewis* (London, Oxford University Press, 1948. Grand Rapids, Eerdmans, 1974).

That Hideous Strength: A Modern Fairy Tale for Grown-ups (London, Bodley Head 1945. New York, Scribner, 1996).

They Stand Together: The Letters of C. S. Lewis to Arthur Greeves (1914–1963), Walter Hooper (ed.) (London, Collins, 1979).

Till We Have Faces: A Myth Retold (London, Geoffrey Bles, 1956, Fount, 1998).

The Voyage of the Dawn Treader (London, Geoffrey Bles, 1952. HarperCollins, 1980).

The Weight of Glory and Other Addresses (New York, Macmillan, 1949). Revised and expanded edition edited by Walter Hooper (New York, Macmillan, 1980, Touchstone, 1996).

The World's Last Night and Other Essays (New York, Harcourt, Brace, 1960. San Diego, Harvest, 1973).

Unpublished Sources

'Great War' correspondence with Owen Barfield. Held at the Bodleian Library, Oxford: C. S. Lewis Collection, MS. Facs. c. 54.

Letter to Bede Griffiths dated 8 January 1936. Held at the Bodleian Library, Oxford: C. S. Lewis Collection, MS. Facs. c. 47.

Letter to Bede Griffiths dated 20 February 1936. Held at the Bodleian Library, Oxford: C. S. Lewis Collection, MS. Facs. d. 263.

Letter to Bede Griffiths dated 24 April 1936. Held at the Bodleian Library, Oxford: C. S. Lewis Collection, MS. Facs. d. 263.

Letter to Bede Griffiths dated 23 May 1936. Held at the Bodleian Library, Oxford: C. S. Lewis Collection, MS. Facs. c. 47.

Letter to Bede Griffiths post-marked 26 February 1931. Held at the Bodleian Library, Oxford: C. S. Lewis Collection, MS. Facs. c. 47.

Letter to Bede Griffiths post-marked 27 June 1937. Held at the Bodleian Library, Oxford: C. S. Lewis Collection: MS. Facs. c. 47.

Letter to Corbin Scott Carnell dated 10 December 1958. Held at the Bodleian Library, Oxford: C. S. Lewis Collection, MS. Facs. c. 48.

Letter to Miss Stillwell dated 29 October 1957. Held at the Bodleian Library, Oxford: C. S. Lewis Collection, MS. Facs. c. 48.

Typewritten mauscript and handwritten additions and corrections of Letters to Malcolm: Chiefly on Prayer held at the Bodleian Library, Oxford: C. S. Lewis Collection, Dep. d. 808.

Other Sources Consulted

Adey, Lionel, *C. S. Lewis: Writer, Dreamer & Mentor* (Grand Rapids, Eerdmans, 1998).

Alain De Lille, *The Complaint of Nature,* Douglas Moffat (tr.) (New York, Henry Holt and Co., 1908).

Alonso Schökel, Luis, *The Inspired Word: Scripture in the Light of Language and Literature*, Francis Martin (tr.) (Montreal, Palm Publishers, 1965).

Athanasius, *On the Incarnation*. Translated by a religious of C. S. M. V. (London, Mowbray, 1982).

Augustine of Hippo. *Against the Academicians and The Teacher*, Peter King (tr.) (Indianapolis, Hackett Publishing, 1995).

_____, *Concerning the City of God Against the Pagans*, Henry Bettenson (tr.) (Harmondsworth, Penguin, 1972).

_____, *Confessions*, E. M. Blaiklock (tr.) (London, Hodder and Stoughton, 1983).

_____, *De doctrina Christiana*, R. P. H. Green (ed. and tr.) (Oxford, Clarendon Press, 1995).

_____, *The Literal Meaning of Genesis: A Commentary in Twelve Books*, J. Hammond Taylor (tr.) (New York, Newman Press, 1982).

_____, *The Soliloquies of St. Augustine*, Rose Cleveland (tr.) (London, Williams and Norgate, 1910).

_____, *The Trinity*, Edmund Hill (New York, New City Press, 1991).

Barfield, Owen, *Poetic Diction: A Study in Meaning* (Hanover, Wesleyan University Press, 1973).

Barth, Karl, *Church Dogmatics*, Volume 2: *The Doctrine of God*, G. Bromiley and T. Torrance (eds), G. Bromiley, J. Campbell, I. Wilson, J. Strathearn, H. Knight, and R. Stewart (trs) (Edinburgh, T & T Clark, 1957).

Bauckham, Richard (ed.), *God will be All in All: The Eschatology of Jürgen Moltmann* (Edinburgh, T & T Clark, 1999).

_____, *The Theology of the Book of Revelation* (Cambridge, Cambridge University Press, 1993).

Bettenson, Henry, *The Early Christian Fathers: A Selection from the Writings Of the Fathers from St. Clement of Rome to St. Athanasius* (Oxford, Oxford University Press, 1969).

Bloch, Ernst, *The Principle of Hope,* Neville Plaice, Stephen Plaice and Paul Knight (trs) (Oxford, Blackwell, 1986).

Boyd, Ian (ed.), *The Chesterton Review,* XVII (1991): *C. S. Lewis Special Issue.*

Brown, Raymond, Joseph Fitzmyer and Robert Murphy (eds) *The New Jerome Biblical Commentary* (London, Geoffrey Chapman, 1990).

Browne, E. Martin, *Two in One* (Cambridge, Cambridge University Press, 1981).

Butterworth, G. W., *Origen on First Principles,* (London, SPCK, 1936).

Carnell, Corbin Scott, *Bright Shadow of Reality: Spiritual Longing in C. S. Lewis* (Grand Rapids, Eerdmans, 1999).

Carpenter, Humphrey, *The Inklings: C. S. Lewis, J. R. R. Tolkien, Charles Williams and their Friends* (London, HarperCollins, 1997). Reprinted by permission of HarperCollins Publishers Ltd. © Humphrey Carpenter, 1978.

Catechism of the Catholic Church (London, Geoffrey Chapman, 1994).

Catherine of Genoa, *Purgation and Purgatory: The Spiritual Dialogue,* Sergé Hughes, (London, SPCK, 1979).

Chapman, Mark, *The Coming Crisis: The Impact of Eschatology on Theology in Edwardian England* (Sheffield, Sheffield Academic Press, 2001).

Chesterton, G. K., *The Everlasting Man* (San Francisco, Ignatius Press, 1993).

Como, James, *Branches to Heaven: The Geniuses of C. S. Lewis* (Dallas, Spence Publishing Company, 1998).

_____ (ed.), *C. S. Lewis at the Breakfast Table and Other Reminiscences* (San Diego, Harvest, 1992).

Congar, Yves, *La foi et la théologie* (Tournai, Desclée, 1962).

Copleston, Frederick, *A History of Philosophy*, Volume 2: *Mediaeval Philosophy: Augustine to Scotus* (London, Burns and Oates, 1949).

Daley, Brian, *The Hope of the Early Church: A Handbook of Patristic Eschatology* (Cambridge, Cambridge University Press, 1991).

Dante Alighieri, *The Divine Comedy*, Allen Mandelbaum (tr.) (London, Everyman, 1995).

Doctrine Commission of the Church of England, *The Mystery of Salvation: The Story of God's Gift* (London, Church House Publishing, 1995).

Dodd, C. H., *The Parables of the Kingdom* (London, Nisbet & Co. Ltd, 1946).

Duriez, Colin and David Porter, *The Inklings Handbook: The Lives, Thoughts, and Writings of C. S. Lewis, J. R. R. Tolkien, Charles Williams, Owen Barfield and their Friends* (London, Azure, 2001).

Duriez Colin, *The C. S. Lewis Encyclopaedia: A Complete Guide to his Life, Thought, and Writings* (Wheaton, Crossway Books, 2000).

Edwards, Mark, 'Origen's Two Resurrections', in *The Journal of Theological Studies*, 46/2 (1995): 501–18.

Farrell, Frank, *Subjectivity, Realism, and Postmodernism – the Recovery of the World* (Cambridge, Cambridge University Press, 1994).

Fergusson, David and Marcel Sarot (eds), *The Future as God's Gift: Explorations in Christian Eschatology* (Edinburgh, T & T Clark, 2000).

Feuerbach, L., *The Essence of Christianity*, George Eliot (tr.) (New York, Harper and Row, 1957).

Feuillet, André, 'Eschatologism', in *Sacramentum Mundi*, Volume 2: *Contrition to Grace*, Karl Rahner (ed.) (London, Burns & Oates, 1968).

Fiddes, Paul, *The Promised End: Eschatology in Theology and Literature* (Oxford, Blackwell, 2000).

Filmer, Kath, *The Fiction of C. S. Lewis: Mask and Mirror*, (London, Macmillan, 1993).

Flannery, Austin (ed.), *Vatican II*, Volume 1: *The Conciliar and Post Conciliar Documents* (Dublin, Dominican Publications, 1988).

_____, *Vatican II*, Volume 2: *More Post Conciliar Documents* (Dublin, Dominican Publications, 1982).

Ford, Paul, *Companion to Narnia: A Complete Guide to the Enchanting World of C. S. Lewis' The Chronicles of Narnia* (San Francisco, HarperSanFrancisco, 1994).

Gibb, Jocelyn (ed.), *Light on C. S. Lewis* (London, Geoffrey Bles, 1965).

Gilson, Etienne, *Being and Some Philosophers* (Toronto: Pontifical Institute of Medieval Studies, 1952).

_____, *The Christian Philosophy of St. Augustine*, L. E. M. Lynch (tr.) (London, Victor Gollancz Ltd., 1961).

Goffar, Janine, *The C. S. Lewis Index: A Comprehensive Guide to Lewis' Writings and Ideas* (Wheaton, Crossway Books, 1995).

Graham, David (ed.), *We Remember C. S. Lewis: Essays & Memoirs* (Nashville, Broadman & Holman, 2001).

Gray, William, *C. S. Lewis*, (Plymouth, Northcote House, 1998).

Green, Roger Lancelyn and Walter Hooper. *C. S. Lewis: A Biography* (London, HarperCollins, 2002). Reprinted by permission of HarperCollins Publishers Ltd. © R. L. Green and W. Hooper, 1974.

Haffner, Paul, *The Mystery of Reason* (Leominster, Gracewing, 2001).

Hawkins, D. J. B., *A Sketch of Medieval Philosophy* (London, Sheed & Ward, 1946).

Hayes, Zachary, *Visions of a Future: A Study of Christian Eschatology* (Delaware, Michael Glazier Inc., 1989).

Hein, Rolland, *Christian Mythmakers: C. S. Lewis, Madeleine L'Engle, J. R. R. Tolkien, George MacDonald, G. K. Chesterton and Others* (Chicago, Cornerstone Press, 1998).

_____ (ed.), *The Heart of George MacDonald: A One-volume Collection of his Most Important Fiction, Essays, Sermons, Drama, Poetry, Letters* (Wheaton, Harold Shaw Publishers, 1994).

Honda, Mineko, *The Imaginative World of C. S. Lewis: A Way to Participate in Reality* (Lanham, University Press of America, 2000).

Hooker, Richard, *The Laws of Ecclesiastical Polity: Books I–IV* (London, Routledge, 1888).

Hooper, Walter, *C. S. Lewis A Companion & Guide* (London, Fount, 1997). Reprinted by permission of HarperCollins Publishers Ltd. © Walter Hooper, 1996.

Howard, Thomas. *C. S. Lewis, Man of Letters: A Reading of his Fiction*, (Worthing, Churchman Publishing, 1987).

Huttar, Charles (ed.), *Imagination and the Spirit: Essays in*

Literature and the Christian Faith presented to Clyde S. Kilby (Grand Rapids, Eerdmans, 1971).

International Theological Commission, 'Some Current Questions in Eschatology', in *The Irish Theological Quarterly*, 58 (1992): 209–43.

Jordan, Mark. 'Augustine', in *The Cambridge Dictionary of Philosophy*, Robert Audi (ed.) (Cambridge, Cambridge University Press, 1999).

Kelly, J. N. D., *Early Christian Doctrines* (London, A & C Black, 1977).

Kilby, Clyde, *The Christian World of C. S. Lewis*, (Grand Rapids, Eerdmans, 1964).

King, Alec and Martin Ketley, *The Control of Language: A Critical Approach To Reading and Writing* (London, Longmans, Green and Co., 1940).

Knowles, David, *The Evolution of Medieval Thought*, D. E. Luscombe and C. N. L. Brooke (eds) (London, Longman, 1988).

Komonchak, Joseph, Mary Collins and Dermot Lane, *The New Dictionary of Theology* (Dublin, Gill and Macmillan, 1990).

Kraut, Richard (ed.), *The Cambridge Companion to Plato* (Cambridge, Cambridge University Press, 1992).

Küng, Hans, *Eternal Life?*, Edward Quinn (tr.) (London, Fount, 1985).

Ladaria, Luis, 'Eschatology', in *Dictionary of Fundamental Theology*, René Latourelle and Rino Fisichella (eds) (New York, Crossroad Publishing, 1994).

Lane, Dermot, 'Anthropology and Eschatology', in *The Irish Theological Quarterly*, 61 (1995): 14–31.

_____, *Keeping Hope Alive: Stirrings in Christian Theology* (New York, Paulist Press, 1996).

Lindsay, David, *A Voyage to Arcturus,* (Edinburgh, Cannongate Books, 1998).

Lindskoog, Kathryn, *The C. S. Lewis Hoax* (Portland, Multnomah Press, 1988).

_____, *Journey into Narnia* (California, Hope Publishing House, 1998).

_____, *Sleuthing C. S. Lewis: More Light in Shadowlands* (Macon, Mercer University Press, 2001).

Lowenberg, Susan, *C. S. Lewis: A Reference Guide 1972–1988.* (New York, G. K. Hall & Co., 1993).

MacDonald, George, *The Complete Fairy Tales* (London, Penguin, 1999).

_____, *Phantastes: A Faerie Romance* (Grand Rapids, Eerdmans, 2000).

Marshall, Cynthia (ed.), *Essays on C. S. Lewis and George MacDonald: Truth, Fiction, and the Power of Imagination* (Lewiston, Edwin Mellen Press, 1991).

Marshall, John, *Hooker and the Anglican Tradition: An Historical and Theological Study of Hooker's Ecclesiastical Polity* (London, A & C Black, 1963).

Mertz, D. W., *Moderate Realism and its Logic* (New Haven, Yale University Press, 1996).

McCool, Gerald, *From Unity to Pluralism: The Internal Evolution of Thomis* (New York, Fordham University Press, 1989).

McDannell, Colleen and Bernhard Lang, *Heaven: A History* (New Haven, Yale University Press, 2001).

McGrath, Alister, *A Brief History of Heaven* (Oxford, Blackwell, 2003).

McReynolds, Sally Ann, 'Imagination', in *The New Dictionary of Catholic Spirituality*, Michael Downey (ed.) (Collegeville, Liturgical Press, 1993).

Meilaender, Gilbert, *The Taste for the Other: The Social and Ethical Thought of C. S. Lewis* (Grand Rapids, Eerdmans, 1998).

Menuge, Angus (ed.), *C. S. Lewis, Lightbearer in the Shadowlands: The Evangelistic Vision of C. S. Lewis* (Wheaton, Crossway Books, 1997).

Milton, John, *Paradise Lost,*   John Leonard (ed.) (London, Penguin, 2000).

Moltmann, Jürgen. *The Coming of God: Christian Eschatology*, Margaret Kohl, (London, SCM Press, 1996).

_____, *God in Creation: An Eschatological Doctrine of Creation*, Margaret Kohl (tr.) (London, SCM Press, 1985).

_____, *Hope and Planning*, Margaret Clarkson (tr.) (London, SCM Press, 1971).

_____, *Theology of Hope: On the Ground and the Implications of a Christian Eschatology*, James Leitch (tr.) (London, SCM Press, 1967).

_____, *The Trinity and the Kingdom of God, The Doctrine of God*, Margaret Kohl (tr.) (Minneapolis, Fortress Press, 1993).

Myers, Doris, *C. S. Lewis in Context* (Ohio, Kent State University Press, 1994).

Navone, John, *Seeking God in Story* (Collegeville, The Liturgical Press, 1990).

Neuner, Josef and Jacques Dupuis (eds), *The Christian Faith in the Doctrinal Documents of the Catholic Church* (New York, Alba House, 1996).

Newman, John Henry, *The Dream of Gerontius*, (Oxford, Family Publications, 2001).

Nicholi, Armand, *The Conflicting Worldviews of Sigmund Freud and C. S. Lewis* (Oxford, Oxford Kaiser Lectures, 2000). Cassette.

Niebuhr, Reinhold, *The Nature and Destiny of Man: A Christian Interpretation,*Volume 2: *Human Destiny* (London, Nisbet & Co., 1943).

Ogden, C. K. and I. A. Richards, *The Meaning of Meaning: A Study of the Influence of Language upon Thought and of the Science of Symbolism,* John Constable (ed.) (London, Routledge, 2001).

Otto, Rudolf, *The Idea of the Holy: An Enquiry into the Non-rational Factor in the Idea of the Divine and its Relation to the Rational,* John W. Harvey (ed.) (London, Oxford University Press, 1950).

Pannenberg, Wolfhart, *Theology and the Kingdom of God,* Richard Neuhaus (ed.) (Philadelphia, Westminster Press, 1969).

Patrick, James, *The Magdalen Metaphysicals: Idealism and Orthodoxy at Oxford 1901–1945* (Mercer, Mercer University Press, 1985).

Phan, Peter, 'Current Theology: Contemporary Context and Issues in Eschatology', in *Theological Studies*, 55/3 (1994): 507–36.

Plato, *The Republic*, Desmond Lee (tr.) (London, Penguin, 1987).

_____,*Timaeus and Critias*, Desmond Lee (tr.) (London, Penguin, 1977).

Polkinghorne, John and Michael Welker (eds), *The End of the World and the Ends of God: Science and Theology on Eschatology* (Pennsylvania, Trinity Press International, 2000).

Polkinghorne, John, *The God of Hope and the End of the World* (London, SPCK, 2002).

Pseudo-Dionysius, *The Complete Works*, Colm Liubheid (tr.) (New York, Paulist Press, 1987).

Rahner, Karl, 'Concerning the Relationship Between Nature and Grace', in idem, *Theological Investigations*, Volume I: *God, Christ, Mary and Grace*, Cornelius Ernst (tr.) (London, Darton, Longman & Todd, 1961).

_____, 'Death', in *Encyclopedia of Theology: A Concise Sacramentum Mundi*, edited by idem (London, Burns & Oates, 1975). Reproduced by kind permission of the Continuum International Publishing Group.

_____, 'Eschatology', in *Sacramentum Mundi*, Volume 2: *Contrition to Grace*, edited by idem (London, Burns & Oates, 1968). Reproduced by kind permission of the Continuum International Publishing Group.

_____, 'Eternity from Time', in idem, *Theological Investigations*, Volume XIX: *Faith and Ministry*, Edward Quinn (tr.) (London, Darton, Longman & Todd, 1984).

_____, 'The Hermeneutics of Eschatological Assertions', in idem, *Theological Investigations*, Volume IV: *More Recent Writings*, Kevin Smyth (tr.) (London, Darton, Longman & Todd, 1974).

_____, 'Ideas for a Theology of Death', in idem, *Theological Investigations*, Volume XIII: *Theology, Anthropology, Christology*, David Bourke (tr.) (London, Darton, Longman & Todd, 1975).

_____, 'The Intermediate State', in idem, *Theological Investigations*, Volume XVII: *Jesus, Man, and the Church*. Margaret Kohl (tr.) (London, Darton, Longman & Todd, 1981).

_____, 'Last Things', in *Encyclopedia of Theology: A Concise Sacramentum Mundi*, edited by idem (London, Burns & Oates, 1968). Reproduced by kind permission of the Continuum International Publishing Group.

_____, *Spirit in the World*, William Dych (tr.) (London, Sheed & Ward, 1968).

Ratzinger, Joseph, *Eschatology: Death and Eternal Life*. Michael Waldsten (tr.) (Washington, Catholic University of America Press, 1988).

Roberts, Alexander and James Donaldson (eds), *Translations of the Writings of the Fathers: Down to A. D. 325*, Volume XIV: *The Writings of Methodius, etc*, William R. Clark (tr.) (Edinburgh, T & T Clark, 1869).

Robinson, J. A. T., *Honest to God*, (London, SCM Press, 1963).

Russell, Jeffrey Burton, *A History of Heaven: The Singing Silence* (Princeton, Princeton University Press, 1997).

_____, *The Prince of Darkness: Radical Evil and the Power of Good in History* (New York, Cornell University Press, 1988).

Sachs, John R., 'Apocatastasis in Patristic Theology', in *Theological Studies*, 54/4 (1993): 617–40.

_____, 'Current Eschatology: Universal Salvation and the Problem of Hell', in *Theological Studies*, 52/2 (1991): 227–54.

Sacred Congregation for the Doctrine of the Faith, 'The Reality of Life after Death', in Austin Flannery, *Vatican II*, Volume 2: *More Post Conciliar Documents* (Dublin, Dominican Publications, 1982).

Sauter, Gerhard, *Eschatological Rationality: Theological Issues in Focus* (Grand Rapids, Baker Books, 1996).

Schakel, Peter and Charles Huttar, (eds), *Word and Story in C. S. Lewis* (Columbia, University of Missouri Press, 1991).

Schakel, Peter, *Imagination and the Arts in C. S. Lewis: Journeying to Narnia and Other Worlds* (Columbia, University of Missouri Press, 2002).

_____, *Reason and Imagination in C. S. Lewis: A Study of 'Till We Have Faces'* (Grand Rapids, Eerdmans, 1984).

Schultz, Jeffrey, and John West (eds), *The C. S. Lewis Readers' Encyclopedia* (Grand Rapids, Zondervan Publishing House, 1998).

Schwarz, Hans, *Eschatology* (Grand Rapids, Eerdmans, 2000).

Stanford, Peter, *Heaven: A Traveller's Guide to the Undiscovered Country* (London, HarperCollins, 2002). Reprinted by permission of HarperCollins Publishers Ltd. © Peter Stanford, 2002.

Swedenborg, Emanuel, *Heaven and Hell*, George F. Dole (tr.) (New York, Swedenborg Foundation, 1979).

Tennyson, G. B. (ed.), *Owen Barfield on C. S. Lewis* (Middletown, Connecticut, Wesleyan University Press, 1989).

Thomas Aquinas, *Summa contra Gentiles*, translated by English Dominicans (London, Burns, Oates & Washbourne, 1934). Reprinted by kind permission of the Continuum International Publishing Group.

_____, *Summa Theologiae*, translated by Fathers of the English Dominican Province (London, Burns & Oates, 1981). Reprinted by kind permission of the Continuum International Publishing Group.

Tillich, Paul, 'Existential Analyses and Religious Symbols', in *Contemporary Problems in Religion*, (ed.) Harold Basilius, (Detroit, Wayne University Press, 1956).

_____, *Systematic Theology*, Volume 3: *Life and the Spirit, History and the Kingdom of God* (London, Nisbet & Co., 1964).

Urang, Gunnar, *Shadows of Heaven: Religion and Fantasy in the Writings of C. S. Lewis, Charles Williams, and J. R. R. Tolkien* (London, SCM Press, 1971).

Urban, Wilbur, *Language and Reality: The Philosophy of Language and the Principles of Symbolism* (London, Routledge, 2002).

Vanauken, Sheldon, *A Severe Mercy: C. S. Lewis and a Pagan Love Invaded by Christ, Told by One of the Lovers* (London, Hodder and Stoughton, 1979).

Van der Walle, Anton, *From Darkness to the Dawn.*, John Bowden (tr.) (London, SCM Press, 1984).

Vass, George, *The Mystery of Man and the Foundations of a Theological System: Understanding Karl Rahner*, Volume 2 (London, Sheed & Ward, 1985).

Von Balthasar, Hans Urs, *Dare We Hope 'That All Men Be Saved?': With a Short Discourse on Hell* David Kipp and Lothar Krauth (trs) (San Francisco, Ignatius Press, 1988).

_____, *Theo-Drama: Theological Dramatic Theory*, Volume 5: *The Last Act,* Graham Harrison (tr.) (San Francisco, Ignatius Press, 1998).

_____, *The Von Balthasar Reader*, M. Kehl and W. Löser (eds), Robert J. Daly and Fred Lawrence (trs) (Edinburgh, T & T Clark, 1982).

Von Rad, Gerhard, 'Life and Death in the Old Testament' in *Bible Key Words*, Volume 14: *Life and Death,* Gerhard Kittel (ed.), P. Ballard and D. Turner (trs) (London, A & C Black, 1965).

_____, *Old Testament Theology*, Volume 1: *The Theology of Israel's Historical Traditions*, D. Stalker (tr.) (London, Oliver and Boyd, 1962).

Walker, Andrew and James Patrick (eds), *Rumours of Heaven: Essays in Celebration of C. S. Lewis* (Guildford, Eagle, 1998).

Walsh, Chad, *C. S. Lewis: Apostle to the Skeptics* (New York, Macmillan, 1949).

Weiss, Johannes *Jesus' Proclamation of the Kingdom of God*, Richard Hyde Hiers and David Larrimore Holland (trs) (London, SCM Press, 1971).

White, William Luther, *The Image of Man in C. S. Lewis*, (London, Hodder and Stoughton, 1970).

Williams, Charles, *All Hallows Eve* (Grand Rapids, Eerdmans, 1968).

_____, *Charles Williams: Essential Writings in Spirituality and Theology*, Charles Hefling (ed.) (Boston, Cowley Publications,1993).

_____, *A Charles Williams Reader: Descent into Hell, Many Dimensions, & War in Heaven* (Cambridge, Eerdmans, 2000).

_____ , *The Figure of Beatrice: A Study in Dante* (Cambridge, D. S. Brewer, 1994).

Willis, John, *Pleasures Forevermore: The Theology of C. S. Lewis* (Chicago, Loyola University Press, 1983).

Wilson, A. N., *C. S. Lewis: A Biography* (London, Flamingo, 1991). Reprinted by permission of HarperCollins Publishers Ltd. © A. N. Wilson, 1990.

Zaleski, Carol and Philip Zaleski (eds), *The Book of Heaven: An Anthology of Writings from Ancient to Modern Times* (Oxford, Oxford University Press, 2000).

Index

CPSIA information can be obtained
at www.ICGtesting.com
Printed in the USA
BVHW030222290121
599078BV00010B/61